IDIOT'S GUIDES.
AS EASY AS IT GETS!

Management
Skills

by David Rohlander

ALPHA
A member of Penguin Group (USA) Inc.

ALPHA BOOKS

Published by Penguin Group (USA) Inc.

Penguin Group (USA) Inc., 375 Hudson Street, New York, New York 10014, USA • Penguin Group (Canada), 90 Eglinton Avenue East, Suite 700, Toronto, Ontario M4P 2Y3, Canada (a division of Pearson Penguin Canada Inc.) • Penguin Books Ltd., 80 Strand, London WC2R 0RL, England • Penguin Ireland, 25 St. Stephen's Green, Dublin 2, Ireland (a division of Penguin Books Ltd.) • Penguin Group (Australia), 250 Camberwell Road, Camberwell, Victoria 3124, Australia (a division of Pearson Australia Group Pty. Ltd.) • Penguin Books India Pvt. Ltd., 11 Community Centre, Panchsheel Park, New Delhi—110 017, India • Penguin Group (NZ), 67 Apollo Drive, Rosedale, North Shore, Auckland 1311, New Zealand (a division of Pearson New Zealand Ltd.) • Penguin Books (South Africa) (Pty.) Ltd., 24 Sturdee Avenue, Rosebank, Johannesburg 2196, South Africa • Penguin Books Ltd., Registered Offices: 80 Strand, London WC2R 0RL, England

International Standard Book Number: 978-1-61564-624-1
Library of Congress Catalog Card Number: 2014941126

16 15 14   8 7 6 5 4 3 2 1

Interpretation of the printing code: The rightmost number of the first series of numbers is the year of the book's printing; the rightmost number of the second series of numbers is the number of the book's printing. For example, a printing code of 14-1 shows that the first printing occurred in 2014.

Printed in the United States of America

Note: This publication contains the opinions and ideas of its author. It is intended to provide helpful and informative material on the subject matter covered. It is sold with the understanding that the author and publisher are not engaged in rendering professional services in the book. If the reader requires personal assistance or advice, a competent professional should be consulted. The author and publisher specifically disclaim any responsibility for any liability, loss, or risk, personal or otherwise, which is incurred as a consequence, directly or indirectly, of the use and application of any of the contents of this book.

Most Alpha books are available at special quantity discounts for bulk purchases for sales promotions, premiums, fundraising, or educational use. Special books, or book excerpts, can also be created to fit specific needs. For details, write: Special Markets, Alpha Books, 375 Hudson Street, New York, NY 10014.

Publisher: *Mike Sanders*
Executive Managing Editor: *Billy Fields*
Senior Acquisitions Editor: *Brook Farling*
Development Editorial Supervisor: *Christy Wagner*
Production Editor: *Jana M. Stefanciosa*

Cover Designer: *Laura Merriman*
Book Designer: *William Thomas*
Indexer: *Brad Herriman*
Layout: *Ayanna Lacey*
Proofreader: *Claudia Bell*

Contents

Appendixes

Introduction

The role of a manager is changing, and you have an awesome opportunity to show how well you can adapt, improvise, and overcome any obstacle or circumstance in your role as a manager. If you're not feeling confident you can do that, rest assured you can—and this book can help.

In *Idiot's Guides: Management Skills,* I've culled all the tips, advice, and essential information I've learned firsthand from my years of management experience. In easy-to-understand terms, I tell you how to build a team of dedicated and loyal people and get them to work together successfully to achieve common objectives. I explain how the field of management has changed and outline what you need to do to succeed in this leadership position. I also offer advice on how to organize and lead a team and how to communicate effectively in the hiring interview and the regular one-to-one meetings necessary to keep your people on track and focused on the big picture. Throughout the following chapters, I teach you what actually *works,* not provide mere theory or platitudes.

With this helpful guide by your side, you will thrive in your role as manager.

How to Use This Book

I've divided this book into six parts. I recommend you read from beginning to end, as each part complements the others.

Part 1, From Employee to Manager, explains the problems and dilemmas of transitioning from worker to manager. In these first chapters, I point out the primary signposts along the way and introduce you to all the different types of people you must deal with as a manager.

In **Part 2, Engaging and Retaining Your People,** I share how to bring out the best in your team, how to measure their performance, and the best ways to provide feedback to help your people improve.

Part 3, Finding the People You Need, reveals myriad ways to find and recruit good people. You also learn how to design a comprehensive orientation program and implement that program so your new-hires will succeed in your company.

Part 4, Your Management Toolkit, covers how to communicate, conduct meetings, employ delegation to maximize your impact, and manage operations and technology.

In **Part 5, Management Challenges,** I offer advice on managing change, becoming the referee and diplomat between all your people, and managing remote workers. Terminating employees or laying off workers is never easy, but in this part, I give some guidance on how to go about both.

Part 6, The Well-Rounded Manager, reminds you that managers are people, too, and need balance. As a manager, you must successfully interface with the world outside of your business and think about your future.

In the back of the book, I've included a glossary of common manager-related terms, helpful resources, tips for reading people, and more.

Extras

Throughout, I've also included sidebars to highlight special information. Here's what to look for:

> **DEFINITION**
>
> These sidebars share the meaning of particular words and concepts related to managing people.

> **LEADING THOUGHT**
>
> These sidebars contain tips from people who have been there and done that. Learn from their mistakes—and their successes.

> **MANAGER MINEFIELD**
>
> You want to avoid anything that will produce disastrous results. These caution sidebars identify those things so you can avoid them.

> **SKILL BUILDER**
>
> These tips help you cut to the chase, save time and money, and find the information you need to succeed.

Acknowledgments

Producing a book is a big project. My special thanks go out to Carole, Cindy, and Brook for their professionalism, skill, and good ideas while putting this book together. It has been great privilege to work with you all.

A special thanks to you, the reader, as well. I trust this book will serve you well as you experience the trials, tribulations, and rewards of becoming a manager. I wish you nothing but success.

Finally, a word of appreciation to my clients over the last several decades: without your faith, encouragement, and shared wisdom, I wouldn't have much to say. You have given of yourselves and helped educate me. I am honored to pass it on.

Trademarks

All terms mentioned in this book that are known to be or are suspected of being trademarks or service marks have been appropriately capitalized. Alpha Books and Penguin Group (USA) Inc. cannot attest to the accuracy of this information. Use of a term in this book should not be regarded as affecting the validity of any trademark or service mark.

From Employee to Manager

Becoming a great manager doesn't happen overnight. It takes time and effort, but the end result is very rewarding.

In Part 1, I share several different approaches to becoming a manager so you can review each and determine which one fits you best and can build your management career around your own personal strengths. I explain what you need to do, beginning on your first day, and how you need to look, talk, and behave. You discover the importance of people, productivity, and profits; understand the key traits of all good managers; and learn how to avoid the common mistakes new managers make. I also offer an explanation of ways to identify the main behavioral characteristics of all your people and how to learn their goals and fears. With this information, you can develop a solid communications plan, establish standards, share expectations, and build commitment.

After reading Part 1, you'll have a great start on your path to becoming an excellent manager.

You're a Manager Now

Over the last few decades, the trend has been to flatten out the levels of management and supervision in organizations. The focus of top management, boards of directors, and shareholders is to get the most productivity and revenue from the least investment. Companies are hesitant to hire new people because it's expensive to find, select, hire, and train good workers. Therefore, effectively managing people and resources is critical—and still the best way to get great results with groups of people.

By becoming a manager, you are embarking on a career that has unlimited potential. You might well have specific technical, practical, or system skills that have gotten you to where you are today. But management is different and requires a unique skill set.

In this chapter, you discover several different ways to look at the role of manager. I highlight those critical attributes you need to get started on the right track and show you the most dangerous things to avoid to ensure success in your new role.

A Beauty and a Burden

Many, if not all, organizations select managers based on the way they performed in a nonmanagement role. Companies tend to promote those who excel in a specific skill. For example, when I flew fighters in the U.S. Air Force, the pilot who got promoted was the one who flew the best. However, just because you're good at your job—whether it's technical skills, sales, or something else—doesn't mean you know how to manage people. Management is different from simply knowing the job, and it takes special learning, time, and effort to master.

> **DEFINITION**
>
> **Management** is the skill of being able to plan, lead, communicate, control, and execute by utilizing a group of people to successfully achieve the objectives of the organization. A **manager** is the person who guides, coaches, and controls a group of people who are focused on common goals or outcomes.

Management provides a beautiful platform to learn how to work with people. No two people are alike, and each comes with various levels of talent. One of the most rewarding parts of being a manager is that you have the opportunity, and responsibility, to help other people grow, develop, and achieve their goals. When they do well, it reflects well on you as a manager. (Unfortunately, the opposite is also true.)

For some, one of the most difficult adjustments to becoming a manager is that your work is never done. You constantly will be thinking about your people, the goals that need to be achieved, and how best to accomplish objectives. You no longer have the option of just punching a clock or getting out a certain number of orders and then leaving early for a long weekend. Your mind will be continually engaged.

Depending on your jobs and skills before you became a manager, you are either well prepared to be a manager or have a lot to learn. In this book, I try to cover the bases for both the well-prepared and the novice manager. Therefore, some things might appear to be obvious to you, while other lessons and learnings may appear difficult to grasp. Whatever the case, I share all the tools you need to be successful.

And give yourself a round of applause. By picking up this book, you recognize the special work involved in becoming a manager.

People, Productivity, and Profits

There are many ways to look at management and determine how to master it. A very useful model is people, productivity, and profits. These three areas are critical to your success as a manager. Let's go through each one.

People

You probably became a manager because you performed at a high level in your last job. In those nonmanager roles, your focus likely was more on your own personal efforts and how those efforts would produce results. You had the mind-set that things could be done better and faster if you did them yourself.

Now, however, your focus should be on getting things done *indirectly* by guiding your people rather than doing it yourself. This requires you to let go and have others learn how to do things. As a manager, you must continually strive to accomplish more through your people. Your responsibility is to your staff and helping each of them improve his or her own performance level.

> **SKILL BUILDER**
>
> Good communication is like the oil that keeps the machine running smoothly. Therefore, the most important part of working with people is learning how to effectively communicate with them. Each individual is different, so it only makes sense that you must develop the ability to communicate with individual people in different ways. Chapter 13 delves more deeply into the importance of communication.

As you develop your employees, you'll gradually see improved power and new possibilities for achievement. This happens when many people are focused on their own individual jobs and how they relate to others while also pulling and pushing together toward a common objective or goal. In the role of manager, you'll find that you become the coach, referee, and cheerleader for your team.

Productivity

Businesses are usually designed and organized to produce either a product or a service. These two broad categories include virtually all businesses, profit as well as nonprofit. As a manager, you are concerned with producing a specific product or service through other people. You focus on the who, what, when, where, and how of the production process.

Ideally, the manager decides who is on the team, but sometimes a upper management assigns team members and the manager has to determine ways to adjust the rest of the team to accommodate the new person. The company decides the broad vision, goals, and desired outcomes and then depends on the manager to organize, implement, and monitor the people and process carrying out those goals. Every department has different requirements and resources, and each manager makes the decisions on how to allocate resources and organize the design, implementation, and operation of the processes. Assignment of who works on what projects; where they work; and how to train, qualify, and measure their performance is all the direct responsibility of the manager. The ultimate test is to have satisfied workers producing sufficient quality and quantity to meet or exceed the company standards and expectations.

Many factors are linked to developing productivity. You start with a goal that usually comes from top management. You then develop a plan that can range from being very simple to highly complex. As a manager, never forget the adage, "If you fail to plan, you plan to fail." (I discuss planning more in Part 4.)

As part of the planning process, you need to figure out how you're going to measure productivity. For example, imagine how boring a football game, basketball game, or game of any other sport would be if no score was kept. One of your jobs as manager is to design and monitor a scorecard for each player—in this case, each employee—as well as one for your department, unit, or team as a whole. With good measurements, you'll be able to stay on track and correct issues before they become problems. This further ensures you'll stay on schedule.

When you produce what you say you will, when you say you will, you and your team accomplish something that's very exhilarating and worthy of celebration. You win.

Profits

Positive cash flow, or having more money coming in than going out, allows a business to succeed. Profits are a good thing. With profits, people get paid on time and the company can reinvest in new equipment, research, and development, as well as expand. Without profits, there are layoffs, cutbacks, old and dangerous machinery and equipment, and low morale. Everyone suffers. The biggest cause of failure in small and new businesses is poor management, which usually directly relates to unwise use or lack of funds and zero profits.

As a manager, you must always be concerned with operating the business in a profitable way. This includes being helpful with sales and marketing efforts, controlling expenses, maximizing the return on all expenditures, planning and implementing budgets, having a solid grasp of payroll and time allocation of all people and production, and so much more. Knowing the ins and outs of these processes goes a long way toward keeping the business profitable.

Success from the Start

You now have the title of "manager." To start, relax and let it settle in, not only with yourself, but also with your co-workers. You'll have more than enough time to tell them what to do later. For now, you need to start slow and get to know the dynamics of the group, even if you've worked with these staff members before. You have a lot of listening and asking questions to do now that you're a manager.

Listening and Observing

As a new manager, or any time you're in a new or unfamiliar situation at work, it's best to spend most of your time listening and observing. It's very difficult to learn when you're talking, so resist the urge to speak up right now and tell people what to do while you're still new in your manager role. You don't want to be the one with all the answers right now. Your goal should be from the very beginning to be known as a good listener.

If people want answers from you right away on issues you'd like to know more about first, explain that you're still evaluating the job or situation or that you'll get back to them at a specific time with an answer. Don't be forced into saying things or making commitments you might regret later or before you have sufficient information to make an intelligent, informed decision.

SKILL BUILDER

Communication is like dancing; it requires familiarity and works along a progression of steps to create a whole. When communicating with someone, it's best to start with a little self-disclosure and share a little bit about yourself. Then you can ask a few simple yes-or-no questions and listen carefully to what the other person tells you. You can then gradually ask deeper questions that are open-ended, listening intently to the responses. Your ultimate goal is to get to an emotional level. Additionally, modeling the other person's tone, posture, and cadence, and maintaining eye contact inspire confidence in the person with whom you're conversing.

Asking Questions

You might not realize this, but the person asking questions is always in control of the conversation. When you ask questions, you are in charge of the topic, who talks when, and the direction of the conversation. In addition, the quality of your questions can illustrate how smart and capable you are. This doesn't mean you show off or try to embarrass someone by asking trick or clever questions, however. Sincerity and honest curiosity should be your core intention.

A good way to use questions to the benefit of the business and your role is to ask other workers what they think about certain problems and projects. It's okay to ask others how or why they do things the way they do. For example, you can ask a team member how he has done things in the past, how that worked for him, and why he does something his particular way. You'll learn a lot about his job, the way he thinks, and what he believes is the best way to do things by asking these types of questions.

You've probably heard the saying, "The only dumb question is the one that isn't asked." Your questions will reveal how much you know or don't know about people, the job, and the industry. When you've taken the effort to really study and understand people, the job, and the industry, that will show. By the same token, if you haven't bothered or had the time to do your research, that also will show. No one will belittle you if you're diligently trying to learn and understand; however, they won't respect you if you put off more pride and ego or act like you don't really know. If you don't know, *ask*.

This approach also allows you to show respect for the person and let him know you believe he is good at his job and you expect him to help you. You know what you know, and he knows what he knows. The goal is to combine both knowledge banks and produce something better than any one individual's point of view. It's like tug of war, but in this case, you only win when you pull together.

Here are a few examples of the kinds of questions you might ask:

> "Joe, who do you call on when you have a problem?"

> "What kind of things come up that cause you difficulty?"

> "Judy, what's your favorite part of this job?"

> "If you could, what would you change to make it more productive?"

> "Bill, do you have any ideas on how we might improve the way we get contracts approved and implemented?"

> "How could we make the system simpler and still maintain or improve quality?"

Frame your questions with the point of view of what's best for the company and also for the individual and department. Avoid wording that could potentially put anyone on the defensive, or you risk getting defensive responses rather than honest, thoughtful answers. Show by your questions that your focus is the welfare of the people, high productivity, and making profits—all of which are equally important.

 MANAGER MINEFIELD

As a manager, you will be constantly watched by your staff. The most effective way you can influence them is by being professional in your own behavior. This requires setting standards for yourself that you want them to model because they'll often use your behavior as their standard. Otherwise, you won't get the discipline and performance you want. If you come in late and leave early, are sloppy and casual, or focus only on money and profits, your team will likely follow suit.

From Worker to Manager Mind-Set

As a manager, you now have more responsibility than you did before in your nonmanager position. Now you're responsible for getting your group, department, or team structured, focused, and working well to produce results that improve profits.

The most important thing to remember as you transition from worker to manager mind-set is how important the big picture is. It's clearly not just about you anymore. Your focus as a manager is on your people.

In addition, you must remember that you and your people are part of a larger department, division, or company that's striving to make a profit. Your role is to help create and produce that profit.

The Right Attitude

Every individual person is unique and has a specific set of life experiences they've developed over the years. We've all experienced successes and failures. You're no different in this sense than all the people you work with. The difference, however, is that now that you're a manager, you have the opportunity to help shape the people on your team.

You have absolute control of what you choose to think about, and that includes whether you think in positive or negative terms. So rather than having a *What's in it for me?* mind-set, instead think, *How can I help my people grow and do better?* People enjoy, respect, and work hard for a manager who has a positive attitude and outlook. To perform well in this position, you must be comfortable with yourself and your role as a manager.

You also must learn to differentiate between your relationships with your staff personally and professionally. Your friends may still be your friends; however, if they want to keep their jobs, they have to demonstrate the quality of their work and perform in a highly productive manner.

I was speaking with a CEO of a major company I'm working with as a coach for key executives. The CEO's biggest concern was that although a few of his managers were very good team players, had good relationships with customers, and technically were very competent, they didn't see the big picture. They didn't realize that everything they do has to improve profits one way or another. They were struggling with making the hard decisions, the ones they knew wouldn't be popular with everyone. As a manager, you can't always do what makes you most popular; you have to produce a profit.

This type of situation shows why it's crucial to rely on the beauty of measurement, as I discussed earlier in this chapter with the scorecard method. Measurement can take the form of dollars, units of output, closed contracts, or customer service, to name just a few. This allows managers to get past the subjective level of a relationship and instead focus on the objective results of employees and the group as whole.

> **LEADING THOUGHT**
>
> "Build a better world," said God. And I said, "But God, how can I do that? This is such a vast and complex place. There is nothing I can do." And God, in all His wisdom, said, "David, you just build a better *you*."

Others' Motivation

Becoming a manager is a bit like becoming a parent. But these children—your team—are all adults and have established beliefs, values, and ways of doing things that are well ingrained in who they are.

Behavioral scientists have been studying human actions and reactions for decades and coming up with newer and better ways to manage people. I've taught as an adjunct instructor at several universities over the years and have found that it all comes down to a very simple statement: people do things to either gain a benefit or avoid a loss. Some might want money; others might want recognition. Whatever the case, each person has his or her own particular reasons for everything they do.

There's no simple, legal, and guaranteed way you can make somebody do something. Sure, some people use intimidation or coercion to control others. But that doesn't lead to a healthy work environment. If you have children, especially teenagers, think about how you get them to do what you want them to do. Do you have a magic wand that works every time? Especially one for often-defiant teenagers?

My son enjoyed sleeping in late when he was young. It was interesting, however, to see how easy it was for him to get up early when we were on vacation and planned to go fishing. Likewise, your people will get their work done faster on the days they want to leave early, go to the ballgame, or have after-work plans. You need to get to know your people and determine what they really want. Help them connect their personal wants and needs to being able to attain those things by making a contribution to the company, working hard, and being diligent.

I remember one manager at Merrill Lynch who would take young brokers out to lunch and go by the Mercedes-Benz dealership to look at cars. It was fun to watch the eyes of the young broker get wide with desire. The manager would then ask if he or she liked the car. When they said "Yes, sir." He'd say, "Well, as soon as you reach another $100,000 in production, you ought to buy yourself one."

It's important that you translate all this information into a simple, workable formula that fits you, your team, and your job.

Beware the Pitfalls

New managers often make the same common errors, and most directly relate to their self-concept and how they try to exert their influence and power.

The only person you totally are able to influence and control is yourself. Therefore, it's important to invest time reflecting on why you do what you do. Read through and evaluate the following pitfalls to see if any are relevant to how you behave.

Managing Your Ego

People hate an egotistical manager. One of the quickest and surest ways to torpedo your reputation as a manager is to let the title or position go to your head.

As you deal with your people, be aware of these simple things that go a long way toward keeping your ego in check:

- Avoid using the pronoun *I*, and get into the *we* mind-set.

- Become a patient and caring listener when people have problems or concerns.

- Monitor your own behavior, and don't interrupt your people.

- Ask people for their opinion more than you give them yours or tell them what to do.

- Don't brag about yourself, how good you are, or your past successes. Let your intelligence and competence become obvious by the quality of your decision-making and understanding.

- Ask your staff for feedback, such as "How am I doing?" or "What could I do to be a better manager?"

Remember, the secret to your success is going to be how well your people do and how much they're willing to help you do your job. It's amazing how much can be accomplished when you don't worry about who gets the credit.

Managing Your Emotions

Intelligence comes in many forms. Historically, in American schools, the focus has been on reading, writing, and arithmetic. Those subjects are important, but there's a lot more to intelligence than doing well in school.

For example, researchers at Harvard University have many new theories about intelligence and identifying specific types of intelligence, such as musical intelligence, spatial intelligence, and interpersonal intelligence. One form of intelligence that studies have shown the most important for success is *emotional intelligence (EQ)*. EQ is more of a determiner of success than reading, writing, arithmetic, science, or technology. The exciting thing about EQ is that when you understand and are well developed in EQ, you can improve your relationships at home as well as at work.

> **DEFINITION**
>
> **Emotional intelligence (EQ)** refers to the ability to be aware and understand your own emotions, to be aware and understand others, and to be able to control yourself as well as influence others emotionally.

The following are the elements of emotional intelligence:

Self-awareness   *You are able to see and recognize your own emotions and how they affect your behavior. You understand why you react the way you do.* Do you interrupt people? Can you sense when someone is feeling intimidated by your body language? Do you sense when you're nervous, and do you know why you are? Being able to feel and understand these types of emotions and behaviors is what EQ is all about.

Self-management   *You can control and manage your own emotions so they are productive and help you meet commitments and obligations and also adapt positively to change.* When someone makes a *big* mistake, are you able to remain calm and speak in a relaxed tone? As a manager, you'll often need to take a deep breath before you speak or react to problems, recurring issues, and crises.

Social awareness   *You are able to read other people on an emotional level. You recognize their feelings and concerns as well as how and why they behave the way they do in a group.* How do you know when the other person is comfortable and sharing deep, emotional points of view? Remember, the key to understanding other people is to be aware of their behavior and watch what they pay attention to with their eyes, the words they use, and their social interaction.

Relationship management   *You can positively influence a group of people. You are able to affect their behavior, communication, and coordination as a team and defuse conflicts.* The more comfortable you are with yourself and the more you can focus on others, how they behave, and what their concerns are, the better you'll be able to influence them. It's like playing poker; you have to guess and anticipate what the other person is up to, interested in, and trying to accomplish. It takes hard work and study to be able to lead your team emotionally. (I revisit this topic several times throughout the book. Appendix C is also helpful for learning how to read people.)

The final goal of mastering EQ is to create an emotional environment for yourself and others that is positive, empowering, and productive. (I discuss this more in Chapter 9.)

Practicing Self-Discipline

Self-discipline is a foundational building block of being a good manager. One way you show good self-management or discipline is through time management. This means you are on time for meetings and appointments and understand the importance of clearly defined priorities.

You spend your time in four key ways:

Planning   Each day's schedule, meetings, tactics, and strategies all involve the planning process. As a manager, you plan for yourself, your people, and the company's major goals and objectives.

Communicating   This includes communication of every kind—conversations, phone calls, emails, texts, listening, and even just walking around.

Managing   As a manager, a big part of your job is controlling, directing, leading, and measuring performance, production, and results.

Executing   You probably spent a lot of time doing this before you became a manager. It's all about performing tasks.

Time marches on whether you invest it wisely or waste it. You have exactly 24 hours in each day; it's important to invest that time constructively in these four areas and not be careless with it.

MANAGER MINEFIELD

Be careful about what you say and how you say it. Credibility can be instantly destroyed if you allow yourself to get involved with or make a contribution to office gossip and rumors. As a manager, you must rise above petty conversations. Your interest has to be in the work at hand, the welfare of your people, and producing results. Unprofessional conversation dilutes and destroys trust and respect.

Creating Balance

There's a huge difference between passion and being obsessed. Passion is good and relates to having high energy and determination, while being obsessed is overextension of passion or desire. You'll do best if you strive for balance when it comes to your work and home lives.

On the home front, that means being sure you get regular exercise, consistently read books and learn, take care to spend time with your family (especially if you have children), and nurture the spiritual side of your life. If you have health issues or difficulty at home or lose sight of the big picture of what life is really all about, you won't be effective as a manager.

As for work, pursue your goals with passion, and celebrate victory in moderation. The manager who is easily distracted or who isn't able to focus with intensity will have difficulty getting results. By the same token, it's wise to be low key in the way you celebrate your own success. Honor and reward others with enthusiasm, but moderate your personal feelings of success and celebration. Remember, it's not about you; it's about your people.

One of the best ways to ensure a balance for both home and work is to deliberately block out time in your schedule to plan, think, and reflect. Allocate specific chunks of time for everything important in both your personal and professional lives. The real benefit comes when you decide to make worthwhile adjustments to the way you're working and living life. For example, when your significant other knows you have a block of time on your calendar strictly for time for the two of you together, he or she will appreciate it. You'll also enjoy the peace, confidence, and increased productivity you'll gain from the consistent practice of planning your life on a daily basis.

Expressing Kindness

When you take, you diminish yourself and others. When you give, you feel good, you honor others, and you stimulate positive energy with your team.

Many people have a knee-jerk reaction to giving and immediately think, *Money*. Giving money is nothing compared to giving sincerely of your time. Few things are better than giving another person your time and attention.

At a recent National Speakers Association (NSA) convention, I introduced a friend of mine who is new to NSA to a prolific author, highly regarded consultant, and successful speaker. My friend had read the author's book several years ago about how to build a million-dollar practice and wanted to meet him and say thank you.

A while later, I saw my friend and asked him how he enjoyed meeting the NSA expert. He said. "It was unbelievable! He didn't say thanks; he didn't even look at me. He just said come to my session tomorrow." The expert then strolled away into the party. I can't share the rest of what my friend said, but it is consistent with what most people say about this particular expert.

As a manager, you have to realize that people will appreciate simple human kindness. A sincere thank you, "How are you?" or "You did a good job" will be appreciated. You don't have to spend money, give your staff time off, or be rude and narcissistic.

What are some other ways you can give?

- Give others credit whenever you can.

- Give others the benefit of the doubt.

- Give others a chance to achieve great things by ensuring they have all the resources they need, they feel included, and they feel secure and safe.

By giving to your employees, you have the power to create a productive and positive environment. Think about the many ways you can say "thank you" for a job well done. It'll be worth it.

SKILL BUILDER

If you want to be known as a remarkable manager, adopt the habit of doing "random acts of kindness." The key is to be sure the act of kindness is sincere, thoughtful, and unexpected.

Crushing Competitiveness

Legendary basketball player and coach John Wooden, winner of 10 national college championships during a 12-year period, was famous for telling his players to "just do your best."

Your job as a manager is not to try to outdo others. It's about focusing on becoming the best manager and person you can be. When you compete with yourself to be better, you're continuing to learn and grow in a way that increases your integrity and helps you develop a positive attitude. Be sure you encourage your direct reports to do the same thing.

However, competition is a healthy part of American culture. It's good to try hard and win. It's also okay to not like to lose. Good, healthy competition can usually help you focus and cause you to give a bit of extra effort. That's all positive.

The key here is to remember that the most important person you're competing with is yourself. Measure yourself and strive to continually improve against that standard.

And be patient with yourself. It's going to take some time before you're comfortable with some of these ideas. You're going to have to experiment and try a few approaches before you know what's best for you. As you work your way through this book, it will all come together.

The Least You Need to Know

- The three keys to being a successful manager are people, productivity, and profits.
- Listen to your people, practice the art of asking good questions, and deliberately plan frequent opportunities to communicate one on one.
- Each person is unique and has a personal worldview shaped by his or her past experience. Get to know and understand your people as individuals.
- Remember the big picture. It's all about profits and productivity, and your people are the solution to both.

What Makes a Successful Manager?

Have you thought about what you want to do to become a successful manager? Or even what "success as a manager" means to you?

It's hard to hit a target you can't see or that you have yet to define, so in this chapter, we begin to look at exactly who you must become and what you must do to be successful as a manager.

In This Chapter

* Ways to recognize a good manager
* Defining *success*
* How important are your habits?
* Qualities of successful managers

What *Success* Means

> Success is the progressive realization of predetermined, worthwhile, personal goals.
>
> —Paul J. Meyer

Let's look at this definition of success from businessman and motivator Paul J. Meyer for a minute. First and foremost, he says success is *progressive,* or a process, a journey. That also applies to becoming a great manager. It's a process, and you'll be continually making progress—with a few setbacks along the way—but always pressing forward and upward.

Next, *realization* means success is not imaginary or theoretical. It's real and can be seen, measured, and achieved. *Predetermined* suggests that you plan and set the target before you start out on your journey. *Worthwhile* and *personal* indicate that success relates to your own values and beliefs—that you're not doing this for anybody else but yourself. (You'll also see that the only way to achieve the goal is to help others along the way.)

Last but not least is *goals.* The more clearly you define your goals, the higher the probability you'll achieve them. (In Chapter 6, I share specific guidance you can use in any goal-setting process. It's especially helpful for clarifying and measuring your goals.)

There are no tricks or gimmicks to becoming a good manager. The true test is a measure of who you are as a person—the real you. Good management requires that you have *integrity.*

> **DEFINITION**
>
> For our purposes, **integrity** means you know what you believe; you're able to express and explain those beliefs verbally and in writing; and most importantly, your behavior demonstrates your beliefs and values.

In her book, *Thrive,* author and syndicated columnist Arianna Huffington proffers it takes more than money and power to be successful; you have to *thrive.* Like many before her, Huffington experienced her share of issues, but then she realized she had to focus on balance and her personal life to really become successful. As a manager, you'll do better if you integrate your personal goals and dreams with your organizational goals and dreams.

Be—Do—Have

When looking at your own personal development and the journey you're on to become a successful manager, this exercise can be of help. I call it Be—Do—Have. Here's how it works:

1. In a notebook or in a new word processing file on your computer, write or type today's date at the top of the page and label the page "To Be."

2. Under the title, list words that describe who you want to become. What attitudes do you want to exhibit? What beliefs do you want to explore and decide on? (This might get into your spiritual and moral beliefs.) How do you want to relate to your family, friends, and colleagues at work, socially, etc.? What attributes, habits, and reputation do you want to be known for at work and in your personal life? These are all things that relate to your character, personality, and behavior traits.

3. Now make another similar list labeled "To Do."

4. List all the things you want to do as a manager. This list can focus on just the next few months, or it can be broader and look forward years. As you work on your list, it will gradually become longer range. This encourages you to think in terms of the big picture—what you'll be doing in 1 year, 2 years, or maybe 5 years.

5. The last part is usually the easiest. Make another similar list and label it "To Have."

6. Write down all the items you want—a bucket list of sorts.

The following table shows a sample Be—Do—Have list.

Be—Do—Have

To Be	To Do	To Have
Positive thinker	Get to bed by 10 P.M.	New office furniture
Good listener	Earn my MBA	Ski boat
Good father/mother	Travel to Europe with the company	New car
Student of people	Save money for kids' college	Zero debt
Decisive and adaptable	Learn accounting and finance	
	Have a weekly date night with my spouse	
	Get promoted to senior manager	

> **SKILL BUILDER**
>
> Most people are comfortable creating a To Have list but find it more difficult to do the To Be or To Do lists. All three are essential to this exercise.

Franklin's Virtues

It must be a part of the grand American tradition to approach life this way. The first person I know of who used a similar kind of an exercise to work on his self-improvement was Benjamin Franklin.

Franklin wrote a list of 13 virtues he believed were important. He actually carried a small card in his pocket with his selected "Virtue of the Month" as a reminder. Legend has it he would keep one card, with one virtue, with him for 30 days and work on just that one virtue at a time. That's more than a year of specific focus on self-improvement.

As you review Franklin's list, begin to think about how you might "build a better you" as you create your own Be—Do—Have list:

Temperance   Eat not to dullness; drink not to elevation.

Silence   Speak not but what may benefit others or yourself; avoid trifling conversation.

Order   Let all your things have their places; let each part of your business have its time.

Resolution   Resolve to perform what you ought; perform without fail what you resolve.

Frugality   Make no expense but to do good to others or yourself; i.e., waste nothing.

Industry   Lose no time; be always employ'd in something useful; cut off all unnecessary actions.

Sincerity   Use no hurtful deceit; think innocently and justly, and, if you speak, speak accordingly.

Justice   Wrong none by doing injuries, or omitting the benefits that are your duty.

Moderation   Avoid extremes; forbear resenting injuries so much as you think they deserve.

Cleanliness   Tolerate no uncleanliness in body, [clothes], or habitation.

Tranquility   Be not disturbed at trifles, or at accidents common or unavoidable.

Chastity   Rarely use venery but for health or offspring, never to dullness, weakness, or the injury of your own or another's peace or reputation.

Humility   Imitate Jesus and Socrates.

Franklin made his list in 1726 at the age of 20. Isn't it amazing how many of the virtues he listed then relate to management and how to become a great manager now?

Habits, Good and Bad

Researchers say the majority of behavior is habitual. That means you (and each of us) have ingrained habits that are actually a part of the way your brain is wired. The exciting thing about this is that you can change the way your brain is wired and, therefore, change the way you think and act. The key to ending bad habits, or starting new good ones, is to first identify the trigger that caused you to do what has become a habit.

In his book, *The Power of Habit,* journalist Charles Duhigg explains how he would go to the lunchroom every afternoon for a cookie. It wasn't that he was hungry; rather, he was lonely from working alone in his cubicle. He went to the lunch room to socialize—and he was getting fat from eating all those cookies! Once he realized this, he was able to change his habit. He found a healthy trigger, which meant no more need to get a cookie or feed his need for social interchange.

Think about your habits, both the good ones and the bad. Why do you have these habits? Also think about what your triggers are—the little things you do or pay attention to that start you on the cycle of your habit. Change your triggers, and you can start to change your habits.

SKILL BUILDER

Triggers usually relate to your senses. Odor, for example, can cause hunger—think of walking by a bakery in the morning. Sound also can be a trigger, and music with a strong beat may make you suddenly decide to go dancing.

Qualities of a Good Manager

A successful manager can have any number of good habits and qualities. In the following sections, I've narrowed it down to those I feel are the most critical. Use this list to ensure you're approaching your job in a positive, comprehensive, and ultimately successful manner.

Good Managers Are Self-Improvers

Continuous self-improvement is a principle that's long been advocated in business. A good manager endorses this principle and also applies it to his or her personal development. This is much more than going to an occasional seminar or reading a motivational book. It's a habit good managers are always working on.

Ideally, self-improvement is a constant part of the culture of your organization. However, it's also (and primarily) each individual's responsibility to work on his or her own self-improvement. You must use your own time to complete your own personal agenda. As a manager, you can share enthusiasm and set a good example. You also may encourage your team members to share new knowledge and insights as a normal part of meeting and lunchroom conversations. The more you focus on self-improvement in your words and deeds, the more it will become a part of your culture.

Some companies sponsor, or at least share the cost of, formal education. Others send their employees to conferences or special courses to learn new technology, popular management approaches, the latest methods of manufacturing, or the current thinking in financial models. Encourage your organization's upper management to set up company-provided training available for all employees, from management to frontline workers.

When management dedicates funds, time, and attention to helping people improve, the return is profitable in several ways:

- Employees become more loyal because they know the company cares about them.

- Everyone can improve his or her knowledge and work skills and bring that knowledge back to the workplace in the form of increased productivity and innovation.

- Retention is improved and makes the organization a preferred place to work.

All this will become a real advantage when hiring new people, as word will get out and people actually will *compete* to get hired by your company.

Education does not have to be expensive or extensive. You're reading this book to improve your management skills, for example, and the price tag on it isn't all that high. Here are some other simple self-improvement ideas you might try:

- Learn another language.

- Sign up for on-job-training in another department, division, or country.

- Listen to books on CD or MP3 when you're driving or flying.

- Read ebooks on your smartphone or tablet.

- Attend seminars and workshops from associations or training companies.

- Take advantage of free webinars and podcasts.

- Explore the internet to see what new or interesting information you can find that might lead to some kind of self-improvement.

SKILL BUILDER

One of the very best ways to find out what you should focus on is to seek feedback. Develop the habit of requesting feedback, both formally with surveys or by using a coach and informally in everyday conversation. It could be as simple as asking "Hey, how do you think we did?" This helps you focus on the areas where you need to improve, new things you might need to learn, and how well you're making progress.

Remember, work on self-improvement for yourself, and encourage your group to do the same thing. It really helps when you set the example.

Good Managers Are Relatable

Some people are naturally good at relating to people, while others have to work at it. Certain principles can help you become more relatable. Try some of the following ideas, and you might enjoy getting to know people better, no matter how good you already are at relating to people.

Two fundamental problem areas in many organizations, teams, or relationships are lack of money and poor communication. To become a great manager, no single skill will have a greater impact on your success than your ability to effectively communicate. One way to measure if you're making progress in communication is to see how much people are willing to give you suggestions and feedback. The process of giving and taking ideas, sharing suggestions, and expressing feelings is a sure sign of healthy communication. Throughout this book, I'll continually come back to helping you develop your communication skills. It's the common denominator for everything in these pages that will help you improve.

When you meet someone, do a brief amount of self-disclosure and then focus mostly on asking open-ended questions. Sharing information about yourself breaks the ice and helps put people at ease. Talk about where you're from, where you went to school, your spouse or children, your hobbies or your favorite sport, or other personal information. Keep it informal and conversational, not a sales pitch. Then you can start with simple small-talk questions like "How's the weather?" "Did you have a good weekend?" or "That was some game Saturday, wasn't it?"

Monitor your dialogue, and be sure you're listening more than 50 percent of the time. After each encounter with a colleague, take a minute to review in your head how the exchange went. *Did I listen? Was he or she at ease? What kind of questions did each of us ask? What would be the best follow-up to the conversation? A note? An email? A phone call? Talk to the boss and get back to them? Write a note to check back with them next week?* You decide what's best for the situation.

In Chapter 1, I compared good communication to a dance. Start small and simple, with yes-or-no questions, and be gentle in your tone and manner. Use eye contact and focused body language to show you're interested in what the other person is saying; pay attention when he or she is speaking; and mimic or model their body language, tone, rate of speech, and expressions. Strive to get to an emotional level of exchange. As you both get more comfortable, you can increase the depth of your questions: "How are you doing with your new assignment?" "What's working best for you on the job?" or "I'm just curious—what are the primary concerns people have about the changes we've made?"

Realize, too, that sometimes it's better to be silent than talk. Listening can be much more valuable and respectful, so resist the urge to talk all the time and embrace the pause and silence as you honor the other person's point of view and comments.

Another part of relating well with people is the ability to "read" other people. By that, I mean to look at them and be able to understand what they're feeling, even if they're not speaking. One of the best ways to improve your skill at reading others is by the use of assessments.

SKILL BUILDER

One simple and straightforward assessment that can help you understand yourself and others is a four-quadrant model of behavioral styles called the DISC (dominance, inducement, steadiness, or compliance) model. Developed in the 1920s by Harvard psychologist Dr. William Moulton Marston, it's a great way to read people based on their actions and then learn how best to interact with that person's style. It's readily available online, including at my website, DavidRohlander.com/assessments.

Good Managers Are Organized and in Control

The well-organized manager is able to be calm, focused, efficient, and effective. A calm and confident manager's demeanor has a very positive impact on his or her team. Confusion, waste, and frustration are minimized, and people feel secure and confident with the direction and competence of the manager's leadership, often with increased respect and trust for that person. Being in control includes emotional restraint; discipline and administrative control; and clear and accurate measurements of their people, production, expenses, and revenue.

An organized and in-control manager is prepared to handle the inevitable crisis as well as adapt to change, making adjustments smoothly and easily to deal with the unexpected. Dysfunction is prevalent when a manager is at his or her wits' end, confused, and stressed.

Focus on being organized and in control, know what to pay attention to, and keep an eye on the big picture. Don't waste time on trivia or items of little consequence. Remember, your goal is to focus on your people, production, and profits. Do that well, and you'll have little time for gossip, idle chitchat, or constant complaining.

Good Managers Are Proactive

A good manager makes his or her own manager's job much easier by taking initiative, anticipating problems, and creating change. Being proactive is different from adapting or reacting to situations; the proactive manager leads thought and action by looking into the future or at least striving to anticipate every eventuality with preparedness.

Former world chess champion Gary Kasparov said he thinks five or six moves ahead when he plays chess. The proactive manager plans ahead similarly. He or she is continually asking "What if?" and thinking of plans to answer that question. Work at expanding your worldview beyond just right now, and strive to see the big picture for your department and your company. Ask yourself and your team: "What do we need to do to win now? In two years? In five years?"

Every day, assess your team's abilities and knowledge. Send them to training before a crisis hits so the inevitable change doesn't become a crisis. Budget and control current expenses, and anticipate future expenses for research and development, repairs, training, and the prep work you need to do now to get ready for what might come.

MANAGER MINEFIELD

Being reactionary is the opposite of being proactive. Don't get caught playing catch-up—or as pilots often say, "Getting behind the power curve." In an airplane, getting behind the power curve refers to when a pilot overextends the plane's capabilities relative to airspeed, altitude, and position of the aircraft. Serious accidents happen when there's not enough altitude, speed, or power to recover from an aggressive maneuver. The reactive manager overcommits his people, resources, or time. Know the limits and capabilities of your people, the required time to complete projects, and the resources at your disposal and then manage all these pieces well.

Good Managers Are Focused

It's okay to focus on one goal at a time. In fact, studies have shown it's not always wise to multi-task. When you do, it can compromise your memory, quality of performance, and decision-making abilities. When you focus on just one thing, you can give that thing your undivided attention—and often yield better results.

Think how you felt when you were talking to someone in their office and their phone rang. Did they cut you off in the middle of a sentence and answer the phone, ignoring you were even in the room? This rude behavior shows lack of social etiquette and compromises mutual respect. Good managers don't do that.

No matter what your politics, you have to admire former President Bill Clinton for his ability to connect with people and focus on them. Several of my clients have met him, and they all agree: when you meet him, you feel as if to him, there's no one else in the room but you.

Adapt the same thinking in your own role. Arrange your office so you can focus and concentrate on work. Position your desk facing a corner, wall, or window, not the door. If you face the door while you're sitting at your desk, you invite interruptions. An open-door policy is great, as long as your people realize that when your door is shut, you don't want to be disturbed.

Managers who have difficulty focusing usually can't do so because they're uncertain about what's important and what their priorities need to be. The more organized you are, the better you'll be able to focus.

Good Managers Are Planners

Consistent and comprehensive planning is essential for managers. Make time for planning to identify your highest-pay-off activities and the best time to do each. By planning regularly, you're forced to reflect and review your opportunities, options, and obstacles to success.

The most damaging events we experience are the ones we didn't anticipate. When you plan, you design a way to handle and recover from almost anything. Without a plan, the result is far more likely to be failure. But have a good plan in place, and you'll maintain a healthy balance on the job and in your personal life.

To be effective, your plan must be in writing or on your computer, tablet, or smartphone. Keep it with you at all times if you can, and develop the habit of planning every day. Write down anything you want to remember or do in the future. Say this affirmation to yourself often, and it will help you develop the planning habit:

> I do it now, or I write it down!

Write down anything you want to remember or do in the future, from getting gas in the car to planning next year's budget. Every time you think of a new task, question, or idea, write it down. You'll do much better as a manager if you're always writing things down than if you try to commit your "To Do" list to memory.

 LEADING THOUGHT

The shortest pencil is longer than the longest memory.

When you sit down to plan, you decide when and how to do all those things you've written down during the day. The ideal time to do this is first thing in the morning and again as the last thing before you leave work at the end the day. If this is a new habit, start with a list of the things you need to do. Prioritize the list numerically, from 1 to 10, based on importance, and then alphabetically, A to Z, based on urgency. When you finish your list, go to item 1-A first and don't do anything else until that first, highest-priority task is complete. Then move on to 1-B and so on until you finish your list.

In addition, develop the habit of blocking time for the activities you need to do each day. Dedicate a chunk of time for planning in the morning and evening, set aside time for meetings, create a set time to make phone calls, etc.

Good Managers Are Communicators

After planning, the next most important activity a good manager does is communicating. However, this can be a neglected area, especially for more established managers who mistakenly seem to think people don't need communication once they know their job. But nothing could be further from the truth. Everyone needs some form of regular communication. The way you communicate with each person on your team depends on his or her behavioral preferences.

The best managers have a reputation for being receptive to feedback and having an open-door policy. You'll find that people are more willing to go along with your suggestions and requests if you're open to their input and feedback. It's a two-way street—each receives information by listening and shares by talking.

Levels of communication may vary in their intensity and quality. A very useful type of communication to improve your awareness of the state of the company and the condition of your people is *MBWA,* or "manage by walking around." Occasionally stroll through the office or plant and simply greet; make small talk; or talk about the weather, production, or a team member's child's latest soccer game. This helps you put a "human" face on the office of manager. It also gives you great insight into what's going on and how well systems and people are working.

> **DEFINITION**
>
> **MBWA** stands for "manage by walking around." It's a simple method in which you literally walk around and interact with your team.

Other forms of communication are very useful as well. You can use email, text messages, memos, announcements, handouts, brochures, and many other hard copy and verbal approaches. To communicate a lot of information with many details, it's best to do it with a written format such as an email or memo. A written document can be reviewed and studied later and can have more lasting impact. You can keep people informed and fulfill legal requirements for posting information on safety, emergency procedures, or hiring practices by putting up notices or posters in the break room, cafeteria, or employee lounge.

Meetings are another option. The highest and best use of a meeting is to build consensus or facilitate a discussion where you are seeking feedback, discussion, and innovative ideas. Meetings are very expensive because of the value of everyone's time. Minimize the use of meetings unless there is a specific purpose with an agenda and defined time constraints. (More on meetings in Chapter 14.)

The ultimate form of communication, one that will change the culture and direction of your organization in a very positive way, is the "one-to-one." This is a regular appointment you have with people who report directly to you, one at a time, during which you review current status, goals, and plans for the future. This is where you, as a manager, play the role of coach. It shows how much you care, clarifies any uncertainty about objectives, and gives you an opportunity to inspire and coach each of your direct reports. When done on a consistent basis, this personal technique can have amazing results.

Good Managers Are Delegaters

On a long-term basis, nothing increases your impact more than a well-managed *delegation* program. By delegating, you can work on higher-priority items only you can do. This is very different from "dumping" unpleasant tasks on someone else, however. Delegation is a way to grow your people's capability, improve their self-esteem, and plan for the future—yours, theirs, and the team's.

> **DEFINITION**
>
> **Delegation** is a process in which you enable others to learn and develop skills by helping you accomplish necessary and worthwhile tasks.

During your planning sessions, analyze what functions and duties you have that you can delegate. Then assess your people and their potential, based on their past performance, and match the right person with the right job.

One little trick to help you do this is what I call the four D's. Each time you approach a task, piece of paper, or request, ask yourself "Shall I *do, defer, delegate,* or *destroy* this item?" This goes back to the "I do it now, or I write it down" aspect of daily planning. Where you write it down will now be either in the calendar or file for deferred items or in the delegation file. Your last choice is to destroy it.

Good Managers Are Controllers

When I was flying fighter aircraft in the Air Force, we had many emergency procedures. One was regarded as the fundamental emergency procedure. It went like this:

1. Maintain aircraft control.

2. Analyze the situation.

3. Take appropriate corrective action.

I have since added a fourth step:

4. Learn from the experience.

Your job as a manager is to above all maintain control of the situation. The best way for you to do this is to "inspect what you expect" on a regular basis. This is actually a very positive process. Regular and consistent follow-ups with your team provide an opportunity to congratulate them when they're doing well, assist them if they're stuck or confused, or give them a boost if they're behind.

It's difficult to know how things are going in a business if no accurate measurements are taken of all essential tasks, processes, and outputs. As I touched on in Chapter 1, everyone, in every role, should be measured in some form on a daily basis. You can call these measurements *key function indicators* (*KFIs*). Each team member should be keeping track of these measurements themselves as well. It's great if you have systems to monitor performance; however, there's a special ingredient added when people are able to measure themselves.

Here are some examples of key function indicators:

Accounts receivable	Write downs
Cash flow	Revenue per inquiry
Customer acquisition	Process time measures
Inventories	Quality measures
New orders	Order ship cycle times
Unit sales	Customer retention
Backlog	Sales profitability

> 📖 **DEFINITION**
>
> A **key function indicator** (**KFI**) is a measurement that that indicates the direction, volume, and quality of a given task.

When you have a fair and honest measurement system in place, people can go home at night and know if they won, lost, or broke even each day, which also is helpful for building morale. You'll find that winners like the idea of being measured while losers don't.

Each day when you plan, you can review the measurements. This helps you identify where you need to focus your attention. It might mean you'll discover the need for a training program for some people. It shows it might be you who needs remedial assistance. And it will clearly identify the people who are high achievers.

Resist the temptation to micromanage your people. Give them generous thank-yous when they do well, and based on the measured results, reward your people for high performance.

Good Managers Are Executers

To *execute* means you do something, and do it on a regular, timely basis. Don't become a manager who says one thing and then does another—or never does what you say you'll do. A good manager believes that their word is their bond. If you say it, you do it.

It's worth noting that people will notice the little things. Did you return the phone call in the morning like you said? Were you on time to the meeting? Were you polite to the stranger you ran into on the street? How's your driving? Do you drive responsibly and carefully? You might not think these things matter, but they do, because your people will be watching you all the time and making judgments about what kind of person you are. That's why a good manager is always working on self-improvement.

Be sure to write things down—write everything down. That way, nothing will fall through the cracks, and you won't forget things you should be doing. Answer your calls promptly, and keep your inbox or message center clear. Be sure to follow up on a regular basis as well.

It is a good idea to have a chart of each person, project, and initiative with dates and a place to check off each time you "inspect what you expect." Frequency of contact is much better than long afternoons building relationships on the golf course. Smile a lot, think good thoughts, and mentally give yourself positive feedback. You are going to be a great manager.

The Least You Need to Know

- Success is a journey; persistence and dedication will result in you becoming a fantastic manager.
- Clearly defined values and beliefs are your best foundation for building your career, and your life.
- Habits make or break you. With effort and practice, you can change your brain's neural pathways and, therefore, your habits.
- Communication is the common denominator to building your team and creating a productive environment.
- If you can't measure it, you can't manage it. Every day, everyone needs to know if they won or lost.
- Inspect what you expect.

CHAPTER 3

Finding Your Management Style

You are unique, you have certain behaviors that have worked for you all your life, and you will always be the most successful when you lead with your strengths—in life and in managing. Sure, as you (or any of us) mature and get more experience, you'll likely modify and refine your way of doing things. However, the core of who you are probably won't change that much.

The good news is, there's no one single method of managing, and you can be successful as a manager in many ways. Knowing what your preferences, biases, or prejudices is helpful, however. People can work with all kinds of managers; problems occur when you're not consistent in your behavior or when you change your behavior without warning. You'll have the most success as a manager if you're transparent, consistent, and predictable.

Trust and respect are intangible attributes that take time to develop, but you must nurture them with your people. Both are required if you want to be successful. Don't assume you have trust and respect just because you have the "manager" title. You have to earn them.

Your team will be watching all your behaviors, and in time, you'll be able to demonstrate that you deserve to be trusted and respected, and it will be the natural by-product of your efforts.

It Takes All Types

Each person is unique and, likewise, so is each manager. Think of the managers you've known in the past. Remember how some were really adept at making friends with their staff and seemed to work at socializing with their own boss, too? Maybe other managers were focused on what was "right" or "proper" and sometimes involved in religion, charities, or special causes. Others likely were driven to get ahead in their career, make money, or win at all costs.

Each manager's style of management is ultimately based on his or her belief system and strengths and weaknesses, but there are basically three types of managers:

- The value-driven manager

- The political manager

- The results-driven manager

It's important to repeat, however: there is no one type of manager that's best.

The Value-Driven Manager

First let's review the value-driven manager. A manager with clearly defined and strong values believes them to be the most important criteria for how he or she manages. The value-driven manager will share his or her values with everyone and often expects others to find them important as well. Values will then become the scale of measurement used in making decisions. This approach can build a strong and tightly knit organization.

If you were a manager in Johnson & Johnson in the 1980s, you'd be well supported by CEO Jim Burke if you made decisions based on company values. In 1982, seven people in Chicago died from cyanide poisoning. Quickly, the FBI and the FDA discovered the victims had ingested the poison from adulterated Tylenol capsules. Burke immediately issued a recall of all Tylenol—31 million bottles. He then took steps to let the public, medical community, and press know what happened and what he was doing about it. His decision was made based on values. The Johnson & Johnson credo, or statement of beliefs, clearly says the company's responsibility is first to its customers (doctors, nurses, patients, mothers, and fathers), then to its employees, then to its community, and finally to its stockholders. Burke was open and transparent with the media, the public, and law enforcement and did not base his decision on monetary results or politics.

Do you know the values of your leaders and your organization? How important are they in day-to-day operations? How much do your values determine your own management behavior? I'm sure you care about your values, but when you're forced to make hard decisions, what else comes into play for you and your team? Do they know your values? How important is it to you that your people buy into your value system?

If this doesn't seem like you, let's look at two other ways to think about the kind of manager you are and which management style you have.

The Political Manager

Economics is all about the fundamental economic problem: unlimited wants and limited resources. Politics is all about who gets what, when, and how. The driving goal in politics is to create ways for people to agree or work together. This happens when they learn the fine art of compromising.

> **LEADING THOUGHT**
>
> Politics is the ability to foretell what is going to happen tomorrow, next week, next month and next year. And to have the ability afterwards to explain why it didn't happen.
>
> —Winston Churchill

Recently I interviewed a partner for a major accounting firm, asking for feedback on another partner, my client. This is usually a part of my process of coaching executives. One of my questions is: "How is his political savvy?" The response was fascinating. First the partner talked about the firm and shared his view of the firm's culture—"Everything has a political orientation." Then he made an assessment of my clients' political savvy. For him, political savvy means how well my client takes into consideration the feelings and interests of the other partners. As my grandmother used to say, "You catch more flies with honey than with vinegar." Politics is not primarily about results or values; it's about how you deal with people's wants and the distribution of benefits.

You can see why a strong political culture in an organization wouldn't lend itself well to being highly profitable. The focus rather would be internal—sharing resources and keeping people cooperative. This would often outweigh the uncomfortable or tough decision to let someone go or to reprimand a coworker.

Managers need to understand politics and learn to be sensitive to the needs and desires of others. The challenge is one of balance and degree: just how political do you want to be, and what is in the best interest of the organization, the customer, and the stockholders (owners)?

The Results-Driven Manager

In business, getting results usually directly relates to making money, and profits are the holy grail for the results-driven leader. He or she works 25 hours a day; seeks every way possible to create an advantage; and pushes, pulls, and squeezes people to make it happen. The results-driven manager's goal is to exceed expectations and make tons of money.

Examples of such managers include celebrity bosses like Donald Trump and Martha Stewart. A more traditional example is Jack Welsh, CEO of General Electric (GE) for more than 20 years who consistently created record profits. The drive for results at GE under Jack Welch was also characterized by firing the low performers, leading in a product category or getting out of it, and creating training centers in Groton, Connecticut, and then all over the world. Many successful executives started out with GE and worked their way up in management. Friends of mine who worked for Jack Welch said it was a grueling ride but worth it if you wanted to be a winner.

What Type Are You?

Can you imagine being only one of these three types of leaders? It's more likely that you're a combination of all three, with the unique characteristics of each type in varying amounts. It might be that you want results but you're also really dedicated to your values. Maybe you have a knack for being able to see political solutions but you also drive hard for results. It's rare to find someone who is only one type of manager—value-driven, political, or results-driven.

> **SKILL BUILDER**
>
> Make a point to reflect whenever you can. It's one of the most valuable uses of your time. Also ask people for feedback on what they like or don't like about the way you manage.

To be an effective manager, you need to determine which type you are the most and which type you shy away from. If you have difficulty deciding which type you are, think how hard it is for your people to know what you want. They're continually watching your behavior, what you say, and the way things play out for other people in the workplace who are influenced by you. Your people might be asking themselves, *What does it take to get fired? What happens if I don't make my quota? Will there be any consequences if I come late or miss a meeting?*

Remember, there are many ways to be a manager and be successful. However, if you aren't transparent, consistent, and fair with people, you won't do well, no matter which type you are. People learn to cope with each type, but problems arise when you change your style in the middle of a project, problem, or when you're dealing with other people. Your personal behavior needs to be consistent.

Let's look at an example. Say a family-owned business has an owner who is clearly a results-driven manager. One of his children starts to work for the company, feels entitled, and doesn't produce well. When the manager slacks off on the requirements for his child, he's not staying true to being a results-driven manager. This destroys the morale of everyone except the child and causes the rest of the employees to lose trust and respect for the owner.

Here's another example. A value-driven leader makes a big point of doing what's right, being honest, and staying above board in all dealings but then takes shortcuts with his or her taxes or takes advantage of perks like fancy lunches or outings paid for by the company when everyone else is encouraged to be frugal and watch expenses.

I've seen real problems develop in organizations when the boss bought a really expensive bottle of wine on a special dinner with one employee. Word got out among the rest of the company about the expensive wine, and this became the beginning of a campaign that branded the manager as being guilty of favoritism.

You have to be consistent to earn trust and respect.

You're Not Alone

Every manager has some amount of self-doubt. Based on your past experience, you'll be somewhere between highly confident and full of self-doubt. It takes real courage to try new things. Reading this book is hopefully giving you answers and encouragement to try being a great manager. Knowing you're not alone, that other managers have felt what you're feeling, might help.

I always did something that I was a little not ready to do. I think that, that is how you grow. When there's a moment of "Wow, I'm not so sure that I can do this," and you push through those moments, it's then that you have a breakthrough. Sometimes that's a sign that something really great is about to happen. You're about to grow and learn a lot more about yourself.

—Marissa Mayer, CEO of Yahoo!

If you lose money, you can always replace it, but when you lose time, it is gone forever. Time is the essence of what life is really all about. How do you spend your time now? Are you spending it with your family, staying in shape, and nurturing your knowledge? When you have a written plan in place and have blocked out time to plan, you dramatically increase the amount of time you're productive and working on accomplishing your goals. And when you have clearly defined goals, you don't have time to waste. Keep asking yourself, *Is this the best use of my time right now?*

The question I ask myself like almost every day is, "Am I doing the most important thing I could be doing?" … Unless I feel like I'm working on the most important problem that I can help with, then I'm not going to feel good about how I'm spending my time. And that's what this company is.

—Mark Zuckerberg, CEO of Facebook

People crave positive feedback from their boss. Are you in the habit of giving your people a simple "thank you" or "way to go, good job"? If not, it's a good habit to have. Do you express to your people how much you believe in them and let them know you expect them to win? It's absolutely amazing how you can influence morale as well as performance by being optimistic and affirming the good things people do.

High expectations are the key to everything.

—Sam Walton, founder and CEO of Walmart

Manager as Specialist

The specialist is a manager who knows a particular subject, skill, or system with a high degree of competence. This focused knowledge can be used to great advantage in many ways.

Having such knowledge is one thing; but now that you're a manager, you need to learn how to *transfer* your knowledge to others. The best way is to help those who report to you learn to think the way you do when solving problems. Don't simply tell people what to do because "I said so"— or because you're the specialist and you know best.

Instead, speak to your people in a tone and manner that makes them feel like they're capable of doing great things. Show them respect and empathy as they struggle to learn. Treat your people as if they already hold the position or knowledge you want them to hold, and they'll most often rise to the occasion.

As a specialist, you have the potential to lead a team of highly skilled and competent people. You'll be considered much more valuable to any organization if you can grow your people than if you're only a highly skilled individual and can't share your skills. Teach others, and you'll have a win-win situation for you, your people, and your company.

 MANAGER MINEFIELD

Resist the temptation to be proud of how good you are. Instead, think about how you can help others learn what you know.

One of my recent coaching clients is a highly skilled PhD from Eastern Europe who now works in a Fortune 500 company. He was a university professor in Europe and carried out state-of-the-art research in his field of engineering. He is clearly a specialist, and because of his superior knowledge and skill level, he was promoted to department manager. When I started to work with him, things were a bit rocky in his department.

There was a minor issue because of his accent and the attitude he brought to his work environment. He had very high standards, his mind was amazingly quick, his cultural background was vast, and he spoke several languages in addition to English. Working with the typical American worker was frustrating for him because the people around him had a rather narrow range of interests and knowledge compared to him. He never said so, but as we worked together, I was able to see this, and soon it became apparent to him as well. He was smart, knowledgeable, a former professor and now a manager and was treating people with a bit of disdain. Once we identified this behavior, we could address it by beginning to look at why he felt the way he did.

My client came from an Eastern European country, grew up under communism, and as a professor, organized resistance against the Communist rulers. This got him into trouble politically, and he had to be constantly on guard to avoid getting into trouble with the government. This unique background influenced his attitude toward people, especially the people he managed. He was short and impatient with them, and he had no tolerance for mistakes or deviation from his standards. He would often do something himself rather than try to train and develop his people. He was aware his group could easily rally together and set him up for a fall. This feeling again triggered in him the angst he felt while living in Europe.

In response, his staff felt nervous, inferior, and frustrated with the way he spoke to them. They often blamed his accent to cover for any mistakes or problems.

Once my client was able to get past his emotions and take a look at the bigger picture, he was able to make progress. The first issue was his internal attitude, so he decided to shift from looking down at his people to trying to find commonalities with them. They liked baseball, while he was into opera, classical music, art, literature, and history. So he started to learn and understand baseball.

Next, he began to ask his people questions—not about how to do an engineering problem, but also how they felt and what they thought might be a good solution. They then discussed the issues together, and he listened intently to their ideas. The professor began to listen to his students.

Finally, they all began to work together. He would inspect what he expected but not to find fault, and he checked in frequently to look for good things, innovations, and solutions. He decided to open his mind and his heart to different ideas and ways of doing things, and he explored ways he could help his people learn and develop. Rather than be the expert and specialist with the right answer, he helped his staff discover within themselves the resources to analyze problems and solve issues.

SKILL BUILDER

My son is a gifted artist. An honors graduate from the Art Center College of Design in Pasadena, California, with a Master's degree, he is a winner of many awards and has done very well with his professional art career. However, on more than one occasion, he has remarked how much more he has learned when he started teaching. The best way to really learn something is to teach it. When you're trying to get someone to learn something, have them teach others. When you're a specialist, you'll gain an even deeper understanding of your subject by teaching it and enabling your people to become teachers as well.

Manager as Supervisor

A supervisor approaches management primarily with a focus on the team or unit—more of an internal orientation. There's a lot of crossover between a supervisor and a manager. Both are concerned with their workers' performance, proper fit of skills with tasks, and production. There may also be crossover during the hiring and evaluation of workers.

Often a supervisor works on the line with workers and helps solve specific problems with them. The manager is a bit more removed from the details of jobs and spends more time and effort interfacing with other managers, executives, or even customers.

As you transition from supervision to management, you'll find the biggest difference is your point of view or focus. Supervisors are focused on production and the team, while managers are additionally involved with plans, interfacing with other departments, and the big picture. If you approach management as a supervisor, you'll probably earn the reputation of micromanager. Realize that you must be more removed from daily production tasks as a manager so you can keep an eye on the bigger picture and interface with other departments.

 MANAGER MINEFIELD

> Resist the urge to become too involved in the routine of production. This will become a disincentive to your workers, and they'll tend to not become good decision-makers. Instead, they'll rely on you to make all decisions and then lack any feeling of responsible for their own performance and results. At its worst, you'll have people thinking or saying, "It's not my job" when asked to help or think outside the box.

If you have a supervisor mind-set from your previous position, strive to focus on your people and not the specific functions they're doing on the job. Have them share with you how they're doing rather than critically looking at the way they're doing things. Remember, that as a manager, you should focus on your people and the results they produce. They have to figure out how they're going to to achieve those results.

You want to be sure they get adequate training and instruction (which ideally will be a delegated task). You are the orchestra leader; resist the urge to pick up the horn or the violin and play the music. That's the job of your group.

Once your staff is trained and perform for a reasonable amount of time, they should be coming to you with suggestions on how to improve the processes and methods used to get things done. You are concerned with their attitude, the level and quality of their activities, and their skill development. If they get stuck, you can help them figure out how to solve a problem. *You don't solve the problem for them.* You want to teach them "how to fish," as the saying goes, and not catch the fish for them. Those who show potential and are able to demonstrate they can work well with others, help others learn, and get results are your future managers.

As a manager, you want to be involved with your people so they can come to you with issues without hesitation. This is very different from having them rely on you to make decisions and say exactly what they should do and when they should do it. Your people will be happier and more productive when you reward them more for taking initiative, making decisions, and even making mistakes. Mistakes are one of the best ways to learn and grow.

Manager as Supporter

You were not hired to be a psychologist, but chances are, you'll find that people come to you with problems and you'll wish you *had* been trained to be a counselor. You are the emotional core and driver of your team. You are the one who needs to be looking and planning for the possibilities and solutions to all the problems you might face—business problems as well as people problems.

People, in reality, can be fragile. Your boss has entrusted you to take good care of the people who report to you. You need to be their advocate and their source of support when they need it.

The preferred way to offer support is to give your people the truth. When they're starting a new job, they need to be told what to do. To hire someone and not give them the proper training and guidance creates a major problem. As the manager, you are responsible for ensuring new employees get all the training and instruction they need so they can master their job. I've seen managers hire really sharp people and think they'll figure it all out by themselves. This is a very foolish way of thinking. Most people won't pick up things on their own without your guidance, and they also won't know the official, company way to do things.

Be sure you give thorough instruction and training to new people. One of the best ways to know if you have succeeded in this task is to personally observe their work and give them qualification tests. This isn't a negative or punitive measure; it's in everyone's best interests. When you test, be prepared to do more training if the level of understanding isn't where it needs to be. Your direct reports need to apply themselves, and if they don't, be sure you clearly tell them and document the conversation.

 MANAGER MINEFIELD

It's much easier to be tough at the beginning and lighten up when your team is performing at an acceptable level. Never start soft or easy. Your goal is not to win a popularity contest; you are a manager looking for results.

Being a supporter is a wonderful attribute. You want to believe in your people, and you want to be optimistic with the possibilities and their ability to achieve great things. You should constantly encourage them and give them sincere, truthful, and positive feedback. You ideally want to be their biggest fan.

As a supporter, you want to cover their position and their reputation within the company. You need to brag about your people. If they're not doing well enough to brag about them, tell them you're disappointed and ask how you can help them become better. If they don't want to become better, you are responsible for helping them move on to another company.

When a person comes to you with a personal problem—be it a marriage conflict, difficulties with children or relatives, or possibly even substance abuse—show empathy and concern. Remember, you are not a psychologist, nor are you or your company a charity. Your concern is to share human concern and then focus on what must be done at work. Refer the employee to human resources for problems that aren't directly work related. Many companies have insurance or special services to help employees with emotional-, physical-, psychological-, or drug-related needs. Educate yourself on what resources are available so you can share that information with your people when necessary.

Employment has to be a two-way street. Your people have to produce for you, and you need to protect, encourage, train, and develop their abilities by providing opportunities for them. Reward, support, and give new opportunities to your good people. Encourage and develop your less-than-satisfactory performers, and eliminate those who aren't able to rise to the needs of the job.

The Least You Need to Know

- You must be authentic and transparent to be a great manager.
- Value-driven leaders focus on using their values to make decisions, even if it costs more or isn't the same way others might do things.
- The primary goal of a political manager is to build a compromise between as many people as possible—sometimes at the expense of results or values.
- A results-driven leader will sometimes be willing to shortcut values and be controversial to gain the desired result.
- Use your strength as an expert, director, or empathetic manager with moderation. Avoid letting an overextension of your strengths become a weakness.

The Introverted Manager

Self-confidence is an acquired habit, not something you have or don't have from birth. Psychologists believe a great deal of our personality is genetic or inherited. They also believe we have the ability to mold and change our personality to some extent, but there's a huge debate about exactly which part of our personality is "nature" and which part is "nurture." Fundamentally, we are each given a set of attributes we can choose to use or not use. Every person is different and able to change in differing amounts.

When you compare introverts to extroverts, you'll find that self-confidence is not the determining factor. You're totally able to be an introvert and still be very self-confident. Likewise, you might be an extrovert and have very low confidence.

In this chapter, we explore the fine differences in several styles of behavior and how you can get the maximum benefit for your job as a manager, no matter if you're an introvert or extrovert.

In This Chapter

- Why you might feel uncomfortable
- Ways to overcome your fears and doubts
- Success as an introvert (or extrovert) manager
- The four fundamental behavioral styles
- The power of speaking softly

Some Discomfort Can Be a Good Thing

As a professional speaker for more than 30 years, I still get uncomfortable just before I'm about to give a presentation. I've been in front of groups and even on TV and radio since I was a child, yet I still get a bit edgy. My experience shows that it's good to be a bit on edge. If you're too comfortable, you might not try as hard nor will you do as well.

Have you noticed when you're in a strange or new situation that you get a bit uneasy? As I'm writing this, my mind has wandered back to how I felt the first time I took off in an RF-4C fighter aircraft in combat. That was a bit uncomfortable. But that was a good thing because it meant I tried very hard to do well and, therefore, I came back alive. Likewise, getting a new job with more responsibility and diving into uncharted or new territory can make anyone nervous. Embrace that feeling. It will actually help you do a good job.

> **LEADING THOUGHT**
>
> It is not the strongest or the most intelligent who will survive but those who can best manage change.
>
> —Charles Darwin

Last year, I had an opportunity to test myself in a very uncomfortable situation. I share this because the simple solution I used can work for you in the new, tight, unique, scary, and uncomfortable situations you might find yourself in.

A client, who became a friend and then years later a business partner in a marketing and technology company, called me one day and gave me an update on the condition of his wife, who was fighting multiple forms of cancer. Unfortunately, it wasn't looking good. There was a pause in the conversation and then he said, "Dave, Christine wants you to sing at her funeral."

I was stunned. At first I declined because I didn't think I could handle the emotions. They wanted a eulogy and a song—not easy to do for someone you really care about and have known for decades. But I finally agreed to do it, and it went fine.

Now here's the important part of the story for you: I arrived at the church more than an hour early; met the custodian; toured the facility; and checked out the stage, microphones, and acoustics. Then I sat alone in the front row (no one else had arrived yet), and rehearsed, visualized, and played through in my mind what I was going to say and sing. I also very deliberately relaxed my body and practiced slow and deep breathing until the service began.

I was first taught this lesson in pilot training. When a pilot gets in an emergency situation—missiles or antiaircraft fire, fire in flight, or failed landing gear—the normal human reaction is to begin to breathe rapidly and shallowly. This reaction, hyperventilation, actually depletes the oxygen to the brain, a condition known as hypoxia. For a pilot, this can be deadly. For you as a manager, it can cause you to make rash decisions, lose control of your emotions, or say something you might regret later.

Science has proven that you can control your nerves, emotions, and reactions. The single best way to get control is slow and deep breathing. This works in any kind of conflict, stress, or uncomfortable situation. When you feel uneasiness creeping in, stop, take a minute, and check your breathing. Breathe slowly and deeply several times before you do or say anything.

Please remember this in your role as manager. It will help you maintain control in all kinds of situations.

Overcoming Fears and Doubts

Courage is having fear and moving forward anyway. We all have fears and doubts, managers included. The courageous manager decides to tackle the daunting project; approach the difficult customer or employee; and with head held high, stand up to upper management. Sure, that's easy to think about, but how do you actually do it?

First think through the situation and all the possible outcomes. Then run through scenarios of what might happen and what would be the best course of action for each scenario.

This is a great time to share your concerns with others who you respect. I often run tough decisions by my wife or my son. In addition, over the years, I have nurtured many business associates who have vast and varied experience and who are willing to give me feedback and perspective. You likewise should cultivate people in your personal and business lives with whom you can interact as a mastermind group. You may be able to help them just like they help you. Plus, you'll likely develop some good friendships. The act of sharing and talking about your fears and anxieties is very healthy. You'll find that everyone has fears, and most will appreciate a safe environment in which to openly discuss those fears. Soon your mastermind group will become a nurturing support group.

Once you've defined all the different options of what might happen, rehearse and role-play your reactions to each possibility. Actually create a "what if" scenario, and practice your response—what you'll say and do and how you'll say and do it.

> **LEADING THOUGHT**
>
> I have learned over the years that when one's mind is made up, this diminishes fear; knowing what must be done does away with fear.
>
> —Rosa Parks

In Hollywood, stunt people spend days and weeks practicing a stunt, be it a car crash, a leap off a building, or a fight scene. They like to think of it as *managing* risk—not *taking* big risks, but rather *mitigating* the risk.

The only problem that will "get you" is the one you didn't anticipate; develop a plan for handling the risk; and practice, practice, practice for it.

Successful Introvert and Extrovert Managers

The debate rages on: is your personality from your natural gene pool, or is it developed from the nurturing of your environment and childhood? Whichever point of view you favor is fine. The good news is, you can become a great manager as an introvert or as an extrovert.

Anyone who has the willingness to learn, try, fail, and try again can master the keys to management. Remember, you learn more from your mistakes and failures than from your successes. And victory goes to those who persist and are resilient.

Your natural tendency might be to speak loudly and boldly, and if so, people probably think you're an extrovert. Or you might be more mild-mannered and speak softly. It doesn't matter what your natural behavioral style is; to become a great manager, I'm going to ask you to learn four new languages. (More on this in a minute.) You need not change your values nor your natural style. In fact, you even can keep your prejudices if you like. The key is that you learn to communicate and relate to people who are very different from you yet still stay true to your own beliefs and be authentic with everyone.

Have you ever travelled to a foreign land? A place where you don't speak the language? I have, and I've figured out a secret: if you try to speak the language, it's not only disarming to those you try to communicate with, it also often opens their hearts and minds and they'll sincerely try to relate to you. The secret is *you* set the tone and make an effort to relate to *them* on *their* turf, in *their* language.

For this to work, you have to be able to identify the different behavioral styles of different people. It's just like learning foreign languages (hence that reference earlier). Once you can identify the other person's "language" or behavioral style, you are better equipped to talk to and relate to them. Hippocrates, born in 460 B.C.E., was the first we know of who began to recognize and record these differences in people. Since then, our understanding has been refined a great deal.

You (and every one of us) have various amounts of each of the four behavioral styles in your normal way of relating to people. This isn't personality or deep psychology; it's simply the way you prefer to relate to others. Most people use one or two of the styles of behavior more than the others, while some focus mostly on a single style.

Let's look at each of the four behavioral styles:

> **D**   Directive and dominant
>
> **I**   Influencing and interested in people
>
> **S**   Steady and stable
>
> **C**   Competent and cautious

(The actual behaviors I describe in the following sections might be extreme or weak. It's a matter of degree.)

Directive and Dominant

Directive and dominant behavior is characterized by boldness. This behavior is also consistent with being an extrovert. D people want to be in control and will seek that control by telling others what to do—and even by forcing their view or opinion upon others.

You'll often hear D people say, "What's the bottom line?" They're often impatient, especially when they're presented with lots of details or when they're blocked from doing what they want to do, when they want to do it. At the extreme, they may be perceived as pushy and arrogant.

The following table shines a light on directive and dominant styles.

D Characteristics	Goals	Fears
Prefers to take control	Results	Losing control
Impatient	Control	Being taken advantage of
Action-oriented		
Bottom line/results focused		
Uses telling behaviors		

Influencing and Interested in People

Influencers are primarily interested in people and relationships. They tend to be very expressive and often exhibit lots of big smiles, emotion, and fun. They're often the life of the party.

I styles talk more than any of the other styles and are able to read others' emotions well. Because they love people, they can get very personal and intimate easily.

The following table offers more information on I people.

I Characteristics	Goals	Fears
Talkative	Recognition	Rejection
Outgoing	Approval	Social disapproval
People-oriented		
Enthusiastic		
Persuasive		

Steady and Stable

In any group of people, the majority are primarily S behavior types. S's enjoy being on a team and part of a group. They are family-oriented and seem to be mellow because they get along with other people easily, often trying to accommodate others.

These folks can be hesitant to act if they're not sure of the way to do something. They might wait to be told rather than take a risky chance.

The following table gives you further insight into S styles.

S Characteristics	Goals	Fears
Supportive	Stability	Sudden change
Easygoing	Security	Loss of security
Process-oriented		
Like people, relaxed		
Unemotional, low key		

Competent and Cautious

The competent behavioral style is also heavily interested in control. However, they use precision and rules to establish control over others. Their favorite slogan is, "a place for everything and everything in its place."

C's pride themselves on being accurate and competent. If they don't believe they can be outstanding at a task, they'll often decline to participate. They think in numbers, focus on what's correct and proper, and sometimes see things in black or white.

The following table explains more about C styles.

C Characteristics	Goals	Fears
Perfectionistic	Precision	Violation of rules
Cool and distant	Order	Criticism of performance
Fact-oriented		
Evaluates pros and cons		
Self-disciplined		

Which Style Is Best?

The easy answer to that question is, no single style is better if you want to be a manager.

SKILL BUILDER

People who favor D and I behavior styles tend to be extroverts, while those who favor S and C styles tend to be introverts.

Before they were bought by Carnival Cruise Lines, I conducted a captain's conference for Cunard Cruise Line for about 15 of their captains as well as another 15 or 20 executives from England and New York. I was surprised when all but one of the captains turned out to be S styles. The one captain who was a D unfortunately was released the next year because he didn't blend well with the cruise line management.

Nobody is just one style. The cruise line captains were mostly S styles. That really means they favored the S style but also had various amounts of the other three as well. We are all a combination of all four styles, each in varying degrees.

It takes practice to be able to recognize these four behavioral styles, but the reward is well worth the effort. Imagine if I understand, better than you do, what you fear and what your goals are. Also imagine I just met you and have figured this out by your facial expression, tone of voice, body language, and what you say and pay attention to as we get acquainted. This is entirely possible for you to do if you study this information and practice. (For more information, log on to DavidRohlander.com/assessments.)

Reading People

When you're able to identify peoples' preferred behavioral styles, you can better understand how to read them and relate to them in their preferred language. To do this, you don't have to change who you are, what you believe, or what you say. You merely need to adjust the *way* you say it.

It's easiest to talk in extremes, so let's look at each of the styles in the following sections using a hypothetical person who happens to be an extreme example. How do you quickly identify the style and then how do you relate to that person?

The D's

Extreme D behavior is pushy, impatient, domineering, and harsh. Recently, I was at a meeting and met an executive born and raised in New York City. His natural style fit this description perfectly. He and I were discussing how many people from that part of the world seem to have an "edge" in their style or behavior, and I could easily recognize it in him, as that's where I lived until I was 19 years old.

The best way to relate to what I like to call "flaming D's" is:

- Give direct answers.
- Focus on goals and outcomes.

- Ask "what" questions.

- Yield control.

- Be brief.

SKILL BUILDER

When first meeting a brash and bold D, it can be helpful not to engage as they try to establish their position. Instead, try just looking them in the eye with a calm and cool stare. It will unsettle them, and they'll probably try and make an attempt to soften up their approach.

The D is concerned with getting results and being in control, and they fear losing control or being exploited. When you give long and convoluted answers or responses, you drive them nuts. Cut to the chase, be short and sweet (forget the sweet), and if you're courageous, tell them what to do. Be bold with D's, and you'll be amazed how they'll back down and yield. Look them straight in the eye, and give a direct answer.

The I's

Extreme I people are a lot of fun to be with anytime … unless there's lots of work to do. I's would rather plan a party than work intensely for a long period of time. You can recognize extreme I's when you see someone who is undisciplined, manipulative, excitable, and vain.

Some of your best sales promoters have strong I behavior. Former president Bill Clinton is one such example. Watch his behavior, how he charms people, and the way he loves to talk, and you'll witness classic I behavior.

To relate to a "high I," try this:

- Be kind and friendly.

- Allow them to talk.

- Show the benefits of high risks.

- Give details in writing.

- Give genuine compliments.

> **SKILL BUILDER**
>
> When you see a smile, give a smile back; when you notice open arms, open your arms. A big smile and open arms will probably get you lots of hugs from high I's.

Above all else, high I's want you to love them. They'll sometimes be late to meetings and appointments—not because they don't care, but rather because they're so concerned with having a good relationship with the last person they were with, they ignore being on time. People matter more to I's than other things.

The S's

Extreme S behavior may be a surprise to you. Remember, the majority of people are primarily most comfortable with S behavior. A small percentage of people have extreme D and C behavior, so if you're one of them, you might perceive someone with extreme S behavior as insecure, conforming, possessive, and unsure.

With more than half the population mainly S style, it might be a good idea to treat most people you encounter as S's. Here's how:

- Be sincere and warm.

- Ask "how" questions.

- Be patient.

- Explain thoroughly.

- Minimize their risks.

> **SKILL BUILDER**
>
> Breathe slowly, smile gently, and listen when you're not sure what the other person's style is. Chances are, they're probably an S and will appreciate your pleasant demeanor.

Most people are concerned with being safe and secure. They also have a tendency to resist or get nervous with sudden change. As a manager, you need to be sure you explain things well, are patient, and treat your people with warmth and sincerity. They'll appreciate you when you act this way.

The other interesting thing is the D and I folks will let you know if they're frustrated or want a different approach. They have extrovert tendencies; the S is more of an introvert.

The C's

Extreme C behavior, like the extreme D's, can be a challenge. Both D's and C's want to be in control—the D's will say so and talk about it, while the C's will be more reserved. When they're offended or feel violated by another person, it might be a while before you realize it or reap the consequences. But they will get even, someday.

Strive to be accurate when dealing with a "high C" because they believe precision is important and a sign of your intelligence and ability. You'll see these behaviors in the extreme C person: critical, slow to decide, picky, and stuffy. You can take advantage of these strengths when you have a need in quality control or want things to be precise and accurate. For example, I work with a lot of accountants, and they almost always have high C tendencies. That's good if you want the books to balance!

You'll do best when you relate to high C's this way:

- Provide pros and cons.

- Use accurate facts.

- Show a step-by-step approach.

- Agree with specifics and disagree with facts.

- Avoid surprises.

SKILL BUILDER

Next time you're late and someone doesn't react, smile, or show displeasure with you, it could be you have a C in the room. Study them closely. Are they feeling disdain for having to meet with an incompetent? If you don't do what you say exactly, a high C will be quietly annoyed and try not to show it ... until later.

When you're having meetings and want to have everyone contribute, be sure the S and especially the C folks have time to prepare and think about the agenda. They both desire to be accurate and prepared and will refrain from participating if they're not confident with their point of view because they haven't had time to check and verify the information.

Hazards to Avoid

You can't control the way other people will perceive and react. As you relate to them, you need to be aware of potential hazards that may interfere with smooth communications.

The following table identifies hazards to avoid when relating to each of the four primary styles.

Style	Don't ...
D	Tell them what to do.
	Attack who they are.
I	Ignore or reject them.
	Give them negative feedback.
S	Rush or confuse them.
	Offer them high risks and competition.
C	Criticize their performance.
	Give them inaccurate information.

Speak Softly, and People Will Listen

Recently, I was coaching a senior executive and the conversation drifted to his personal life. He and his wife were having a difficult time with one child, a girl who got very emotional in public when she wasn't getting her way. It was frustrating and embarrassing for the parents.

We discussed it for a bit and then I offered a simple suggestion. I recommended the next time she started to act up, he take a deep breath and very deliberately look her straight in the eye and speak in a very soft and controlled voice. I told him to explain to her that her behavior was unacceptable and if she couldn't control herself, he would remove her from the restaurant/store/theater/etc. and wait in the car with her until the family finished their meal/shopping/the show/etc.

LEADING THOUGHT

Speak softly and carry a big stick.

–Theodore Roosevelt

This might be simple common sense, yet how often do you see parents losing control of their emotions or tone of voice when a child acts up in public? The same thing happens at work.

You are the manager. You are the boss. You do not need to yell, swagger, or demonstrate how powerful you are. You simply have to take a deep breath, look them straight in the eye, and explain how it is going to be. Period.

The Least You Need to Know

- Embrace the fear and discomfort you might feel, and use it to help you do your very best.
- To survive as a manager, you must develop the ability to adapt and improvise.
- Everyone is different because of unique past experiences. You need to spend time and effort getting to know your people's strengths and weaknesses.
- Study and learn to read people's behavioral style. When you know their goals and fears, you know how to communicate with them and lead them.
- When you use silence combined with direct eye contact, it can be very intense, so use it judiciously.

Getting to Know Your Employees

When you don't know someone well, it's easy not to trust them or to at least be suspicious of them. As a new manager, you are the stranger in town. And even if you worked with your team before as peers, they're going to be concerned about how you'll be as a manager. You need to set the right tone from your first day on the job.

First impressions are difficult to change, so it's important that they be good ones. The impression you have of your team will be based on your first impressions. The same is true of their impression of you. A person can form an opinion or impression of someone in as little as 7 seconds based on what they see, feel, and hear. People also have a tendency to prejudge others.

There are a few fundamental guidelines you need to honor immediately. Dress the part of manager. Be sure your clothes are clean, neat, and appropriate for the work environment. A well-groomed person creates a positive first impression. Remember also to smile, greet people in a pleasant tone, give a firm handshake, and look the people you're talking to in the eye. Carry yourself with good posture, and be polite. You only get respect when you first give respect.

In This Chapter

- Ways to understand your people
- Establishing standards and expectations
- Creating open and honest communications
- The importance of trust, respect, and loyalty
- Crafting agreements and commitment

I begin this chapter sharing this very basic information because my job of speaking and coaching puts me in front of many people, companies, and associations every month, and I continually see people who don't know how important these basics are—or just don't do them. I trust you know and already practice these basics, but if you don't, here's a reminder of how essential they are. Now let's move on to how you get to know your people.

Watching Their Behavior

People are going to tell you things, show you things, and try to persuade you. Be polite, listen well, and see what they want to share with you. This is all valuable.

However, the most important way you'll get to know your people is to watch their behavior. What really matters is what they do, not what they *say* they'll do. Do they show up on time? Do they help others with difficult tasks? Do they complete their jobs in a neat and orderly manner?

People who are high achievers perform. Some talk about what they're going to do and actually do it. Others talk about it but never get around to it—and often explain how it isn't their fault. Still others don't talk much; they just do their work.

You need to become a student of people and learn to read their behavior. This means paying attention to what they say and do as well as the way they say it, to whom they say it, when they say it, and why they say it. For example, when someone gives a someone else a compliment, do they say it in private to share appreciation for the good deed? Or do they say it in front of others, with a loud voice, to show off? Maybe they don't say anything complimentary to others. Perhaps they have a habit of catching people doing good things and compliments just naturally flow as a sincere comment. Become attuned to how your people behave, and begin to look for patterns.

Each one of us has unique habits and behavior patterns. Your job now is to observe, identify, and categorize the individuals on your team into patterns while identifying their strengths and weaknesses. First impressions are important, but even more important are the attributes you identify by observing their behavior patterns over time.

SKILL BUILDER

Remember that your people are watching your behavior, too. They might not be consciously observing and quantifying your behaviors as I recommend you do, but they are paying attention. Take time to reflect, plan, and be deliberate in the way you spend your time and manage your own behavior.

Setting Standards and Expectations

People always do their best when you have high expectations for them. It actually hurts their performance when you accept less and they sense you don't believe in them. One of the most valuable things you can do for your people is to believe in them and let them know you believe in them and are counting on them to perform well.

Your faith in their ability to perform needs to be grounded in reality, and that reality is established based on their past performance. This is one of the main reasons you want to measure performance. That measurement gives you the foundation for setting standards and expectations.

As a manager, you have a hidden power you need to use carefully—the ability to influence what people do simply by paying attention to the right things. If you want people to be on time for work, pay attention to when they arrive and let them know you're watching and are aware of when they come and go. If you want to increase production, pay attention to specific production results. Ask your people how many widgets they're putting out per hour. Later, come back and ask again. It's that simple and straightforward. What you're doing is "inspecting what you expect." If the rate is too low, show concern and interest by asking how you can help them improve and increase their production rate.

This communication process may reveal roadblocks or shortcomings in the system, the way resources are allocated, or unrealistic expectations. By working with your people on a common and clearly defined goal and desired result, you'll learn more about your people, the process, and what you can do to help them.

Also encourage your group to measure themselves on a daily basis. Each day, everyone needs to know if they have won or lost. If they don't make their numbers, they've lost. If they meet or exceed their numbers, they've won, so be sure to congratulate them.

I remember consulting with a rep from a large manufacturing company that sold all kinds of durable fabrics like canvas for outdoor awnings, shades, and sign materials. The company had an established group of salespeople who had been working there for many years. The pace they worked at was modest.

The company was interested in increasing sales, so it hired a new salesperson. He was young, sharp, and full of energy. Within 2 months, he was the lead salesperson. That might sound like a good thing, but eventually the other salespeople started to figure out ways to slow down the young tiger because he was rocking the boat of their modest pace. This can create a difficult situation for a manager. You need to be sure your people are producing well, even if, as in this case, you have a long-established group who are comfortable working the way they've been working for a while. Change can be a good thing, especially when it means a company creates profits.

 MANAGER MINEFIELD

Israel's Sea of Galilee is famous for its beauty and bounty of fish. Filled with water from mountains to the north, at the south end of the sea, the water spills into the Jordan River, where it travels more than 70 miles into the Dead Sea. Befitting its name, the Dead Sea—which is filled with the same water as the living Sea of Galilee—supports no fish or plant life. With no other outlet, and with an elevation that's the lowest point below sea level of anywhere on Earth, the Dead Sea's water is some of the saltiest on Earth. It's a stagnant, lifeless body. It's not healthy to have a stagnant company. A vibrant organization needs new people to join, grow, and move up or on to another opportunity.

Establishing Open and Honest Communication

You don't have to lie to be successful in business. No businessperson must lie to be successful. Instead, the easiest way to remember what you said, develop trust in your group, and earn the respect of your people is to have open and honest communication. It's important that your "yes" means "yes" and your "no" means "no."

When you have a sensitive matter that cannot be discussed yet or has confidential ramifications, it's okay to say "I'm not at liberty to discuss that now." Be courteous as you do, and explain that you appreciate the other person's understanding of your position. Then move on. Don't dwell on the subject or get into a conversation in which you try to rationalize your situation or explain all the extenuating circumstances.

As a manager, you have the responsibility to teach your people how to communicate well and at the same time be open and honest. Business has accepted mores and etiquette. Be careful not to interrupt even though you're the boss. Listen more than you talk to everyone. Address people by their name and avoid calling all people "guys." Generously say thank you when people are polite, helpful, or courteous. Use the magic word, *please*, rather than simply tell a person what to do. Use the word *I* as little as possible. This is especially true when you're giving a presentation or announcements. Or simply hold the door open for others (and not just women). You can never go wrong by being a little extra polite, respectful, and considerate.

SKILL BUILDER

Here's a short course in human relationships. The six most important words to remember are *I admit I made a mistake*. The five most important words are *You did a good job*. The four most important words are *What is your opinion?* The three most important words are *If you please*. The two most important words are *Thank you*. The most important word is *We*. The least important word is *I*.

Building Trust

Developing trust takes time and is not earned because of a title, reputation, or pedigree. For you and your people to trust each other, it's going to take some time working together, watching each other, and fulfilling commitments. You probably begin to trust people when they do what they say they'll do and have a tendency to get skeptical when they don't finish a project on time.

Are you encouraged when people keep the small commitments or promises they make, and do you get annoyed if they talk a good game but don't come through when needed? That's typically the same point of view for many other people. It's also how people often decide if they trust someone. Isn't it refreshing to know that if you just do what you say you're going to do, people will trust you? At least, it's a great place to start.

Open and honest communication means you share with your people, verbally and in writing, that you will do what you say you'll do and you expect the same from them. You need to ask them to hold you accountable to this standard and explain that you'll be holding them accountable for doing their part and doing what they say they will do. This is a very simple concept, but it's not easy. It will test the true integrity of you as a manager and your people as reliable and trustworthy.

I can't tell you how many times I've heard a manager say "I'll take care of it" … but then they don't. Somehow it seems to fall through the cracks. Imagine what this behavioral failure does to trust, or if a lack of follow-through is a clearly defined pattern of behavior. People will quickly figure out that the manager is a good talker but doesn't come through when a result is required. The best way to ensure this doesn't happen to you is to get into the habit of writing things down. By this, I mean write down *everything:* ideas, tasks, to-dos, conversations, plans, targets, commitments, and promises. If you need to act on it or remember it, write it down.

Every morning and every evening before you leave work, review what you've written down as well as your personal action plan. These two planning meetings with yourself must be non-negotiable. You must do them every day.

As a new manager, pay special attention to keeping your commitments to the little things. Be on time, end on time, answer calls promptly, and get people answers to concerns or questions promptly—ideally the same day. People will notice if you are prompt, efficient, and reliable because anymore, it can be an uncommon set of traits. You'll set yourself apart and above the competition if you're always on top of the details. If you deliberately strive to master the little things, the big things will take care of themselves, or at least become easier to fix.

The reason many managers don't have time to do the little things is because it's easy to ignore them, they don't have a habit of just doing it, and they spend immense amounts of time trying to get organized and fix the bigger problems. Big problems start out as little problems. They become big because when they were little ones and didn't seem important so they were overlooked or ignored.

SKILL BUILDER

When I was in the Air Force and stationed in Germany, we would fly to Turkey, Spain, or Libya periodically for gunnery and bombing training, typically in four-ship formation. When the weather was clear, we could fly in a very loose formation and then come in close if we entered clouds or weather. Fuel consumption was a big concern, and we discovered that if we stayed in close formation and made small corrections during the several hours' flight, we used much less fuel than if we flew loose and then needed increased power to get back together. This principle applies to management as well. Stay on top of the little things and manage for precision and consistency, and you'll get more done with less effort and time.

Giving Respect

Your people deserve respect, even when they don't perform up to standard. They deserve respect simply because respect is a part of human dignity. It's not something you give out to a few, to your favorites, or to those who happen to be well connected within the organization. *Everyone* deserves respect. It's a critical necessity to establish quality communication.

It's uncommon for people to truly give everyone respect, but you aren't a common manager. You're a high-quality, dignified, and respectful manager. It's not necessary for you to receive respect to give it. You are above such small and petty thinking.

Each little thing you do, say, or think reflects whether or not you respect another person. The tilt of your head, the gaze of your eyes, and the tone of your voice all send a signal of respect or disdain. People don't need an advanced degree to be able to read and understand your attitude toward them. It's intuitive, and you can't fake it.

It helps to show respect to others by monitoring your internal dialogue, your self-talk, what you say in your mind about others. One way to take control of and to begin managing your thoughts is by the use of *affirmations*.

> **DEFINITION**
>
> An **affirmation** is a positive statement made in the first person, present tense that declares a positive condition or belief. When repeated often on a regular basis, it can influence your mind-set. For example, "I visualize myself having a positive mental attitude, and I practice being that kind of person." Or "Every day, in every way, I am getting better and better." Some people use negative affirmations: "I just can't seem to figure anything out." The choice is yours. I hope you choose to be positive.

The single most important behavior you can use to show another person respect is to politely listen to them. Quality listening is not a passive activity. Practice *active* listening. This means you're engaged emotionally, your facial expression is attentive and receptive, you give slight head nods, and/or you voice short comments like "Oh," "I see," or "Tell me more."

By being engaged, you can come up with intelligent questions naturally. The quality of your questions will show the other person not only how well you listen, but also how much you care. If you have no questions, the other person probably will assume either you're not interested or you don't really care.

Inspiring Loyalty

Trust and respect lead to loyalty. You might be loyal to a person, an ideal, values, or an organization. The basis of loyalty is your personal values. Open and honest communications allow you to discuss values with your people and your superiors. When shared values are known and expressed, you build loyalty.

Loyalty is being faithful to commitments made between people. In your case as a manager, it means being faithful to the commitments you've made to your people and to your organization. These must be compatible. You can't make agreements with your people that aren't consistent with your commitments to the organization. By the same token, your people have to realize you have obligations to the organization. Your commitments can only be realized if your people are committed and loyal to you.

Loyalty to an individual does not mean you're required to compromise your commitments to the organization to be loyal to your friend or team member. All three—you, the team member, and the organization—need to be on the same track and have the same commitments.

Assume you have a friend and team member who is not producing at an acceptable level. You as manager are responsible to get production up. The team member is not producing. You owe it to the team member to explain that they must produce or there will be consequences. This might be a reduction in pay, a penalty, or possibly even getting fired.

You demonstrate loyalty to nonperforming team members by telling them the truth and exploring ways to help them fix their problem. This might include training, coaching, or an intervention where professional help is needed. You show loyalty to the organization by telling the employee their real status and demanding improvement. You really don't have any choice. People get a paycheck for producing.

You further show loyalty to the team member if they're ultimately fired and you personally make an effort to help them find a more appropriate job in another company. You might share referrals from your personal network or even give an honest yet helpful recommendation. Just because they didn't fit in your company doesn't mean they don't have certain talents. A different type of organization might benefit from that person's talents.

Loyalty means you don't gossip or tolerate gossip. It means you don't spread rumors or generate negative stories about your coworkers or the organization.

Creating Commitment

People ultimately do what they do for their own reasons. Each one of us does what we do to gain a benefit or avoid a loss. Your job as a manager is to discover what's unique about each person on your team, what their prime motivators are, and how best to help each individual align his or her personal motivators with the job or task they need to complete.

Making a commitment is a combination of a promise and an emotional decision. Be sure you clearly define the promise, and the other person has a clear understanding of it. Include specifics, measurement, target dates, and checkpoints along the way. For the emotional part of any commitment, it might take time and sharing explanations of the why and how of the commitment.

Learning how to make decisions is one of the most valuable lessons you can teach your people. The better they become as decision-makers, the easier your job will be and the better the results produced.

A helpful tool to use whenever you're making a decision or asking one of your people to make a commitment (which is also a decision), is a simple T chart. At the top of the chart, write one option and below that, write a + and a − sign on either side. Under the first option and the + sign, list all the positive factors and considerations you can think of if you do it. Under the − sign, list all the disadvantages or negative factors you can think of if you do it. Then do the same thing, on another T chart, for any other options you're considering.

A simple example would be making the decision to buy new software or not to buy new software, as illustrated by the following table.

Buy New Software		Keep Old Software	
+	−	+	−
Increase speed	Cost	No new expense	Slower speed
More capability	Training	No training	Limited capability
Apply to new markets	Unknown potential	Test before market expansion	Lose market share

The process of writing down all the ramifications of your decision or commitment helps clarify the impact and possible benefits gained. You also can use this technique to review the decision with other people to see what they think and help you be sure you're not missing an important consideration.

The beauty of this technique is that it's so simple, you can use it for big decisions as well as small ones you think of over lunch and use a napkin as your writing pad. You can also add numbers and put real costs and projections to start computer analytic approaches to get more complex and accurate results. The principle is what's important—identifying the pros and cons and knowing how to weigh or measure the options.

Many years ago, I used this simple approach to decide if I should leave a successful career with Merrill Lynch to start my own business. I created a T chart and shared it for review with several colleagues from Merrill Lynch, executives from other industries, and my wife, who was not concerned with the money but rather the impact on our relationship and family. That was the emotional side of my decision. Emotion is not something you can simply put in a computer program and measure with numbers.

In sales 101, you learn that all decisions have emotion as the trigger, and most of the time, decisions are based primarily on emotional considerations. I've been in sales for decades. What has always amused me is that very analytical people believe they make rational and logical decisions.

The reality is, the decision is made from an emotional trigger they might not even recognize and then they justify that emotional decision with lots of facts and figures.

Your role as a manager is to encourage your people to commit to helping you build a successful department, team, or company. Remember that the most important element in making a commitment is the emotional side of the decision. People commit to work with people they trust, respect, and with whom they have developed loyalty.

The Least You Need to Know

- Observe your people's behavior, so you'll have more insight into their real goals and motivators than what they say.
- Leadership is the art of influencing other people's behavior. The most impactful way to do this is by setting the example.
- Effective communication requires more than talent. It involves trust, respect, understanding, empathy, and resolution.
- Loyalty and commitment start with shared values and beliefs.
- Teaching your people how to make good decisions should be one of your major goals.

PART

2

Engaging and Retaining Your People

As a manager, you are as strong as the team you lead—no stronger. So it's in your best interests to help develop and make them stronger. The beauty of helping your people grow is that it helps you grow as well. Understanding their motivation is key to helping shape their—and your—future.

In Part 2, the focus is getting to know your people, from what you need to learn about them, to ways to uncover the necessary information to motivate them, and how to manage each individual, including different ways to handle performance evaluations, give feedback, and even reward people.

Remember, though, that one size does not fit all. In these chapters, you also learn about the many ways to see the differences among your staff. I explain how to work with those you easily relate to as well as those who seem to be very different from you because as a manager, you need to be able to communicate with, relate to, and motivate all kinds of people.

Bringing Out the Best in Your Team

Nobody intentionally plans on being a loser; we'd all prefer to be winners. And as a manager, you are in the business of helping your team members become winners. Part of the way you create winners is by believing in your people more than they believe in themselves. When you encourage people to win because you know and can see what they're capable of becoming, you help them achieve great things.

Economics includes the notion of *supply push* versus *demand pull marketing*. Much more success is available when you're able to create demand pull marketing rather than supply push. If you have lots of excess products to sell, you might be tempted to lower the price to entice people to buy. That's supply push. However, if people realize you're selling the best computer money can buy, and with lots of extras, customers will flock to your store or flood your website with requests. That's demand pull.

In This Chapter

- Understanding what drives people
- Tips on encouraging and giving direction
- Determining your goals
- Making the environment motivating
- Assembling a successful team

You want to create an environment in which people will flood you with requests to work on your team or in your department because it's the best place to work and you provide abundant opportunity for team members to grow, advance, and achieve great things. Big opportunity creates demand, and people will try with all their might to work with you. Remember, you are a winner, and you attract people who have winner behavior.

This chapter shows you how to create that environment.

Understanding Motivation

Some people think other people are lazy or unmotivated, but usually this isn't the case. Everyone is motivated to survive and live life as best they can. The problem is often they don't understand what they're actually capable of doing. When you see a person doing little or nothing, it's more a problem of their self-belief than lack of physical energy.

Behavioral scientists have studied *motivation* for many years, and many theories about motivation exist, ranging from economics, physiology, and psychology, to basic needs, hygiene, conscious, and even unconscious theories. I highly recommend you study the various theories. (Several are referenced in Appendix B.)

> **DEFINITION**
>
> **Motivation** is the reason why people do what they do, or their purpose to action.

As a manager, you need to keep in mind that all people are unique and no two are motivated by exactly the same thing. Also know that there's more to motivation than just money. Money is important, but it's not the ultimate motivator.

So if everyone is different, how do you motivate others?

Based on my experience, I believe it's safe to say you cannot motivate another person. Sure, you can force or coerce another person to do something, but that's not motivation; it's *manipulation*. Each person is responsible for his or her own attitude, and they're also responsible for their own motivation.

Your responsibility is to get to know your employees and help them determine what their motivators are, what their goals are, and how best to achieve those goals. It also is your responsibility to clearly understand your organization's goals and match your people, and their unique skills and motivators, with the organization's goals and objectives.

Let's look at an example. Many of my clients love the challenge of technology, computers, and programming, but they don't particularly care to deal with people primarily. I've actually had a CEO express the desire to have all his people replaced by computers—and he was only half kidding. This CEO needs someone else to manage his people because he doesn't care to get involved with the emotions and needs of his staff.

Other managers love working with people and get very frustrated by technology and computers. Of course, most people are a blend of desires and motivations, so it takes time and effort to work with different people and determine their strengths, weaknesses, preferences, and desires. The best way to learn about your group is by observing their behavior and scheduling periodic one-to-one meetings during which you can discuss these issues, work assignments, and performance.

Your work environment, organizational culture, and management style will set the tone and create a place where self-motivated people can thrive. It's tedious and frustrating to work in a situation where you have to continually prod and poke people to get things done. You need to weed out those workers who don't fit the environment you desire to create. Fundamentally, people strive to enjoy their work and get pleasure from it. If they don't enjoy the work and the people in the organization, let them go.

 MANAGER MINEFIELD

A worker is there to make your job easier. If he or she is continually causing stress and difficulties, they need to be released or reassigned.

People also work hard to avoid pain and eliminate negative consequences. They might not be in their dream position, but they need to work and are able to be positive and make a contribution. In time, and perhaps with the right manager, these people can be happy contributors to an organization.

Realize as you work with your people how different they are and how varied their personal backgrounds and life experiences have been. These differences shape their worldview. There's also no one simple thing that can motivate all people. Honor the differences in your staff, and learn to appreciate each person for his or her unique abilities and talents. The joy of managing is matching these unique people with specific tasks and teams to enable everyone to do better and achieve great things.

Giving Guidance and Direction

In Chapter 4, you learned how to appreciate the different behavioral styles and how to speak to each style in their own "language." Now let's examine what those conversations with people sound like as you guide and direct them.

Dr. Paul Hersey and his competitor, Dr. Ken Blanchard, both are advocates of a common-sense approach to leadership they call situational leadership. The two met many years ago at an Ohio university, and they worked together for several years before they decided to split and compete using the same leadership model. (See Appendix B for more information.) Their work, this simple model of how to become productive and profitable while working with others, is well worth your time to study. Let's review the concept.

As a manager, you have two basic forms of behavior to use with your workers: one is *task* behavior, and the other is *relationship* behavior. Task behavior is telling people the what, how, when, and where of doing tasks. Relationship behavior is listening, encouraging, clarifying, and giving emotional support.

Your responsibility is to read your staff's behavior and, based on their behavior while performing a task, determine their level of performance. Then you deliberately increase or decrease the amount of task or relationship behavior you use. The assumption is you give guidance based on the situation. If a person is new to a job, he or she probably doesn't know how to do it so they're unable of performing the job, or at least insecure at it. Therefore, most of your behavior should be in the form of telling or giving precise direction. There's little relationship behavior. I once had a boss who was fond of saying, "Spare us your genius until you have worked here at least six months."

As the person begins to develop confidence and starts to be productive, your behavior should transition more to selling them on their ability and explaining more about the job. This increases the mutual relationship behavior between manager and worker.

> **LEADING THOUGHT**
>
> Treat people as if they were what they ought to be and you help them to become what they are capable of being.
>
> —Johann Wolfgang von Goethe

The next phase of worker development, the situation, is when they are able to do the job, but they're still a bit insecure. You'll relate with your employee a lot during this time, working on problem-solving and also encouraging him or her. Your task-focused behavior lessens as your employee's performance improves.

The final phase is when the worker is competent and confident at his or her job. Now you can delegate to your employee and mostly observe and monitor his or her behavior. Both task and relationship behaviors are reduced.

Dr. Hersey believes leadership is any attempt to influence the behavior of another person. He sees management as working with and through others to accomplish organizational goals. I've worked with Dr. Hersey. He wrote the following note on the inside cover of my autographed copy of his book, *The Situational Leader.* It's a simple but pithy summary:

> David,
>
> READ THEM.
>
> LEAD THEM.
>
> SUCCEED WITH THEM.
>
> —Paul Hersey

Defining and Setting Goals

Goal-setting is one of the most powerful forces you can use to achieve remarkable results. The more clearly you define your goals, the higher the probability the goal will be accomplished. Everyone has goals; however, not everyone is deliberately managing his or her own goals.

A good way to illustrate this is to take an inventory of how you're spending your time and money. Measure your time in 15-minute increments, and keep track of each 15-minute block of time in your day for at least 2 or 3 days. Next, put all your expenses for a month on a spreadsheet. Cash, checks, credit cards, electronic payments—record everything you spend and then categorize the expenses. When you review the way you're spending your time and money, you'll get an indication of what your goals really are.

In business, goals are used to focus activity, increase productivity, and measure results. I'd like to share three operating principles with you and encourage you to use for yourself and when working with your team.

Write Down Your Goals

The process of writing down your goals helps you get clarity and allows you to edit and refine your goals. When you have written goals, you have a stronger sense of commitment to them. Plus, your goals document ensures you remember exactly what your goals are. If they're not worth writing down, they're probably not worth doing.

> **SKILL BUILDER**
>
> There's incredible power in writing. Writing can help you define and organize your thinking as well as help you remember what's important. Use a written journal to keep track of your completed goals. This will build your confidence and self-esteem.

State Your Goals in Positive Terms

When you set a goal in positive terms, you harness your imagination. A negative goal is usually based on willpower. Think about it: which is stronger, your willpower or your imagination? Clearly it's your imagination. That's why the best advertising stimulates your imagination—because it works. Have you ever seen a car ad or a vacation ad with unattractive people? Imagination works, so use it to set your goals in positive terms.

Share Your Goals

Goals are more powerful when they're shared with others, ideally displayed on a chart in plain sight.

Think how great it would be to walk around your office or shop floor and see at each workstation, a chart showing your employees' production. It could be a simple chart with three lines: a red line shows the minimum level they allow themselves to go to, a blue line shows the most likely level of production they need be at to hit the desired result, and a green line indicates a superstar productivity level in which they get into bonus territory.

This type of chart lets everyone know where they've been, where they are currently, and where they're going. This can heighten each employee's emotional intensity toward his or her goal. Every day, as they mark their own achievement before going home, they'll know if they are winning or losing.

SSMARTT Goals

SMART goals is a commonly used goal-setting model where S = specific, M = measurable, A = attainable, R = realistic, and T = timely. I believe this formula is best used with a few improvements. I think you should make your goals *SSMARTT*. Let me explain:

S = self   If everyone does what they do to gain a benefit or avoid a loss, it only makes sense that you need to know what the payoff is for you. No one will be highly motivated to achieve a goal they don't see some benefit in for themselves. Remember this when you ask someone to do something. If there's no benefit for them, they might not be all that excited to do it.

S = specific   Nothing becomes dynamic until it first becomes specific. Think of the diffused, probably fluorescent light in your office ceiling. Now compare that to another form of light, a laser. A laser has amazing power to cut, blind, shoot down missiles, and help surgeons perform the most delicate surgery. A laser is focused and specific light. Your goals need to be equally focused and specific.

M = measurable   If you can't measure it, you can't manage it. By definition, this requires numbers—be those numbers dollars, repetitions, pounds, cycles, units, time, distance, or units like inches, centimeters, or nanometers.

> **LEADING THOUGHT**
>
> When performance is measured, performance improves. When performance is measured and reported, the rate of improvement accelerates.
>
> —Thomas S. Monson

A = attainable   This has a lot to do with your belief. If you don't believe you can achieve a goal, it is, for all practical purposes, unattainable. Therefore, you must set goals that are attainable based on your beliefs. This is why it's so important to measure your goals. Once you achieve a small goal, you're better able to believe that if you set another goal a little bit higher, faster, or better, you can achieve that, too. You'll have a higher level of motivation and faith in achieving your next goal if you achieved your previous, measured, goal.

R = realistic   Realistic has everything to do with resources. Do you have the necessary resources to achieve your goal? In business as well as in your personal life, one of the main resources for goals relates to money and/or credit. If you want to buy a house, first you need to get your finances in order. In business, you must have sufficient cash flow to support debt. Resources can be money, education, training, skills, connections, square footage, research, equipment, or people.

T = tangible   This can be contrasted to *intangible*. An intangible goal might be to provide better customer service. This is a goal that's very worthwhile but must be converted to *tangible* elements so it can be measured, managed, and charted. Some possible tangible aspects of customer service might be the number of complaints, returns, broken goods, positive comments on a blog or Yelp, likes on Facebook, or referrals.

T = target date   Until you have a commitment to a deadline or target date, you just have a dream or fun idea. When you're ready to set a target date, you're ready to set your goal.

Goal-setting can be a lot of fun. Work with your people, and ask them to share their goals with each other. Bring a few people together, and have them help each other set goals that are positive and meet the SSMARTT formula. This is an opportunity to develop teamwork, and motivation is stimulated when people share their goals and help each other craft those goals.

Creating a Positive Environment

Have you ever walked into a room and felt the energy? All your senses are tuned when you're with a group of people; you can feel their energy. In my business, I am continually visiting new and different companies. I can feel the pulse by just walking into a company's lobby.

Recently, I had my first meeting with a new client, a major accounting firm in southern California. The receptionist was refined and friendly as she politely requested I sign in and asked who I was there to see. She then made a quick call and told me it would just be a minute. She offered me a seat in the lobby and asked if I would like some water. Mints sat on the counter, and a *Wall Street Journal* and a few other papers to read populated a table by several comfortable chairs.

A couple minutes later, the receptionist approached me and asked me to accompany her to the conference room where I would be meeting the firm's western regional manager. As we walked into the conference room, I saw a tray with water bottles, an ice bucket, and two glasses. I sat down, and in about a minute, the regional manager's assistant came in and introduced herself. She gave me one of her business cards and suggested I call her if I ever needed anything in the future.

After the meeting with the regional manager, I had to wait a few minutes for the receptionist to return to her desk. While I waited, two different partners in the firm happen to walk through the lobby and noticed me. They both stopped and asked if I needed any assistance. This accounting firm's staff demonstrated a class act from start to finish.

When people visit your company, are they equally impressed with the tone, feeling, and courtesy of your organization? You have the power to create whatever type of culture you want. Is it important to you and your company?

LEADING THOUGHT

Be the change that you wish to see in the world.

—Mahatma Gandhi

When you think about it, most people spend a large amount of their time at work. Sure, they spend time at home, too, but 7 or 8 hours of that time is dedicated to sleeping. Your daily work environment is the reality of how you and your people spend a major part of life. Make it worthwhile and as accommodating as possible.

The best way for you to influence your environment is by your own behavior. Are you neat, courteous, organized, and conscious of how you affect other people? If you behave in a dignified, respectful, and considerate manner, others will follow your example. If you listen well, are thoughtful, and focus on the organization's goals with passion, others will fall in with you. That's the power you have as a manager.

Building a Successful Team

A chain is as strong as its weakest link. A team—whether it's an in-house production team, a group of vendors, or people from other departments—is dependent on the quality and reliability of each member. The higher the quality of each individual, the stronger the potential for the team itself.

Each person on a team brings his or her own set of values, prejudices, and talents to the group. Some are strong D's who want to get control and do it now. Others are strong C's who want everything to be accurate, on time, and in order. You'll have people who are more politically oriented and some who believe values must be preeminent. Talents come in many forms and shapes, too. You might have an IT expert as well as someone who is stellar at customer service. As the manager, you need to respect and understand all these unique individuals and bring them together like strands of a rope. Weave them all together, and you'll have a strong team. Then you can focus them all on the same goal.

Getting everyone on the same page and focused on one common goal is best done by starting with open discussion and then leading all to agree on the team's operating principles. Do this right at the beginning of the team's formation. Write down the operating principles, and focus them on the behaviors all team members agree are appropriate. For example, one principle might be "One person will talk at a time while others listen." Some teams use a talking stick to get this habit ingrained, and you can only talk if you have the talking stick. If you want to say something, you raise your hand and request the talking stick.

Other examples might be punctuality, meeting minutes, procedures for follow-up, and a system of measurements. By posting these agreements in team meetings, you are able to bring everyone's attention to the agreed-upon principles when things get out of hand rather than having to confront or point out an individual. A simple comment like "Let's stick to our agreement" while pointing to the list on the wall can work magic. Try it.

> **SKILL BUILDER**
>
> In 1965, psychologist Bruce Tuckman came up with a clever way to describe the evolution of a team: Forming—Storming—Norming—Performing—Adjourning. You'll probably be able to identify with each stage of this evolution. Realize this is a normal process, and it'll help you adjust and adapt.

An effective team is a cohesive unit composed of diverse individuals. To get the best results, think of your team as your critical co-workers and also as your customers and vendors. In each of these groups, evaluate three considerations:

- Diversity

- Cooperation

- Effectiveness

Let's look at each in a little more detail.

Diversity

There's a natural human tendency to like people who are the same as you are. An outgoing person enjoys other expressive people, and a reserved person is more comfortable with another low-key person. If this tendency is taken to an extreme, it potentially can cause imbalance and weakness for your team.

The same principle applies to technical skills. A research department might focus on scientific knowledge, yet people skills, namely persuasion, might be necessary to acquire funding from the finance department. The best team has a balance of styles, skills, and talents. A good manager will evaluate the strengths of the whole team and hire or train people to supplement any weakness.

With diversity comes possible misunderstanding. Therefore, it's important to ferret out and address problems on a timely basis. Keep communication lines open. Regular contact with customers, even when there are problems, minimizes the depth of problems. Frequent short discussions with co-workers are also necessary.

As you strive to build a diverse team, evaluate your members based on objective results. How much business do you do with each customer? Which vendors deliver on time? What's the actual sales volume of each salesperson? Subjective measures like golf scores, friendships, and images are comfortable but not appropriate for most business decisions.

Cooperation

Along with diversity, you also need to make deliberate effort to have cooperation. Consider these two aspects: willingness and ability. Both are necessary, but they're achieved by different means.

Willingness is primarily an attitudinal factor. As the manager of a team, you can influence the willingness of others. However, this is primarily the responsibility of each individual. You are responsible for your own attitude.

Abilities can more easily be taught. Ability is usually related to skills. With training, an individual can improve his or her ability. This tends to improve their attitude by increasing their self-confidence.

You primarily control the training element as a manager, which influences the attitude element. By observation and good listening, you will be able to identify problems and determine whether the problems are related to willingness or ability.

SKILL BUILDER

Ability is something you can train; willingness is something you hire for. Find the positive, energetic, and willing person.

Effectiveness

You have the responsibility of providing the vision for your team. Organizational goals are more important than narrow departmental goals. You'll be most effective by pushing decisions down the organization as you encourage individual initiative. Organize chaotic situations by using your human relations skills, as outlined in Chapter 4.

An effective worker has a clear understanding of high-payoff activities and does them. The efficient individual does the right things, and does them very well. Make a valuable contribution to the team by clarifying exactly which activities are most important to ensure the desired result is accomplished.

Think of yourself as an orchestra conductor. The conductor determines the score, or the sheet of music, that will be played. He or she then calls upon each instrument—violin, cello, trumpet, drums, etc.—to come in and be silent on cue. The conductor does not play an instrument. Rather, they direct others who actually play the instruments.

You are the manager; the leader of the team; the conductor. You don't play an instrument. Instead, you lead and give direction to the members of your team. You are responsible for the score, for keeping everyone in rhythm, and for ensuring everyone is in the same key. Together, you all make beautiful music.

The Least You Need to Know

- Each person is motivated by different things, and not always just money. Be sure to look for the emotional motivators in people.
- Workers need varying amounts of task and relationship guidance depending on how competent and confident they are in their job.
- Goals need to be written, stated positively, and clearly provide a benefit to the individual.
- The most effective teams are diverse, have clearly defined operating agreements, and are focused on one unifying goal.
- Continually evaluate if everyone on your team is focused on doing high-payoff goals, and work with them if they're not.

CHAPTER 7

Effective Performance Management

Giving your people useful, effective feedback is a one way to guide them, stimulate them to higher achievement, and reward them for their efforts. The performance management process needs to be deliberate, creatively implemented, and a consistent element in your everyday interaction with your people.

A practical way to organize your quality performance management is to get a notebook, file system, or computer program in which to keep track. You should have a section for each key person in which you can take notes, keep schedules, and record comments received from others.

As you read books and magazines, go to seminars, and come up with good ideas, keep a section in your notebook or file to store the information you consider most valuable so you can easily review and use it during your personal planning time. One of the inevitable results of being a manager is that your mind will always be thinking of your people and how to help them improve. A performance notebook or file is a great place to keep all these ideas organized and in one place for future use. (Note that this is different from your files and records required by human resources, by the government, or for disciplinary means.)

In This Chapter

- Satisfied employees are high performers
- Developing the one-to-one habit
- Formal performance evaluations
- Providing frequent feedback
- Sharing meaningful rewards

In this chapter, I give you ideas and practical tools you can use with your people to supplement your thinking and design practical performance management procedures.

The Satisfaction Value Chain

Recently I had my car repaired after a minor collision. The body shop manager did a masterful job of providing good customer service. He sent me periodic status emails and called to let me know how it was going. After I picked up my car, I experienced a minor problem with the engine. I stopped by the shop again, and the manager went with me to my car's dealership, ensured it was taken care of, provided a rental car, and was charming and efficient until everything was perfect. I'm happy to refer his body shop to anyone because they did such a great job.

> **SKILL BUILDER**
>
> There's no higher form of flattery in business than to give a person or a company a referral. Getting referrals is also the wisest and least-expensive way to market your products and services. Referrals are earned by delivering quality.

During this process, the manager and I had several occasions to chat. He's a happy family man, enjoys his work, and believes he works for a quality company. When an employee is happy at home and at work, it's much easier for them to be productive and provide good customer service. Happy employees beget happy customers.

Take Care of Your People

When I was flying U.S. Air Force fighters in Europe, I had occasion to serve on temporary maneuvers with an Army tank unit, and I learned a fundamental lesson from the Army company commander. At chow time, he and I didn't even consider eating or sitting down until all the troops were served their food and provided for. Only then did we get our food. As a manager, you must realize that your first responsibility is to be sure your people are well taken care of.

I highly recommend you take a holistic approach when caring for your people. When a person is suffering from a personal problem such as health issues, marriage difficulties, child learning or discipline problems, or other issues, it can be very difficult for them to function as a high achiever at work.

When a person is under severe stress, they might resort to blaming their job, management, or the company and shift blame from their personal situation. Or they might seek restitution by filing for worker's compensation or take other legal action to resolve their personal issues. This possibility requires that you stay well informed on legal matters.

Be careful how you interact with employees—especially how you approach an employee with performance issues. This doesn't necessitate you being uncaring or void of compassion. You're a manager, and your concern is to have your people be productive. If they all have a positive attitude and the ability to perform in a productive manner, the output will be higher. And that's your goal.

Maintain Your Value Chain

There's a connection between the culture, values, and behaviors of a company's board of directors to the CEO and executive suite through each level of management and all the way to the front-line employee. It's almost like having a string joining a strand of beads—everyone is connected. The attitude and values of the top people affect the whole organization. You are part of that chain. Your responsibility is to instill in your people the caring, behavior, and values of the organization.

When management believes employees are valuable, they take good care of those employees. When employees feel well cared for, they want to take care of each other and the customer well. This is a value chain that needs continual nourishment to remain vibrant.

LEADING THOUGHT

No company, small or large, can win over the long run without energized employees who believe in the mission and understand how to achieve it.

—Jack Welch

There are three things you can do to be sure your value chain stays healthy:

1. On a daily basis, observe how you and others on your team treat each other. Are you all courteous, caring, and thoughtful?

2. Periodically request formal and informal feedback from your people on how they're doing, how they're feeling, and what they're looking forward to in the future.

3. Continually review results and trends. Are people producing at a high level and growing?

As you do these three things, use this formula to determine where you and your people are strong and where you have weak spots:

Attitude + activities + skills = results

It's difficult to measure and influence attitude; however, it's the most important of the elements in the formula. Each person is responsible for his or her own attitude. The real indicator of how good the attitude is is that person's results.

Activities are easy to measure and should be boiled down to key function indicators (KFIs), those critical things that indicate what the results will be. These are the must-be-done things.

Skills are learned over time. They're very important and require the right attitude and activities to be used effectively. A person with great skills is useless if they're not providing a positive attitude and doing the right activities.

If a person has a positive attitude, does the right activities, and is continually improving his or her skill level, you will see results. If any of the key elements are missing, you won't get results. This simple formula is a great test when you're trying to coach or guide a worker to improve.

One-to-One Meetings

If you want to help someone grow and improve, developing the habit of holding quality, one-to-one meetings is invaluable. These meetings are specific, personal, and have a strong emotional commitment component. Plus, you'll derive great pleasure and dramatically improve your own learning curve by being involved with another person at this level.

I recommend you have periodic one-to-one meetings with your direct reports. How periodic your meetings are could depend, in part, on how many people you have on your team. Ideally, a manager has around five to seven direct reports, but this number can vary depending on the size of your organization and the type of work you do. (For example, my editor has three direct reports, and I'm currently working with a senior vice president of a major distribution company who has twelve managers who report to him.)

SKILL BUILDER

Develop the habit of having one-to-one meetings consistently with your direct reports. This is the ultimate cornerstone habit that will dramatically improve your organizational culture. Encourage all other managers in the company to hold these meetings as well.

Try to meet for about $\frac{1}{2}$ hour every 2 to 4 weeks. Even a busy executive can carve out 30 minutes three or four times a week and have quality one-to-one meetings with several people if they're scheduled at the rate of one meeting per person per month.

The purpose of a one-to-one meeting is to help the other person grow, understand the big picture, receive and accept feedback, and increase the level of performance and commitment. A typical agenda might look something like this:

> **Welcome and review**   Greet and discuss the biggest win since last meeting.
>
> **Business status**   Performance—KFIs, team concerns, opportunities, culture, organizational goals.
>
> **Personal status**   Health, significant others, leisure pursuits, life balance, education— continual learning.
>
> **30-day plan**   Most important goals, review of the plan, roadblocks, what success will look like.
>
> **Review**   Status of previous goals, progress on annual plan, ideas and concerns, next meeting schedule as well as future commitments.

During these meetings, you want to be the mentor or coach. Focus not only on performance but also on correcting mistakes. In addition, attempt to help, encourage, and guide the person to future success.

Your employee should do 70 percent or more of the talking during the one-to-one meeting. Resist the temptation to lecture, educate, or push. Ask open-ended questions, seek to understand why they're doing whatever it is they're doing, and guide by your questions rather than by telling them what to do. Your goal is to help the other person expand their thinking to see the big picture. They'll gradually learn how to process problems and develop better decision-making ability. If you just provide answers, you limit their ability to grow.

Your people will treasure this time they get to spend with you. This is especially true if you show trust and respect for who they are. This meeting should be an honor and something that's reserved for people who are highly motivated. Those who are not included should crave the opportunity to meet with you. It's not something that should be forced or used as punishment or an obligation because they're not achieving at an acceptable level.

The ineffective manager spends lots of time trying to persuade and encourage low-performing workers. This is a mistake. Instead, send them to training or counseling. Your job is to pick out the winners, the high achievers, and help them soar to new heights. People who are either unwilling or unable to learn and grow need to be terminated or moved to another position.

Provide a learning environment with opportunities for those who want to improve to learn and become better trained. It's all a matter of acquiring and keeping the right people and getting rid of poor performers.

SKILL BUILDER

Former CEO of General Electric (GE) for 30 years, Jack Welch had the right idea: each year he eliminated the bottom 10 percent of his staff. He also gave bonuses to the top 20 percent. The rest of the people were considered the vital 70 percent. Under his leadership, GE had record profits.

Crafting Effective Performance Appraisals

Many companies have a formalized appraisal process once a year. This is good to do, but for an evaluation to provide the most benefit, it should be part of a comprehensive and continual appraisal process.

As an Air Force officer, I was evaluated using Officer Effectiveness Reports, or OERs. My immediate supervisor conducted these reports at least twice a year with rating factors including knowledge of duties, performance of duties, effectiveness in working with others, leadership characteristics, judgment, adaptability, use of resources, writing ability, and oral expression. The Air Force also rated military qualities and overall effectiveness.

In addition to OERs, we had frequent and continual tests and evaluations involving flying, operational readiness, and weapons. After virtually every flight, we would have a debrief and evaluation of everything we did during the flight. The Air Force believes in, and practices, continuous improvement. I recommend you do the same.

The Benefits of Appraisals

Performance appraisals are important to individuals because they provide specific feedback on their performance from their supervisor, manager, and peers. This gives the person an indication of how well they're aligned with the company's goals and culture. It also provides input on where they stand relative to management's expectations, promotion opportunities, and rewards. This information can be used to make adjustments in behavior and improvements in knowledge and performance, as well as let them know where they're under- or overachieving.

Formal appraisals are useful for management to evaluate how well an employee is performing toward the company's goals. An appraisal also ranks employees relative to their peers and identifies areas where more training or assistance is needed. Additionally, accurate appraisals are a valuable record if there are legal issues relative to an employee and labor laws. All this is helpful in deciding who to promote, reassign, or invest more time and money in for personal or professional development.

Clearly defined expectations are necessary to give credibility to any appraisal. You must establish standards and clearly communicate them to all your people for each of their jobs before you can rank or appraise them.

MANAGER MINEFIELD

When doing an appraisal, be sure to remain objective and use specific numbers. Focus on trends and the entire time period under review, and don't obsess on one incident, either positive or negative. Base your remarks on job performance, not popularity, personal preferences, or a single recent event. Avoid limiting your thoughts to first impressions because people can grow and improve.

What to Measure

When I was chairman and CEO of a marketing and technology company, we developed an internet algorithm that measured the actual level of a manufacturer's performance based on quality, price, responsiveness, and delivery and culled from numbers of deliveries and responses from many customers. As a company established a record, it became obvious that they could put a cost on poor quality, low responsiveness, or tardy delivery. They had to lower their price if any of the other three components were inadequate.

You can use the same concept as a manager. When an employee delivers for you and the company, they can earn a raise or reward. If they don't deliver, by rights, their income should be lowered or they should be terminated. The other, and preferable, option for them is to choose to improve. An appraisal well done will clearly show them this concept.

Let me share a few examples from various fields:

Production goals—output/results:

- A partner in an accounting organization is required to produce a specific dollar amount of revenue.

- A supervisor in a maintenance company needs to run a certain amount of volume with a specific profit margin.

- A manufacturing firm requires machine operators to produce a set volume of parts with certain tolerances and rejection rates.

Personal achievement goals—development:

- A teacher, attorney, or accountant may have educational requirements.

- Executives often are required to participate in community organizations to enhance the company's brand and social footprint.

- Health and life balance relate to company insurance costs, attendance, longevity, and reputation or brand.

Task goals—activities/projects:

- Administrative workers need to collect receivables, make payables, answer the phone promptly, keep records accurate and up to date, respond to customer requests, etc.

- Supervisors might need to lead or participate in a development, training, or technology project or new implementation within budget.

- Salespeople need to network, make calls, close deals, and provide good customer service. The best test of this is to monitor the number of referrals a salesperson gets.

The Importance of Feedback

For several decades, I have been involved in sales—first in the securities and investment business; then in real estate; and finally in consulting, speaking, coaching, and training—and I have trained hundreds of salespeople. A habit I instilled in all of them was to favor team selling and after every appointment, to stop for a minute in the parking lot or grab a cup of coffee and debrief the appointment together. Talk about what went well, what mistakes were made, and how can you improve the process and your technique in the future. Then make specific commitments and write them down.

This should become part of your culture. Everyone can do this type of feedback for all encounters and tasks, not just people in sales. Always seek feedback from all involved to help shape and develop continual improvement. If everyone does this all the time, it actually becomes a fun and desirable way to conduct business and work with your colleagues.

SKILL BUILDER

Feedback is the breakfast of champions!

Another way to think about performance appraisal relates to one of the biggest time-wasters in most companies—meetings. Every meeting should contain a time to provide feedback. Before anyone leaves the room, draw two columns on a flip chart or white board. In one column, write down the pluses, or what was good and productive, in the meeting. In the second column, write specific suggestions for changes to improve any deficient areas of the meeting. You'll find that by using this feedback method, the group will start to monitor each other during meetings. They'll develop a desire to improve the way meetings are conducted as well as discipline their own behavior. Your team also will appreciate the opportunity to give feedback and influence the way meetings are conducted in the future.

Performance appraisals are a good complement to your habit of having one-to-one meetings with your key reports. The appraisal process is focused on other people giving objective feedback to the employee. The one-to-one meetings emphasize developing plans, attitudes, and solutions to help the individual achieve his or her own personal and organizational goals. The notebook or file I discussed at the beginning of this chapter helps you keep track while you grow and develop your employees. The formal performance appraisal gives you another perspective on how to assist your employees desiring to improve.

Rewarding for High Achievement

Rewards are meant to be given for work or achievements accomplished. They can act as an incentive, a thank you, a way to highlight and celebrate special effort. The more creative you are in designing a reward program, the greater the positive impact.

One of the most powerful rewards you can share costs nothing. It's the simple and sincere "thank you." While you're managing by walking around, look for people who are doing things right or giving extra or special effort. When you see such people, make a big deal of it. Take a minute to do a mini-celebration and say a simple thank you. It's okay to let other people in the area hear you and see what you're doing.

Many managers have a unique something they give out when someone does something noteworthy. David Novak, CEO of Yum Brands, gives out a small toy, chattering and walking teeth, to his people who are walking the talk of the company values. Military commanders give out a challenge coin that has the unit's motto and symbol engraved on each side. Others give out ribbons, pins, or hats. Be creative and consistent with the culture and values of your company and department when choosing your reward. This simple gesture will build loyalty and enthusiasm. And those folks who haven't yet earned a gift will strive to figure out how they can get one by working to be part of the team.

You also need to be deliberate with your time. There are few things more valuable that you can share with another person, so don't waste this precious asset. As a manager, you will want to invest quality time with your key people, but they need to earn the right to spend time with you. This isn't something to take lightly. Your first priority is to allocate the proper amount of time to plan and structure how *you* are going to use *your* allotted time. As you prioritize your week, remember that you want to invest in your high achievers, work on plans for improving results, and plan how you're going to shape and conquer the future. This includes what rewards you'll give to those who help you achieve the goals.

MANAGER MINEFIELD

The highest reward you can give another is to share your time. But don't waste it. Be sure you give yourself your own time first, before anyone else.

There's real strength in having a can-do mind-set and acting as if the goals are inevitable. When you meet with your key people, ask them to help you plan how you'll achieve your team or company's goals and also include their feedback on how you're going to reward those who help. Specifically ask what you expect them to do and what and how the rewards will be a part of the plan.

Discard the idea of an "employee of the week." That becomes trite and useless because in short order, people start to make jokes about how they're selected and who's next. Rewards need to directly tied to significant achievement that's measured and takes effort to achieve. Just showing up to work five days a week is not worth a reward.

Instead, create special projects or tasks that go beyond the norm, and reward that achievement. Connect the projects with specific results that align directly with your company's overall goals.

I recommend a five-level appraisal structure for measuring achievement and, therefore, rewards:

Level 1 Unsatisfactory

Level 2 Less than expected

Level 3 Meets expectation

Level 4 Exceeds expectation

Level 5 Consistently exceeds expectation

Be a manager who is always a level 5, consistently exceeding expectation to your manager and also to your own staff. Get involved in the company's objectives and goals, figure out how you and your people can anticipate what will be needed, and achieve great things before anyone else. Real success is more about working *smart* than working *hard*. As a manager, your hardest work effort needs to be in your thinking processes. Continually ask yourself who, what, why, when, where, and why not. Become a possibility thinker—if we did *X,* what would happen? If we did *Y,* what would happen? There's great power in asking questions, especially when you're asking them of yourself.

Reward people for their thinking, and they will think. A friend of mine, Frank Maguire, was senior vice president of FedEx at the beginning of the company's life. He loved to tell the story of conducting some focus groups to try to discover exactly what customers wanted. They were having trouble building the market and were trying to clarify their mission. During one of the focus groups, a New Jersey airplane mechanic made a comment: "absolutely, positively overnight." That simple comment became FedEx's slogan, "When it absolutely, positively has to be there overnight!"

The best part of the story is when Frank explained how FedEx said thank you and rewarded the mechanic who helped them dramatically change the FedEx game and produce remarkable profits with his "absolutely, positively overnight" idea. Frank personally went to New York City and took the mechanic and his wife out to dinner at a fancy restaurant. During dinner, while the husband went to the restroom, Frank and the mechanic's wife talked about their children, and she mentioned how expensive college was going to be. Frank then explained that in appreciation for the value of her husband's idea, FedEx was going to pay for college for each of their children.

Frank attended each graduation.

The Least You Need to Know

- Feedback is a way to catch people doing something right. Praise them in public, and reprimand them in private.
- Activities are the easiest thing to measure, but attitude is the most important. Remember, attitude + activities + skills = results.
- The best reason for a meeting is to debate and share ideas. Don't let your meetings become an expensive waste of time.
- Make annual appraisals part of a comprehensive continual feedback system. Eliminate review surprises by providing frequent feedback and measurement.
- One of the most important rewards you can give an employee is your time.

Developing Your Talent

You'll grow as a manager in direct correlation to how well you grow your people. Your job no longer depends on you being super productive at performing tasks; now it's how well you can develop your people into being top producers.

Growing people is just like growing a garden. You need to prepare the soil, plant good seed, water and fertilize your crop, pull out the weeds, nurture and trim your plants, and know when to harvest. It's actually a lot of fun and can be very rewarding.

In this chapter, I teach you how to identify your people based on their talent and contribution to the organization. Then I give you a host of ideas on how to develop and nurture each of your direct reports' talent and skills. As a manager, you also play the role of coach and mentor. There's a difference between coaching and mentoring, and I clearly define that distinction in these pages.

In This Chapter

- Identifying high potentials
- Ways to nurture budding talent
- Coaching from the sidelines
- Mentoring that means something

You're about to discover the primary difference between being a manager and being a person who only produces individually with no responsibility for others also producing results. This requires more than a mind-set change; it requires a new awareness and skill set.

Categorizing Performance

Jack Welch, former chairman and CEO of General Electric for 20 years, divided his employees into three categories: top producers (20 percent), vital workers (70 percent), and low performers (10 percent). He developed the nickname of *Neutron Jack* because of his lack of empathy and his proclivity to fire people. Over time, the growth of GE under his leadership was remarkable. Welch also insisted his company be a leader, number one or two, in any segment it participated in or else leave the market. As a chemical engineer of small stature (5 foot, 7 inches), he was small but mighty and focused on the numbers.

When I worked at Merrill Lynch, we used a quintile system, in which everyone was ranked based on commission dollars into one of five groups, each representing 20 percent of the total group. The first quintile was the place to be.

Initially, I was rated only with my entry class and same year, but as time went by, the range was adjusted to groups of years—1 to 3 years, 4 to 7 years, etc. The size of each group got smaller and smaller over the years as people quit or were fired. This meant it became more and more difficult to stay in the first quintile. It also meant that the quantity of production that got you in the first quintile when you first started wasn't sufficient to keep you out of the fourth or fifth quintile after a few years. Obviously, this was a strong incentive to encourage continuous improvement.

SKILL BUILDER

I encourage the use of open-book management, wherein you share with your people the performance numbers and results in units, dollars and cents, profits, profit margins, and numbers comparative to other departments and companies. Educate your team on how to read the numbers, and they'll try harder to improve them. And in time, they'll help figure out ways to boost the numbers even more. People want to be involved.

The easiest way to evaluate and identify talented people is by simple, straightforward performance numbers—how much did they produce, measured in units, dollars, customers, market share, or whatever is most appropriate to your business? As a manager, two of your own key measurements of success are going to be (1) whether you attract and keep the top, talented people, and (2) how many leaders you produce. You'll also be measured on the productivity of your unit, team, or department.

Improve Efficiency and Effectiveness

Pure production can be measured well with various computer programs or evaluation tools or by collecting statistical input. Ideally, these numbers are displayed on a chart that's posted out in the open and updated by the individual responsible for the production. This is very useful when you're focused on tasks or units, such as in a manufacturing production line. Even more interesting is the process of measuring run rates, setups, changeovers, machine failures, and downtime for breaks and cleanup. As a manager, you're always looking for ways to improve efficiency and effectiveness.

Modern Postcard in Carlsbad, California, has a 75,000 square-foot facility and is currently in expansion mode. The company has managed to automate printing and yet maintain the highest quality of their products. Management spends a great deal of time figuring out how to combine runs and develop efficiencies while at the same time deliver high customer satisfaction. The company now has highly-trained artists and designers communicating with customers to develop mailers and marketing programs. Modern is a good example of management really studying production and making it effective and efficient while increasing the connection with customers.

The company began in 1976 by Steve Hoffman, a photographer. As his business grew, he joined forces with a designer, Jim Toya-Brown, and they started printing postcard products in small runs. Photography, design, and printing are all tasks originally done by individual producers. Ideas from management created a company that combines these tasks efficiently and effectively while focusing on the big picture—growing their customers' marketing ability to generate sales.

Watch Individuals

You'll observe people who focus on specific tasks and master the ability to produce high quality in high volume. They might love what they do in part because they've become very good at doing it. These people are prime candidates to teach others how to do that particular task. Not only will they teach them how to do it, they'll probably share a positive point of view because they enjoy their work. Usually they take pride in their work as well.

 MANAGER MINEFIELD

When a person isn't able to master something, they have a tendency to not enjoy it. Fill your team with people who are good at and enjoy specific tasks.

Next, observe how well these employees do at teaching. You might find they enjoy helping others. If this is the case, you might want to write yourself a reminder that they could be a good candidate for more training in team building or leadership training. This is one way you find the managers of the future.

Another type of person you need to look out for is the person who might not be the king of production but who is very good at working with others and managing communication issues within your team. Management is all about bringing people together as a team, so people who are naturally good at dealing with people sometimes can be better at management than your top producers.

It's a natural tendency to want to promote the top producer from production to management. This might be appropriate but only if that person is also good at dealing with people. Management is all about achieving results through others, and this requires people skills and administrative competence, not only being a star or top personal producer. The best manager gets more excited about her people winning than her own personal successes. Think about the proud parent or grandparent in your life.

Last but not least, look for people who are thinking and sharing ways to improve production, processes, and company results. These people are the most valuable asset you have in your company. People who are thinking about the big picture and trying to make things better, smoother, more efficient, and more effective with a desire to help others become more successful.

Building Your People

Have you ever thought of yourself as being in the people-building business? That's exactly what you are as a manager. The better you become at building up strong, competent, productive people, the easier your job will become and the more successful everyone will be.

You now have several ways to become more aware of your talented people (see the preceding section). So how do you go beyond talent? Real success requires a lot more than that. It also requires awareness as well as the right attitudes, knowledge, skills, and behaviors.

SKILL BUILDER

You can use these five areas—awareness, attitudes, knowledge, skills, and behaviors—to stimulate your thinking and discussion when you're doing one-to-one meetings with your key people, too.

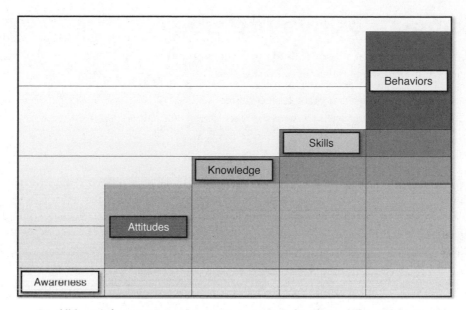

In addition to talent, success requires awareness, attitude, knowledge, skills, and behaviors.

Awareness is developed by first of all being comfortable and confident in your own skin. Then you are able to focus on others. As you manage by walking around, chatting with people, and reviewing personal performance charts, you'll see trends and patterns. If you're giving guidance, rewarding good deeds, reminding people of their goals and the company's objectives, as well as offering an occasional course correction, you'll become aware of their attitudes.

You'll quickly see those who look for a scapegoat or those who try to slip by unnoticed and avoid taking personal responsibility. This attitude is unacceptable. You need to call these people on their behavior and give them a course correction. Do this in private, but don't let it slip by unnoticed. Part of your job is to inform your people what your expectations are relative to attitude.

Choosing a Positive Attitude

I highly recommend you share the kind of attitudes you expect. Opt for a positive, winning attitude—and encourage your staff to do the same.

Here are a few suggestions to practice and share:

A winner says, "Let's find out"; a loser says, "Nobody knows."

A winner makes commitments; a loser makes promises.

A winner sets goals daily; a loser doesn't know what goals are.

A winner has plans and goals that can be measured; a loser hates measurements.

A winner asks questions and listens to the answers; a loser never asks and never listens.

A winner discusses opportunities; a loser complains about problems.

A winner repeats behavior that works and avoids behavior that doesn't work; a loser repeats behavior simply because he or she is comfortable with it.

Please feel free to duplicate these. Put them on the lunchroom wall. Work them into the course of everyday conversation. Above all, incorporate them into your personal behavior.

Attitude is the most critical characteristic to lead to success. It's totally the personal responsibility of the individual, and it's not something that's easily taught. You can encourage, guide, and reinforce a positive attitude in your staff, but ultimately, each individual has to decide for him- or herself what they will be.

Encouraging Continual Learning

Your most valuable people have a thirst for knowledge. Those who want to do the same thing for the rest of their lives might be useful for mundane and repetitive tasks, but those who choose a limited, long-term vision and are not concerned about personal growth will never be your star performers. Hopefully, in time, you can convert them to wanting to change, learn, and grow. As the manager, you want to believe in your people and always strive to encourage your people to improve. Never give up on them.

However, given that your time is limited, you must strategically plan and invest in the people who are trying hard and making the most contribution. Encourage your low-performing people, but don't invest a lot of time trying to convince them. Ultimately, they have to accept responsibility for their own destiny.

Don't ever give up on encouraging those who do want to grow. Focus on them, and determine ways to support them. Ask how they're doing, reward their accomplishments, and let others know how proud you are of those team members who are growing, learning new things, and showing initiative. Remember, others will notice who and what you pay attention to.

Keep Them Learning

Think about how much easier it is to steer a car that's moving than one that's parked. A person who is continually learning is like the moving car. If you're lucky, you'll have a hard time keeping up with some of your people in the education department. That's a good thing! Seek out and encourage those members of your team who are smart, capable, and show promise to become leaders. They're not a threat to you or your position; they're actually the future of the company. A competent manager has several people on their team who are smarter than they are.

When people are learning new things, have them share what they're learning and teach other people in your department, too. Encourage this team work and sharing. When one person is able to help another, it's wonderful for morale, so be sure to reward it.

LEADING THOUGHT

It is one of the most beautiful compensations of this life that no man can sincerely try to help another without helping himself.

—Ralph Waldo Emerson

Cross-training is another way to extend continual learning. When one of your key workers is temporarily reassigned to another department or section of your organization, he or she can share ideas and connections between the two departments. If your company doesn't already participate in cross-training, encourage upper management to implement the practice. Talk to other managers in your company, and volunteer to bring some of their workers into your department.

Have you seen the TV show *Undercover Boss?* I first heard about this idea from Peter Drucker, a professor of mine at Claremont Graduate University. Many years ago, around 1923, Al Sloan, president of General Motors (GM), regularly went undercover at auto dealerships and manufacturing plants within the GM organization. Sloan was known to actually work as a mechanic on some of these covert visits. His objective was to increase his awareness of what was really going on in the company and learn how to fix or improve the processes and procedures.

In 1946, Drucker wrote a book about GM called *Concept of the Corporation.* This seminal work describes what a corporation is and how it works. Drucker's views expressed in the book caused friction between him and GM's leadership. In spite of this, he continued to meet with Sloan regularly for many years to give counsel.

Drucker believed organizations and individuals have a moral and ethical responsibility to society, and in 1959, he coined the phrase *knowledge worker.* One of his highest values was education and continual learning, and he believed the more you learn, the higher you can go, and the more value you can bring to yourself, your organization, and society.

During the nineteenth century, the prevailing attitude was one of exploitation of natural resources and of people. With the advent of the industrial revolution, the focus was on machines, factories, and steam power, and many were excited about the invention of cement, advances in metallurgy, and the potential of mass production. Canals, railroads, roads, and eventually cars and trucks changed markets dramatically. Little focus was given to workers, who were given minimal wages, performed piece work, worked 10 or more hours a day, and often included children.

Drucker was concerned about the behavior of people. Now considered the father of management, he always had a heart for working with charities and religious groups in addition to his extensive work with corporations. His efforts to focus on people rather than machines and technology naturally gave birth to his concept of the knowledge worker. A worker is more than a human machine, he claimed. A worker is flesh and blood, emotions, and an amazing intellect. Now companies are realizing the power of engaging workers emotionally and intellectually; hence, the knowledge worker.

Keep Encouraging

While you're encouraging continual learning, remember a few simple guidelines. Everyone is different and will be interested in different types of learning. Some are oriented toward technology, some to mechanical things, and some to learning about people or customer service. A good team has many different types of people and interests. When they communicate well, it makes the team stronger and more capable.

Also, ask for volunteers. People will be happy to volunteer if they clearly see the benefits of helping out or making a contribution. As a manager, your job is to explain to people the benefits of being a volunteer, the consequences of being away or being involved, and the ramifications of mistakes and risks. When you create a safe and forgiving environment, people tend to try new things, volunteer for new projects, and realize that mistakes are not fatal but rather learning opportunities.

A good but not scientifically proven theory is that for every negative reprimand or correction you give, you must share four or more positive strokes to get the person back to normal or to recover from that one negative. And that negative can be something as simple as a snide comment or joke that makes fun of someone's mistake. I can still remember my fourth-grade teacher making a negative comment about me in front of the whole class. I was a slow reader, and she simply said, "David, are you only on page nine?" A lot of it had to do with her tone of voice.

LEADING THOUGHT

I've learned that people will forget what you said, people will forget what you did, but people will never forget how you made them feel.

—Maya Angelou

Be Their Coach

The beauty of approaching your job of manager with the idea of being a coach is that you may or may not be able to do what your employee does, but by watching them, understanding what needs to be accomplished, and having the ability to see possible solutions, you can help them improve. And your focus is on them, which they'll like, especially if you sincerely care about them and are able to help them. However, they won't appreciate it if they perceive you are nagging or leaning on them.

You can approach a coaching mind-set in several ways. I suggest the first thing you do is realize that for your employee to improve, he or she is going to have to discover some of their own solutions. Your role is not to dictate or tell them exactly what to do. A brand-new employee might need very specific direction; however, coaching is best reserved for people who are well on their way to knowing their job and who are trying to refine their abilities.

The best way to help someone discover a solution by themselves is to guide their thinking by the questions you ask. A very effective technique is to ask big-picture questions and then ask how they see themselves fitting into that big picture. For example, ask, "Where do you see our department a year from now?" and then follow with, "How do you see yourself making a contribution to that?" Then try, "How can I help you get ready for that role?"

Do this all in a very easy and conversational way. Adjust your tone, style, and pace to match the individual you're talking to. This isn't an attempt to push people; rather, it's more a joint discovery process. Be patient, and don't get into mechanical or memorized questions. Remember, management is like a dance, and you are sharing time and interest with a colleague.

You also can encourage and stimulate thinking. When you see someone doing something well, take note and compliment them. Then, at a later date, mention the incident again and tie it to something else that will help the person see how they might grow, change, or try new things. For example, say "Sally, I noticed last week how well you handled the customer with the returned item. You were very helpful and courteous." Wait for a response and then suggest, "I was wondering if you would be interested in going to a seminar on X, Y, or Z. Maybe you could go for the department and then share with us what you learn. You might get some ideas that will help all of us get better." Whether they say "yes" or "no," express thanks and encourage your employee to continue doing good work. Share that you appreciate their effort.

LEADING THOUGHT

It is no use saying, "We are doing our best." You have got to succeed in doing what is necessary.

—Winston Churchill

A third approach is becoming an accountability partner. This encourages people to pull together. Ideally, this will be done based on a voluntary agreement—or your direct report asks for and wants you to hold them accountable. First you need to figure out what the goal of your agreement is and then design a plan and agreed benchmarks along the way. After that, it's a matter of checking in, following up, and encouraging your staff to catch up, keep up the good work, or maybe adjust the target date because of unforeseen developments.

Having an accountability partner works somewhat the same way as having workout buddy. You both want to get in better shape, so you form a pact or agreement to help and encourage each other. Try it; I think you'll enjoy the process. It also will help build closer relationships between you and your colleague because you share a mutual goal.

Meaningful Mentoring

Mentoring is different from coaching in several ways. The biggest difference is that a mentor has been there and done that. They have extensive experience and typically have accomplished many things in which the mentee has little or no experience.

Another difference is that the mentor may be from a completely different department, company, or organization. I mentor graduate students enrolled at the University of California, Irvine. The students have various areas of expertise but are new to the level of business and knowledge offered by the university. A colleague of mine who is an experienced attorney mentors young attorneys. This type of mentoring is usually done pro bono, or for free.

I'm a grandfather. Mentoring is a lot like being a grandparent. You care a lot, you know a lot because of your years of experience, and you're willing to spend time to help a young or inexperienced person. The rewards are huge.

Many companies assign a mentor to young or newly appointed executives. It might be advisable for you, if you are a new manager, to seek out a mentor to work with you as you grow in the role of becoming a manager.

A mentor will share perspectives and explore ideas and options that might or might not relate to producing direct results for the company. They'll take a personal interest in the development of the mentee as a person, parent, worker, or friend. Mentoring can get a lot more personal than coaching.

A mentee can also share at a different level with a mentor. They may get into more emotional and psychological areas than the typical coach. It's not uncommon for a mentor to give direct and tough feedback or advice that someone "needs to hear."

 LEADING THOUGHT

> The true secret of giving advice is, after you have honestly given it, to be perfectly indifferent whether it is taken or not, and never persist in trying to set people right.
>
> —Henry Ward Beecher

Mentors also might get into career counseling and give the mentee suggestions and referrals that have little to do with the job tasks. A good friend of mine from college—he's a grandpa, too—loves having a parade of young people come by his office to tap his brain and wisdom. It's been so rewarding for him, he has decided to write a book about how to nurture, guide, and help young people through mentoring.

Several major accounting firms where I coach partners have a program to help new partners negotiate through the politics and procedures required of a partner. These firms are working with Fortune 100 companies and have significant legal, financial, and ethical issues that have to be handled judiciously. For example, it's wise to run decisions by someone who has already done scores of Securities and Exchange Commission filings before you finalize a report as a new partner. Having a mentor is a perfect solution.

You're probably thinking a lot right now about how you can personally benefit from these ideas. That's good. Coaching and mentoring have become a mainstay of the modern progressive organization. I heartily recommend you suggest a comprehensive program of coaching and mentoring to your upper management.

Think about who has coaches. Every top athlete, actor, and high-functioning team has a coach. The only people who don't need a coach are those who prefer to be mediocre. Think about it: if you want to really soar and do great things, you want to have a coach. So do your people.

The Least You Need to Know

- Measure everything. If you can't measure it, you can't manage it.
- Your highest calling as a manager is to be a teacher and a coach. It's all about getting things done through others.
- Develop a positive attitude, and be a continual learner.
- People will remember how you made them feel more than anything else.
- Every employee could benefit from having a mentor.

Managing Differences

You have the power to relate to anyone you want to relate to. The mystery of not being able to relate to some people is often simply that you don't know them as well as you might know others. The better you get to know another person, the easier it is to relate to them—if you want to. Granted, you might not want to relate to some people. However, if you are the manager, you can't just relate to those members of your team you like.

In this chapter, I reveal numerous ideas, concepts, and simple practices you can incorporate into your daily routines to become a master at connecting with people.

In This Chapter

- Adapting and adjusting
- Connecting with anyone
- Understanding the generations
- Building relationships
- Being credible
- Celebrating diversity

Individualized Management

Here in southern California lives an old Swedish fellow I've known for years. At one time, he owned a very successful import business. During World War II, he worked with U.S. forces as a translator because he spoke and read seven languages. He now has trouble hearing, uses a walker, and moves slowly.

Recently, I saw him at a restaurant, being assisted by his daughter as they were leaving. From the other side of the room, I called to him in Swedish, *"God dag, god dag."* ("Good day, good day.") He stopped dead in his tracks, got a firm grip on his walker, and lifted his head to see who had spoken. When his daughter pointed me out, he smiled, and with a big grin, waved and said *"God dag."*

I lived in Europe for 3 years and traveled to many countries. Fortunately, I spoke German fairly well, but I also learned a little bit of several other languages while I was there. It was amazing how much friendlier people were when I tried to speak the language, even if I didn't do it very well.

The successful manager applies this same principle to managing people. You need to speak to each individual in his or her own language. (In Chapter 4, I mentioned this concept as it relates to behavioral styles—direct, influencing, steady, and cautious. If you haven't been practicing using that model, make a note to review Chapter 4.) Each person is unique, special, and different. The better you become at seeing these differences and using that knowledge to modify your speech and the approach you take with individuals, the better you'll do as a manager.

You can "speak the language" in numerous ways besides using words, including behavioral styles, values, learning styles, types of natural intelligence, cultural background—the list goes on. Let's start with reading the simple forms of communication—tone, body language, and speaking style.

> **LEADING THOUGHT**
>
> People fail to get along because they fear each other; they fear each other because they don't know each other; they don't know each other because they have not communicated with each other.
>
> —Martin Luther King Jr.
>
> I don't like that man. I must get to know him better.
>
> —Abraham Lincoln

During my nearly 10 years as a broker with Merrill Lynch, most of the selling I did was on the phone. When you use the phone, you can't see what's going on around the other person or what they're wearing, nor can you get any signals from their facial expressions or their body language. Yet if you practice and try hard, you can visualize most of those things by doing quality listening.

The words people choose to use, their grammar, their enunciation, and their tone of voice can all paint a picture of who they are. With practice, you can tell what part of the country a person is from, if they're in a good mood, if they're distracted, how much education they have or haven't had, and myriad other things just by listening.

You want to be careful to look at the whole picture before you make any judgments, though. Many elements combine in each individual to make the whole person. It's not until you really listen, absorb, and spend time with a person that you get to know them.

The manager who thinks he's really smart and is able to quickly judge a person is probably making a mistake. People are complex. That's why it's important to spend time with and have numerous encounters with people in various situations. Be slow to judge; however, once you believe you know what's going on, act. There's an old adage that relates to this concept: "Hire slowly, and fire fast."

Body language is another area that's prone to be misunderstood. There's no single position, movement, or stance that alone gives you much insight into what a person is thinking or feeling. It's only when you observe a person in the totality of their mannerisms, posture, movements, and positioning that you start to understand them from their body language. Yet body language is one of the most revealing aspects of how people communicate.

When you understand who the other person is based on tone, body language, and speaking style, you are able to communicate best if you model their behavior. Modeling the other person's behavior is an effective way to make them comfortable. If they're standing, you should stand, too. If they talk in quiet tones, lower your voice and get in synch with their rhythm and pace. If they like small talk and want to chat about the recent World Series game, you'll do well to be able to discuss the game and other sports they're interested in. When I was with Merrill Lynch, I subscribed to *Sports Illustrated* for the express purpose of being able to discuss sports with clients.

SKILL BUILDER

If you know the people on your team love country music or mariachi music, learn about this type of music and play it in in your office from time to time. Skip the classical music if you know that's not what your employees like. It's amazing how many managers just don't think about these simple but important aspects of relating to people. Ask yourself what other things you can do to relate to your own people more.

The important lesson is to adapt and adjust the way you communicate and relate to your people. It will make them more comfortable, and when you ask them to adapt and adjust the way they're doing their job, it will be much easier to win them over. People like to associate and be with people like themselves. The more you're able to have in common with your people, the easier you can relate to them and get them to contribute to the team.

The responsibility for initiating this leaning toward each other is yours as the manager. It's the same as extending your hand to shake hands when you meet someone. If you stand there with your hands in your pockets, the other person will be uncomfortable, think you aren't friendly, and will probably become defensive.

Making Friends of Strangers

The more genuinely interested you are in people, the more they'll be interested in you. It's wonderful when people perceive you as interested and interesting. An international speaker, trainer, and friend of mine, Boaz Rauchwerger, tells the story of his mother coming to America—not speaking a word of English—and over a short time, becoming a successful business person.

As a child, Boaz remembers his mother asking five magical questions. They are brilliant in their power and simplicity. If you want to get to know your coworkers or be the life of the party, learn Boaz's five questions:

1. Where are you from originally?

2. *If not from here:* What brought you here?

   If from here: Have you lived here all your life?

3. Do you have a family?

4. What do you do?

5. What did you want to be when you were growing up?

Start the five questions by saying "I'm just curious …" to put the other person at ease. As you ask the questions, relax and ask follow-up questions as appropriate. You'll find this a fun, insightful, and very helpful way of meeting strangers or getting to know coworkers better. For more helpful ideas from Boaz, visit BoazPower.com.

Understanding Generational Differences

Most people agree that we are in unusual times because several distinct groups of people are all working together, separated by unique generational differences. With the fast and always-accelerating pace of change, the span of worldviews, values, and behaviors called *generational differences* has become chronologically shorter and shorter.

DEFINITION

Generational differences are the areas influenced from different points of view of varying generations, such as change, values, attitude toward discipline, competitiveness, self-reliance, trust, and adaptability.

We develop our worldviews, values, and beliefs over our lifetime but primarily when we're young. As youngsters, we absorb and believe what our parents tell us as truth and reality without question, but as we approach adolescence, our peers start to influence our thinking and beliefs. During adolescence, the impact of family, relationships, peer groups, and society in general are the incubator for developing self-concepts and beliefs. Any significant emotional events during youth will have a lasting impact on who a person turns out to be and what they believe.

Traditionalists are those people born before 1946. Their worldview was shaped by the Great Depression, two World Wars, and the Korean War as well as the growth of major corporations like General Motors.

Baby boomers are those born between 1946 and 1964. Commonly called the "me" generation, boomers grew up during the Vietnam War, civil rights demonstrations, and man launching into space. Divorce rates rose dramatically among the boomers, and they pursued money, material goods, and personal gratification.

Next came *Generation X*, born between 1965 and 1980. Divorce rates have continued to rise in this generation; both spouses typically work; and kids are more casual, free, and independent. They're skeptical of and not impressed with authority, yet they strive for education, balance, and good jobs.

Millennials are those born before and after the turn of the twenty-first century. This group has grown up during worldly disruptions like terrorist attacks, AIDS epidemics, and school shootings, and divorce has become the new normal. Education is emphasized, tolerance is expanded, and the internet is omnipresent.

In its own way, each generation is characterized by its desired rewards:

- Traditionalists value doing a quality job. They respect authority and rules and look for security.

- Baby boomers want status, money, and titles. They often work long hours and sometimes expect special treatment.

- Generation X strives for independence and time off, and members are prone to change jobs. They want to be listened to and deferred to.

- Millennials strive to change the world and be unique individuals. They expect people to pay attention to them.

Many studies have been conducted to determine what each generation wants. The surprising facts have revealed that all four groups have three things in common: they want to feel valued, receive sincere appreciation and recognition, and be in a healthy and supportive environment.

With so many ways to understand and assess your people, you could be forever learning more. This is a good thing! Remind yourself that you desire to adapt, improvise, and overcome no matter what the circumstance. This is best done by becoming a master at asking questions and listening attentively to the answer given by words, tone of voice, actions, and body language.

 MANAGER MINEFIELD

Be aware of what's *not* being said. Sometimes the most important thing to notice is what a person avoids saying or talking about.

Nurturing Relationships

Developing relationships requires time, work, and pure intent. There's no substitute for having quality time with another person if you want to develop a significant relationship. But this isn't accomplished by just being in the same room or on the same team as another. The only way to develop quality time is to be alone with the other person and be focused on one-to-one communication.

Reach Out

People pay attention to who initiates contact. If you want someone to know you care, take the initiative to make contact with them. If the only time you talk to or meet with a person is when they call or contact you, they'll know you don't have much invested in the relationship. Some people get a kick out of having people call or request time with them; they have their secretary or assistant make all their appointments and confirm their schedule. I've worked with hundreds of CEOs and executives, and most who do this are on a constant ego trip or not very competent. Not all of them; just the majority.

If you plan well and know how to utilize today's technology, you can manage your own schedule very easily. That doesn't mean you can't have an assistant help and coordinate your schedule. Assistance is invaluable, and you should properly utilize it when it's available to you. Just remember to use your planning, and schedule to plan and communicate effectively. Keep in mind the power of personal contact and how to relate well with people.

Listen, Listen, Listen

When you're with a person, give them your undivided attention. Have you ever been at a conference and been talking to someone in the hall between meetings and the whole time they're looking around to see who else more important is there they might want to talk to? I've been a member of the National Speakers Association for more than 25 years, and it's a common joke among members to watch people in the hall craning their necks while trying to talk to someone, looking for a famous speaker to talk to instead.

The other sad joke is how speakers sometimes walk up to two people who are talking and jump into the middle of their conversation without even an "Excuse me" or waiting for an introduction or invitation. Speakers love to speak; unfortunately, they often don't know how to listen or be polite. You'll do much better as a manager if you're a disciplined listener who is polite and respectful of others.

Has someone ever said to you, "Thanks so much for your time. You are a great listener"? The way you'll know you're listening well is when people comment and thank you for listening. It's just like if you're in sales: if you're good, you'll get referrals. Likewise, if your company is a good place to work, people will be applying for jobs and workers will be referring friends and relatives to work at your company.

Make Better Meetings

You nurture relationships when you develop the habit of having frequent meetings or encounters with people. It's not as effective to have very long sessions together, like a day of golf, that are only once in a great while. Numerous short encounters are better. The key is to make the frequent encounters focused and productive as well as casual once in a while. Mix it up.

Think about reasons to contact another person. This shows your interest and sincerity because to create a worthwhile reason to contact another person, you have to have been thinking about them. This also demonstrates your intention. It might be an article that relates to their interests, an idea that can help them improve their team effort, or something specifically about their work specialty. Maybe it's feedback from upper management, and instead of just sending an email, you meet and have coffee together while you talk.

> **LEADING THOUGHT**
>
> No one cares how much you know, until they know how much you care.
>
> –Theodore Roosevelt

It's hard work to nurture relationships. To help yourself in this task, make a list of the people with whom you want to develop significant relationships. Across the top of the page, put dates and ideas for contact. Use this simple list to keep track of who you reached out to, when you made contact, and what type of contact it was. This helps you stay in touch, adds variety to the types of contact, and ensures nobody get lost or falls through the cracks.

You are now managing your relationships. Remember, if you can't measure it, you can't manage it.

Establishing Your Credibility

The most obvious way you demonstrate credibility is by the way you talk. What you say and how you say it create an important and lasting impression with other people.

When you go to a restaurant with your spouse, does the waiter say, "What do you guys want?" or is it something more like, "Good evening, Mr. Smith. It's nice to see you and Mrs. Smith this evening"? Based on only this exchange with the waiter, can you guess which restaurant has the better food and costs more?

The way you speak can reveal how well educated you are, where you're from, and whether or not you have credibility. Even if you're brilliant, if you can't express yourself, your talking will create a permanent impression. If English is your second or third language, that's all the more reason to really work on your diction, articulation, and facility with the language. It might not be fair for people to judge you by the way you talk, but they will. Your speaking ability is something you cannot hide, so you must continually work at improving.

> **SKILL BUILDER**
>
> Toastmasters International (toastmasters.org) is a nonprofit international educational organization that can help you improve your ability to present ideas and speak in front of a group. It also can help increase your self-esteem when you practice speaking before groups. Membership is very inexpensive, and clubs can be found all over the world.

No matter what your age, the ability to speak with confidence is a sign of competence and credibility. Pay attention to the types of things you talk about. People have a tendency to first talk about *things*. This is a very basic and elementary form of communication. The next level of communication deals with people talking about *people*, as in, "Did you hear what Joe said?" Often the source of this information is gossip and can easily be petty. It's a notch above conversations about things; however, it's usually not uplifting. The highest form of communication is about *ideas*.

Notice which level of conversation you are most often involved with at work, at leisure, and whenever you're with other people. Are you mostly talking about ideas? Discussing ways to improve? Sharing your current joys and future plans?

You'll find that people who constantly are talking about the past are typically a negative influence and seem to be old or worn out. People who are in the present and planning for the future are exciting to be around. They seem young no matter what their age. Listen to yourself and others, and see what you discover.

Embracing Diversity

It's uplifting, positive, and energizing to embrace diversity. Many organizations define diversity as including people of color, gender, and sexual orientation differences. This is a very narrow view of what diversity will mean in the future.

Diversity can be approached as an attempt to meet legal and political requirements or it can be used by businesses to expand thinking, innovation, and marketing. I recommend the intent of diversity be in line with abundance and positive thinking rather than legalistic and scarcity impediments.

Teams perform at a much higher level when they're composed of a diverse group of people. Research groups are more creative when they have a diverse group of scientists and researchers. Countries are more vibrant, democratic, and productive when they include people of diverse cultures and backgrounds. The result of all diversity is productive when the group is united with its values and objectives.

LEADING THOUGHT

We need to give each other the space to grow, to be ourselves, to exercise our diversity. We need to give each other space so that we may both give and receive such beautiful things as ideas, openness, dignity, joy, healing, and inclusion.

—Max De Pree

When a group of radicals is focused on forcing diversity to accomplish their own extreme agenda, that's not productive. Such individuals are using another organization to selfishly accomplish their own goals. It's very much like a tree that dies because it's overwhelmed by parasitic plants. You should look at how you can make a contribution to the greater good as opposed to how you can milk the system.

An organization needs to clearly define its values and objectives and then find people of every possible variety who are aligned with those values and objectives. The color of their skin, their country of origin, or any other particular personal attribute they may have doesn't matter.

Any organization is stronger when it embraces diversity. In order for diversity to work, it takes an understanding and appreciation for quality communication. Everyone in the organization must practice this. As a manager, you are responsible to respect and understand people of all descriptions, both on your own and with your group.

I work with a group of CEOs called The CEOs Forum. We meet regularly, and I also meet with each CEO individually to coach them. I have done this for more than 15 years. I'm continually amazed how powerful it is to bring together a diverse group of people who all want to improve and have high integrity. It doesn't matter their gender, education, culture, or even sexual orientation. If they want to improve, are focused on business, and have high integrity, they can make a contribution.

Part of our agenda when we meet is to discuss and solve significant business issues. We all marvel at how often someone who hears and participates in the discussion of a specific problem comes up with a great solution despite not having any experience in the specific business being discussed. Members base their responses on practical experience, intuition, and common sense. Those aren't attributes you can learn in a classroom.

Listen to your people, listen to upper management, and listen to your customers. Hopefully, those groups provide a great variety of people, backgrounds, and experiences you can learn from. After all, you make better decisions when you have a diverse array of points of view to pull from.

The Least You Need to Know

- Each person is unique; therefore, as a manager, you have to treat each member of your team, your customers, and others differently.
- Communication takes more than talent. It requires trust, respect, understanding, empathy, and resolution.
- Short, frequent contact has more impact than long, occasional meetings.
- The way you speak reveals your character, knowledge, and level of sophistication, and you cannot hide it. You need to learn to master communication.
- Diversity is a vital requirement for innovation, creativity, and progressive thinking and planning. Embrace it.

Finding the People You Need

New people are the lifeblood of any organization. In Part 3, I explain the best ways to recruit, hire, and get quality people onboard and up to speed as integral parts of your team.

It all starts with defining exactly who you're looking for, what qualities they possess, and how to find them. You'll be surprised how easy it is to find good people, especially when you know how to get other people to help you. I show you, from the inception of an idea to final result, how to design and implement a comprehensive recruiting and hiring system, including the key questions you need to ask and how to rate the answers.

Once you choose the ideal person and they accept your offer, what comes next? Chapter 12 discusses how you can create the right environment and design short- and long-term plans to ensure your new people get quickly and correctly immersed in your company and become productive members of your team.

CHAPTER 10

Recruiting Basics

The lifeblood of your organization is quality new people. When you bring in new people, you also bring in an energy and anticipation that gets everyone excited. Hiring a new person should be a community celebration, and the process should be designed as an opportunity for your people to participate.

New people provide new ideas, expanded talents, and an increase in responsibilities. The more you involve your team, the better the orientation and assimilation of the new person will be. Remember, first impressions are lasting impressions. You want the new person to go home after their first day so excited they think they've just made the best decision of their life. There's no reason this shouldn't be their reality.

When you have a well-designed process, it will spill over into the organization so everyone becomes more productive and enthused. After the first day, you want to have a learning and welcoming system that ensures the new person feels a part of the team, gets answers to their questions, and knows what the next steps are as they become a vital part of the organization.

In This Chapter

- Who is your perfect candidate?
- Attracting quality people
- Hunt where they feed
- Looking at internal sources
- Looking at external sources

In this chapter, you discover the core competencies you need to hire quality people. I start by explaining how to define the open position, identify your dream candidate, and understand the process for matching that definition with real candidates. I also share specific techniques for evaluating potential, performance, skills, and the intangibles like culture fit and attitude. In the last half of the chapter, I give you a collection of ideas for finding, enlisting help, and making the final decisions to determine who's the best fit for the job.

Defining Your Ideal Candidate

The only thing worse than not finding the ideal candidate is hiring the wrong candidate. It's expensive to find and hire a new employee. If you approach this task casually, you do it at your own risk. Poor hiring practices are one of the most damaging things a manager can have. You'll be rated and evaluated based on the quality of the people you bring into the company and the results they produce. Therefore, quality hiring practices must be high on your priority list. They determine your future.

> **LEADING THOUGHT**
>
> You need to have a collaborative hiring process.
>
> —Steve Jobs

Before you interview or approach anyone about a potential job, you must clearly define exactly what characteristics your ideal candidate possesses. These skills and traits need to cover at least two broad areas: the required background and skills for the job, and the cultural and character traits to blend well in your organization.

Crafting a Job Description

To attract the best candidates, you need to have a clearly defined job description. It should include the position's title, objectives, duties, responsibilities, schedules, activities, authority, measurement, wages, and benefits. If special licenses, ratings, or clearances are required, can they be earned after the hire? Does a person need to have a certain number of years in a certain position to be considered? What equipment, systems, and programs will be used? Are there strength, agility, or other physical requirements, or is specific knowledge of an industry, product, or service required? Also, how will they be evaluated, measured, and rewarded, and what areas might require restrictions or unique disciplines?

All this information must be clearly spelled out in the job description so you can find candidates well suited to the position.

LEADING THOUGHT

If you don't know where you are going, any road will get you there.

—Lewis Carroll

When you have a series of qualifications a new person must attain before they can make a meaningful contribution, you're not done with the job description yet. You also need to add more specifics and be sure you differentiate between training/learning and actual production.

For example, consider the professional services industry. Several test requirements are in place before a person can sell professional services and products—securities, insurance, real estate, accounting, law, and other types of investments. Many people are very good students and can pass difficult tests (the training/learning part), but being successful in selling (the actual production part) is an entirely different skill set.

The attorney or accountant who's a wizard with the law or at crunching numbers may or may not make a good partner in a major firm or as a solo practitioner. Even if someone is the best and brightest in their professional field, it's only once they get established and prove their competence in their particular discipline—real estate, securities, tax, law, audit, etc.—that the real test begins. How well do they deal with people, create solutions, and most importantly, bring in new clients? That's selling.

As a manager, you need to admit and understand that everything in business, and in life, involves selling. You have a successful marriage, raise quality children, find a good job or career, and become financially independent in direct proportion to your ability to convince and persuade others. That's what selling is all about. Whether you're persuading people to do an assembly line task, clean the office well, complete a project, create a solution for a client, or bring in new business, all these things involve being an effective salesperson. Be sure you clearly define these positive attitudes and characteristics and include them in the job description because each one applies to the job opening you're trying to fill.

The final job description should be completely documented, reviewed, and edited by others (your boss, attorney, and human resources) in writing.

The benefits of a good job description are numerous. It clarifies and establishes expectations of both the employer and the employee, and clearly spells out the employee's duties. These elements will eliminate or at least minimize any possible misunderstandings.

With a well-thought-out description comes clarity in communication, allocation of resources, and the structure of responsibility and authority within the company. An organized path to learning, training, promotion, and personal development may also be part of a job description.

Evaluating Backgrounds and Skills

Wherever a person has been in the past influences where they might go in the future. Based on your past experience, you've developed a unique-to-you worldview. Some people see the world as a place where they can function successfully and are in control of their own growth. Others see life as difficult and believe outside factors determine their ultimate outcome. These folks tend to seek security and believe external factors, people, or fate are running the show.

Psychologist Julian B. Rotter studied these viewpoints. Known for his theory of *locus of control,* Rotter believed people are predominately focused either on either an internal or external locus of control. An internal locus of control is characterized by believing you are responsible for your own results. A person with an external locus of control tends to believe his environment and circumstance play a major part in his life's outcomes. Taken to an extreme, this person might have a victim mentality and constantly claim "It's not my fault."

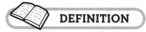 **DEFINITION**

> **Locus of control** is the way a person views his or her life and what controls the outcome.

Most people are a blend of these two perspectives. As a manager, you need to assess the criteria you're looking for in a candidate and then evaluate applicants to determine if they fit your desired profile.

The best way to assess a person's skill level is not by reviewing his or her résumé, education, and past job descriptions. Far better is to actually have the candidate demonstrate their skill in a real-life situation. For example, if you're looking for a new receptionist who will be answering the phone for the company, have the first interview be a phone interview. Ask questions and evaluate the candidate based on the way they talk and respond to problems on the phone. And think about how appealing their tone of voice, diction, and courtesy are.

If you're looking for someone to do bookkeeping or accounting, have them work on a test ledger, journal, or financial statements during the interview process. Maybe ask them to analyze the return on investment or the present value of some assets and explore financial alternatives.

If the job involves dealing with customers, actually take them out in the territory or into meetings with potential customers. Ask them to participate in the presentation or suggest ideas for solutions on how to deal with difficult people.

One of the biggest benefits of this type of involvement and challenge is that you get to observe and evaluate how the candidate approaches problems and handles the unexpected, and you get a hint at how creative and resilient they are.

No matter how many assessments and qualifications you assemble and use, the ultimate test is going to be on-the-job performance. Always hire based on performance and actual development of results on the job. If a candidate isn't able to catch on and produce based on a predetermined schedule of learning and growth, take specific action. Predetermine standards and have benchmarks in place that will automatically trigger a review and possible dismissal. Remember, this is business. You are paying for performance and contribution, and if that's lacking, you have no choice but to let that person go.

Success has a tendency to breed more success. Ideally, you'll be seeking people who have an established success pattern in their background or skill set. When they have duplicated that success while working in the same arena or type of work you're seeking in a new employee, it makes for a good match.

> **LEADING THOUGHT**
>
> The reasonable man adapts himself to the world; the unreasonable one persists in trying to adapt the world to himself. Therefore all progress depends on the unreasonable man.
>
> —George Bernard Shaw

Factoring In Culture and Character

Skills and background are useful measures of a candidate's worth, but a more important indicator of success and compatibility is a person's cultural values and attitudes. Do they have strong character composed of integrity, honesty, and self-discipline? These virtues are valuable, and you should seek out candidates who epitomize them.

Focusing only on skill sets or experience in a particular industry sector is a fundamental mistake. Often I see firms hire for skills and ultimately have to terminate that person because of his or her inability or unwillingness to be a part of the team and assimilate into the culture of the organization. The more clearly you can define the values and culture of your organization and your team, the easier it will be to identify the right person to hire.

People tend to associate with other people who are similar to themselves. People who crave knowledge hang around libraries, schools, and seminars. Party lovers go to clubs, bars, and social functions. Athletes can be found at the gym, on the playing field, or jogging in the park. What are the key interests of people in your industry and profession? What specific evidence are you looking for that indicates a person has the attitude and character attributes you're looking for in a candidate?

Some of my clients look for candidates who have played team sports in school. They're not only looking for the star athletes who have winning aspirations; they're also looking for people who enjoy and have experience being part of a team. Some people are solo operators, prima donnas, or do their best when left alone, and they are able to use self-discipline to achieve meaningful results. Others need a group and accountability close at hand to continue to be productive.

All these various characteristics are different, and you likely have people on your team who are a blend of these attributes. Be sure you clearly know what's required and can assess your people to match the right person with the right job.

 MANAGER MINEFIELD

Remember it is more important to monitor a person's behavior than to rely only on what they say.

Attracting the Best Candidates

Like a campfire on a cold night, people are attracted to warmth, light, and safety. Does that resonate with you? Do you run a group with a positive, warm, and welcoming attitude? Do the people on your team learn to grow, develop, and move forward or upward in the organization? Are you known for an environment that's open, transparent, and fair toward all people? If these questions are all true for you, you probably have no problem attracting new people.

People want to work for managers who believe in them and will help them get ahead and achieve their personal goals. Although a small part of their on-the-job behavior is to please you, the majority of what they do is really for their own reasons. However, once you understand this, it's easier to attract people. Help them get what they want by having them help you get what you want (increased production and profits for the organization). This attitude will breed loyalty. It also will encourage people to tell others about what a great boss they have and why your organization is a great place to work.

I once had an interesting chat with an attorney who was out to dinner with his son. The discussion centered on the son's college plans. In southern California, the University of Southern California (USC) is a very well-known school. One predominate characteristic of USC is its tight and well-connected alumni association—they stick together. If you're in business in southern California, you have a distinct marketing advantage if you're a USC alumni.

It was interesting to hear the father trying to persuade his son to go to USC. USC offers a good education and is a smart choice for developing opportunities after graduation. It would make good business sense for him to attend that school. But the son was interested in another school. It didn't have the quality reputation of USC, and the tuition cost less—convenient because the son was still uncertain what he wanted to study.

The real issue was *why* the son was going to college and what benefits he hoped to attain. Finally it was revealed that the boy's girlfriend was going to the other school.

It's important to understand why a person is making a particular decision. Often it's not obvious and might be difficult to ascertain. When in doubt, ask another question.

LEADING THOUGHT

On an important decision one rarely has 100% of the information needed for a good decision no matter how much one spends or how long one waits. And, if one waits too long, he has a different problem and has to start all over. This is the terrible dilemma of the hesitant decision maker.

—Robert K. Greenleaf, *The Servant as Leader*

When people in your neighborhood are looking for a job, what do they hear from the outside world about your company? Do you have a great reputation locally? What's the social and economic footprint of your company?

One of the best extracurricular things you can do as a manager to attract candidates to your company is to participate in the local community. Join service clubs like the Lions, Rotary, or Chamber of Commerce. Or coordinate with local schools through job fairs, visits to your facilities, and internships. Or get involved with social groups, special interest organizations, or religious groups that need to know about your company.

Promote your organization as a great place to work by honoring your employees. You can do this with awards, promotions, and special assignments. Then share these honors not only within your company but also with your local media. What can you do to help your local radio, television, and print media? Have a science fair or contest for students? Make contributions to, sponsor, or organize charity 5K or 10K runs?

If you want quality people from your community to join your company, make a quality contribution to the community so they get to know who you are while you promote the values and culture of your organization. All these things will contribute to attracting good people to your campfire.

Let the Hunt Begin

If you were going fishing or hunting, it would help if you were familiar with the lake, stream, or woods where the fish and game lived. The same is true when looking for good-quality people to hire into your company. You have to know the neighborhoods, schools, and associations potential candidates frequent.

Every year, major companies go to the finest colleges and universities to recruit talent. Major accounting firms send their top young partners to recruit, and the military uses its best and brightest. Who do you send to college campuses, to job fairs, and to meet and greet people in the community?

Finding new employees is just like finding new customers—you need a strategic plan, committed time, and dedicated funds and then have someone who is bright and sharp lead the charge. Part of the plan needs to be educating all your people on the program and getting them involved emotionally in identifying and finding candidates. This might even include rewards. For example, the broker who referred me to Merrill Lynch received a commission equal to one month's pay when I was hired by the firm.

The single best way to get a new customer or find a new employee is by getting a referral. People are more prone to share a referral when they have confidence in the person or company seeking the referral. It also is beneficial if the person asking for the referral has in some way added value to the person asking for a referral. This could be in the form of outstanding customer service, having purchased a quality product or service from the company, or offering a token of appreciation for the referral.

 MANAGER MINEFIELD

Always be sensitive to and avoid favoritism. When you hire friends or relatives— your own or those of your employees—you risk destroying long-term relationships and creating severe complications within your organization. All candidates, friends and family or not, must clearly earn their income and any promotions, be highly dedicated, and be top performers.

Depending on the culture and style of your organization, determine how you can give to the community, customers, and other employees to show your appreciation for referrals. Once you determine this, design a system to ensure everyone knows about your goal to find quality people and what you're willing and able to give in exchange for them helping you. It should at least be a heartfelt "Thank you."

I heartily recommend you be continually on the lookout for new potential employees. When you find a special person that might fit your organization, develop a way to stay in touch and keep up to date with their situation. You never know when you might need a new person.

With social media, the internet, and a dynamic community action program, it's easy to keep others aware of news and developments in your company. Make all the publicity and public relations efforts fun and entertaining, and be sure you keep them current. A brochure or flyer that's obviously out of date can actually do more harm than good.

Your strategy should include regular updates and a way to easily get feedback. The best way to do that is by including a call to action. Actually ask people to do something. For example, Starbucks' rewards program gives you a free cup of coffee after you earn 12 stars. You earn stars each time you purchase something from the coffee shop. This is a good example of getting customer engagement—they give to get.

Working with Internal Recruiters

The larger your company, the higher the probability you have internal staff charged with finding, qualifying, and hiring personnel. For the hiring function to be effective when delegated to a special group, you need to focus on frequent and thorough communication with the hiring team.

Ideally, when you're looking for a new employee, you'll make a detailed description of your ideal candidate to highlight the primary characteristics you're looking for in a new employee. For example, demographic criteria could include things like age range, nationality and/or languages spoken, gender, location, work from home availability, and veteran status.

The psychological and emotional traits you desire might mean someone who's calm under pressure, mature, and reserved. Or you might want someone who is enthusiastic, talkative, and assertive. A candidate's attitude might be important, too, especially as it relates to the customers or coworkers with whom they'll be working. Their past work experience, including special qualifications, management experience, or supervisory responsibility, are also key to note.

Also clearly define when they need to be available and the details of the required schedule they'll be keeping. Company plans for growth; seasonal demands; and probable vacancies due to promotions, illness, and vacations must be factored in and planned for as well.

I recommend you design a probationary period for the new employee—and for you—to evaluate how appropriate the mutual fit is. That way, you have an easy out, with a precise timeline, if it doesn't work.

 MANAGER MINEFIELD

> The biggest hiring problem with large companies is the lack of effective coordination in defining the needs and requirements of the managers who will be working with the new people. The most direct way to solve this common problem is for the manager to be intimately involved with the recruiting team and participating in the hiring interviews and decision-making.

Be sure all your plans, paperwork, and proposed interview questions are reviewed by human resources and your company's legal department. This is potentially a contentious and legalistic environment, and you want to be well grounded in the law.

Hiring Employment Agencies

Temporary staffing companies, employment agencies, and head-hunters are all available to you as you seek out new candidates for your company. Each is different and fulfills unique needs, but they can be invaluable tools when you're pressed for time, have limited resources to devote to recruiting, or have a very occasional need for hiring new people.

Also consider employee leasing companies. With these groups, the employee legally works for the leasing company, which leases the employee to you to work at your company.

Temporary staffing is used mostly for administrative staff or repetitive work. Several firms lease accounting people as well. One advantage of this type of arrangement is that the cost is incurred only for as long as you have the demand. You don't have to have staff work on recruiting, finding, interviewing, and hiring people. You just put in a request for the type of work you need done, and they send you candidates.

This field is expanding, and agencies are diversifying to include several types of workers, from maintenance to clerical, consulting to legal or accounting.

One side benefit of working with employment agencies is that you might be able way to evaluate an employee while they're on temporary status and if he or she is a good worker, you can arrange with the providing agency to hire the person full-time. This option usually comes with a fee, but it's probably an attractive alternative financially. Additionally, by observing a temporary employee's behavior, you know the quality of the person before you decide to hire them.

Recruiting should be a constant theme within your company. Even if you don't have an imminent need, continually talk up your company in the community, at association meetings, and to vendors and customers. It's just a matter of time until you'll need to fill a position. In all your business and social encounters, let those around you know you're always looking for good people.

> **LEADING THOUGHT**
>
> I am convinced that nothing we do is more important than hiring and developing people. At the end of the day you bet on people, not on strategies.
>
> —Lawrence Bossidy, former COO of GE

The Least You Need to Know

- A complete job description is necessary before you can begin the recruiting process.
- People come and go; this is normal and will actually revitalize your organization.
- A candidate's experience and background are important, but not as important as their culture and how their character matches your team.
- Finding good candidates is the responsibility of everyone in the company, not just human resources.
- You should be on the lookout for good people 24/7, 12 months of the year.

CHAPTER 11

Hiring the Best and Brightest

Your reputation and your future as a manager depend on the quality of the people you hire, train, and have on your team. Staffing your group with top-notch employees starts with the hiring process. The better you learn how to hire winners, the higher the probability you and your team will win.

In this chapter, I show you a definable structure and process that can ensure you get the best and the brightest on your team. I give you all the critical information you need to identify, select, and hire the most qualified candidates.

Hiring people is not a simple mechanical task. Skill and understanding are required, and it's a process that takes time for you to learn, develop, and use effectively. With focus and determination, you can master all the necessary elements, from selection to making an offer the candidate won't be able to refuse.

This is one of the most exciting opportunities you have as a manager. You're creating your own future by carefully and intelligently selecting the people who will be joining your team and working toward common goals.

In This Chapter

* Evaluating candidates
* The hiring process
* Making your choice
* Extending an offer

Meeting Candidates

You might interview many people, but you get to choose who, among all of them, are viable candidates. Not everyone will fit the criteria you've determined you need in a candidate. In Chapter 10, I explained how to create a job description with all the characteristics you're looking for in a candidate. Now let's see how you ferret out and find those folks who meet your criteria.

During the interviewing process, you'll evaluate from various situations (assessments, tests, interviews, etc.) the applicants you have interested in working with you and your company. Likewise, the applicants will be making evaluations of you. All the work you've done to expose your company to the community will help; however, you also need to have available a brochure, pamphlet, or at least a fact sheet about your organization. This should be available to candidates before they're interviewed. Resourceful candidates will take it upon themselves to do research on your company—and maybe even you—before the interview.

To determine who the ideal candidate is, you need to boil down all the criteria you've accumulated to a few primary requirements and qualifications you'll be looking for during this process. You (or perhaps your assistant if you have one) need to define three primary areas as you look through the applicants' initial paperwork: required education, job experience, and credentials or licenses. The filled-in application or résumé should clearly spell out whether or not the person meets the mark.

Once you select those who meet the initial requirements, the real fun begins. I highly recommend you have a series of assessments, tests, and exercises for your interviewees to take. You can have them do these at the beginning of the process or possibly interspersed among other elements such as interviews.

SKILL BUILDER

You'll get the best picture of a candidate by having several different elements to the interview process and be sure more than just you interview each candidate. The combined perspective of several different people and various assessments will help you make a better choice.

Develop a system to collect observations of all the people who interface with a candidate. Include your receptionist, assistant, coworkers, executives, and those you call for references and verification of employment. Record this information on a chart that ranks all the observations so the applicant actually gets a score. Check with human resources and an attorney about anything you plan to write down or use to ensure you're following the letter and intent of the law.

Using Assessments

You'll save time and money if you deliberately structure your hiring process to include assessments. It's possible to use assessments to define the characteristics of your ideal candidate by surveying your current employees. You want to compare your most productive people against the least productive workers. What attributes make for a high-achieving employee in your department? An assessment can be used to identify those characteristics.

You also should use an assessment to determine the behavioral style of every candidate. Certain styles fit best and flourish in certain situations, and combinations of styles are doomed to failure in other situations. For example, asking a high C to work in an unstructured public relations and promotion role goes against all their instincts. The same is true when you ask a low D to close sales; they just don't want to do that to people. (Refer to Chapter 4 for a review.)

Assessments are inexpensive, easy to administer, and customizable to meet your specific needs. They add to the total picture you paint as you review an applicant. Don't use them alone or as the only criteria to evaluate a candidate, however. They're best used as an additional data point.

Employing Exercises

Assume you're looking for a person to do customer service and handle complaints on the phone. Common sense dictates that the first encounter and interview with all applicants for this job should be a phone interview. During the phone interview, have the applicant role-play how they would handle a fictitious situation comparable to what they would be doing if they got the job. Grade them on their voice, diction, tone, attitude, ability to adapt, sensitivity, and anything else you believe is important.

If you're hiring someone for an information technology (IT), position, give the applicant a test about various programs. Using a PC or Mac, have them create a solution to a typical problem they might work on in the new job. Test their ability to develop and design algorithms or find a glitch in a system. If they're in graphic design, have them create a one-page brochure and demonstrate their creativity and speed of execution. Do they ask questions so they understand the big picture? Some technology people are so enamored with code, they lose touch with the real business objective.

Sales positions are easy to fill, but finding a good salesperson is hard. In the first interview, hand them your pen and ask them to sell you the pen. Or actually take the applicant out on a sales call or to a networking event and ask them to prospect for business cards. See how much information they can gather, and watch their style of interfacing with people.

If you're hiring a truck driver, a bus driver, or a pilot, have them demonstrate their ability to drive the truck, bus, or plane. You can also test them for their knowledge of the rules, regulations, and requirements of the specific job. If you're hiring a spokesperson, have them give you a speech. Have a bookkeeper or accountant work with journals and financial statements. Ask them to analyze the strengths and weaknesses of your department's financial status. You can do the same type of exercise for a plumber, carpenter, or any other position. Have a maintenance person repair something.

During all these types of exercises, it's your job to observe and evaluate not only what they do but also how well they do it. Also evaluate their resourcefulness, adaptability, and how they handle things emotionally. Remember to record the results and include the information on the chart you create for each applicant.

Holding Interviews

Getting one on one with a job applicant is the highest-payoff activity you can engage in to determine if they're a good match for your organization. Ideally, you'll have more than one person interview each applicant and have at least three interviews conducted at different times. As with the assessments, remember to combine and evaluate the results of each interview on the chart you create for each candidate.

Hold one of the interviews at your office and near the actual job environment so you can give the applicant a brief tour of where they'll be working if they're hired, and let them see who works there now.

It's best to be open and transparent and avoid all types of games and manipulation. That can only hurt your reputation and compromise your integrity. Imagine how you'd feel if you were hired thinking you'll work locally only to find out that half the time you'll be expected to travel out of town. Or you agree to take a job and then discover you have to pay for training or the real difficulties in the job were whitewashed. If ugly, dirty, or difficult tasks are included in the job, let applicants know up front.

> **MANAGER MINEFIELD**
>
> Many times I have to ask interviewees not to talk about a particular area because they start to share personal things. If you're a skilled listener, you'll have the same problem.

The actual job interview need not be a marathon. If you have well-thought-out questions, you'll learn a lot in a relatively short amount of time. Be sure to have your questions prepared in advance.

I believe it's beneficial to let the applicant know the basic questions you'll be asking before they come into the interview. I've done hundreds of job interviews for my own companies and for client companies, I always let the applicant know the questions, and I still get tons of useful information. By sharing the questions relative to suitability and what kinds of skills you expect in the successful applicant, the person will be able to agree or not agree to submit to the questions. When they have time to think about the question beforehand, they are reassured you're not trying to play games and trick them and, therefore, they'll be more honest and open.

Once you become a skilled interviewer, it's easy to see through false or misleading statements. Applicants might say one thing and then, when you ask to have them share an example of how something worked for them in the past, they could be stuck or unrealistic in their examples and explanation if they're not being truthful.

The interview should be a gentle, flowing conversation using your questions as the agenda. Because you're primarily listening, be sure you pay attention to the candidate's tone, body language, and context of their responses. By context, I mean, how they frame the answer. Do they use the word *I* a lot? How do they refer to their previous boss, coworkers, and company? Are they spoken about in a positive context, or does the candidate tend to belittle and blame others?

Listen well to determine if they're talking about things, people, or ideas. Do they think and talk big picture or more minuscule details and trivia? Can you imagine how they might blend with the other people on your team? Listen for emotion, and notice what they don't talk about. Often a person reveals the most significant things by what they avoid talking about.

Do they have an internal locus of control or an external locus of control? What's the primary attribute they would bring to your team that's currently missing or that you need more of to balance your group?

Have a score sheet on which you can make a mark and very brief note during the interview. After the applicant leaves, take a few minutes and review the interview in your head and make necessary comments and evaluations on your score sheet so you can add the results to the chart. It's critical that all interviewers are well trained so they know what questions to ask, what records to keep, and how to make judgments and evaluations of candidates.

Some attorneys have advised me that it's wise to have a company policy of always destroying any notes you take during an interview immediately after your meeting. They believe, from a legal point of view, it's best to not take any notes while you talk because anything you write down could be used as evidence in the eventuality there is ever a lawsuit. The problem with this philosophy is if that there's nothing written down, the judge will only have verbal testimony to use in deciding the case—"he said, she said."

You might have heard the old adage, "If it's written down, it happened. If it's not written down, it didn't happen." That's why it's so important to have contemporaneous records to support your financial expenses, income, etc. when you have an audit with the Internal Revenue Service. The same principle applies to everything in business, including job interviews, reprimands, and when hiring and firing employees.

Asking Questions

The interview isn't all about the applicant coming in prepared. You have to be prepared as well. And part of that means ensuring you ask the best questions to best get to know the applicant. The quality of your questions determines the quality of information you receive. Your questions also can lead the interview conversation.

 MANAGER MINEFIELD

> I urge you not to expressly or impliedly, directly or indirectly, question the interviewee or engage in conversation regarding religion (except to explain the company's policy regarding religious holidays, e.g., Christian, Jewish, Muslim, atheist, etc.), race, nationality, immigration status, whether the applicant rents or owns their residence, sex or sexual orientation, marital status, pregnancy or the possibility of pregnancy, parental obligations, or physical or mental handicaps (unless the interviewee raises the issue).

There are two primary areas for questions: work related and personal attitude and character questions. A former human resources executive, now a successful trainer and speaker and a dear friend of mine, Phillip Van Hooser with Van Hooser Associates, offers these questions as those best to ask during an interview:

Interest in the organization:

1. What do you know about our organization, including its history?

2. What do you know about our products and/or services?

3. Where or how did you hear about this opening?

4. What made you apply for this position?

Work-related:

1. What do you consider to be your greatest accomplishment?

2. Tell me briefly about your past work history.

3. What previous work experiences do you think have prepared you for this position?

4. Which position has given you the most satisfaction?

5. Which position was the most frustrating for you?

6. Describe one or two of the most important accomplishments in your career to date.

7. What kinds of supervision have you experienced in your previous jobs?

8. Describe your favorite supervisor.

9. What kind of supervisory style would you use with your subordinates?

10. What might your subordinates say are your strengths and weaknesses?

11. What would you say are your work strengths? Your weaknesses?

12. What has been your biggest career disappointment?

13. Why did you choose this career?

14. Why are you leaving your current position?

15. What would make you leave us?

16. What kinds of coworkers do you like best?

17. What kind of organization would you like to work for?

18. How does this open position fit into your career plan?

19. What new knowledge or experience did you gain from your last job?

20. Why should we hire you?

21. What did you do that was innovative or new on your last job?

SKILL BUILDER

Remember, the person asking questions is always in control.

Education and training:

1. What kind of formal training have you had?

2. What special certificates have you received?

3. What special skills do you have?

4. What aspects of your education or training have best prepared you for this position?

5. Which courses did you like most in college?

6. Which courses did you like least in college?

Personal attitude and character:

1. What has been your greatest business success or experience?

2. How much time out of each 24 hours do you devote to …

    Your occupation?

    Sleep?

    Play and relaxation?

    Self-improvement?

    Family?

    Other?

3. For you, the desirable way to deal with most other people is … (Please rate these from 1 to 4 with 1 being most and 4 the least appealing.)

    Logical and restrained.

    Deliberate and patient.

    Open and enthusiastic.

    Direct and decisive.

4. What are some personal areas you would like to improve?

5. If we don't hire you, what are your plans?

Disclaimer: These questions are for informational purposes only and not for the purpose of providing legal advice. You should contact your attorney to obtain advice with respect to any specific question.

Obviously, there's a similarity in some of these questions, and you wouldn't want to ask them all. This is a comprehensive yet partial list; there are many more questions you might ask. Be sure you transfer the notes you take on these interview questions to your chart for each applicant.

Here's a sample of some of your possible criteria with definitions and a rating scale:

Summary of Interview Results

Appearance: Professional attire, neat personal grooming, good posture and body language.

Low   1   2   3   4   5   6   7   High

Eloquence: Executive-style vocabulary, grammar, diction, and proper use of the English language; ability to express ideas clearly.

Low   1   2   3   4   5   6   7   High

Listening: Active listening skills, eye contact, patient, able to grasp ideas quickly. Do they interrupt or have nervous habits?

Low   1   2   3   4   5   6   7   High

Ethics: Is honesty apparent? Do they bend the rules to get what they want? What do they say, value, and pay attention to?

Low   1   2   3   4   5   6   7   High

Team player: Do they share the glory, or is the word *I* used a lot? How do they talk about their old bosses and coworkers?

Low   1   2   3   4   5   6   7   High

Career orientation: How many jobs has the applicant held, and for how long each? Do they talk in terms of helping find solutions and contributing, or is it "What do *I* have to do?" What are their long-term goals: promotion, income, freedom, and desire to learn more? What questions do they ask?

Low   1   2   3   4   5   6   7   High

Motivation: What do they talk about: challenges, money, friendships, pride in accuracy? Are they persistent and achievement-oriented?

Low   1   2   3   4   5   6   7   High

Concept of work: Do they have the big picture in mind, or do they focus on smaller details? How much do they stretch their ideas, stories, and frame of reference?

Low   1   2   3   4   5   6   7   High

Past experience: How valuable is their past experience, and is it on positive terms?

Low   1   2   3   4   5   6   7   High

Use the same low to high scale for each additional criteria and question you have.

MANAGER MINEFIELD

Don't hire someone because they're just like you. Don't get impatient and hire the first or second person you interview based on your gut feelings. Don't ask personal or non-job-related questions during the interview process. Don't slow or hinder the process and cause delays in decision-making. And don't talk too much during the interview; opt for 90 percent listening.

Making a Decision

When you and others in your organization have interviewed several applicants and you've decided on a few good candidates, you're close to making your final decision. But before you do, using your short list, it's time for the last test.

Call all the references your applicants provided, and find out what they're willing to share of a positive and negative nature. Hopefully, they'll be forthcoming in their feedback. Sometimes former employers aren't very helpful because of legal worries or having been burned in the past. Do your best to get information from them, and if you can, probe into areas that seem to be deliberately not spoken about.

You should consider all references, whether good or bad, but it's unlikely that they'll be a deciding factor. If you have doubts, they might confirm your doubts, however. Likewise, they might confirm positive thoughts you have about an applicant. References probably won't give you dramatically unique information if you've done a thorough job in the hiring process. But do call them though. What they have to say could save you from making a very costly mistake.

I suggest you keep a few things in mind as you go through the final decision process. First, there's no single item, characteristic, or reason why you should select anyone. Instead, you should be looking for patterns. It's difficult to get a precise picture of exactly how a person is going to work out once you hire them, but patterns are much more reliable than individual data points or elements in making a decision. Look for clusters of information that help you see a pattern in behavior or attitude.

Also remember to compare the results you attained from the assessments, exercises, and interviews and your chart to the original job description you created before the hiring process kicked off.

> ## LEADING THOUGHT
>
> Your employees come first. And if you treat your employees right, guess what? Your customers come back, and that makes your shareholders happy. Start with employees and the rest follows from that.
>
> —Herb Kelleher

When everything has been evaluated and you're about to make up your mind I suggest you assess two final elements. First, what is their why? Why do they want to join your company? Are they just looking for a job? Is it just about the money? Do they only know your industry and have no other alternatives? Ideally, you want an employee who has passion for the industry, their job, and your organization. It's the candidate's attitude and emotion that will make big things happen. All the knowledge, past experience, and skill is useless if there's no passion or there's a lack of a positive attitude. With passion and a positive attitude, miraculous things can happen. When in doubt, go for the good attitude.

The other final test should be, are they thinking and planning to have a life of significance as opposed to just being successful? Significance is greater than success. It means the person is focused on goals and achievements beyond their own personal gain. They want to make a difference. People who want to live a life of significance make the world a better place, and they'll do that through incredible achievement with you and your company. Such people are a joy to work with, and you'll have to run fast to just keep up.

Remember, you want to hire people who are smarter, are younger, and who have more energy than you do.

Making an Offer

Once you decide who your best candidate is, you really shift into sales mode. The key to this final part of the hiring process is to remember that "Sellin' ain't tellin'; askin' is." So here are a few questions you might ask your candidate:

> Would this schedule work for you?
>
> If we made you an offer, what do you think would be your weak spot in this job?
>
> Is there any reason you wouldn't be able to, or wouldn't want to, work here?
>
> For you, what would be the best part about working here?
>
> If we were able to make you an offer, what would you expect it to be?
>
> What factors would cause you to reject an offer?

When you start to ask this type of questions, the candidate is going to sense that there's a possibility they're going to get an offer. You'll see the excitement rise in their eyes and body language.

When the time feels right, you can simply say, "Well, I am happy to say we would like to offer you this position at *X, Y, Z.*" Now keep your mouth shut, and wait until they respond. If they say "yes," stand up, extend your hand, and welcome them to your organization with a warm handshake and a big smile.

If for some reason they want to think about it, set a specific time for their final decision. Don't do anything else until you get a final decision. Don't make contact with the other candidates until the job is filled. If your first choice isn't available, you can then offer the job to your second choice or continue to seek new candidates and do more interviewing.

Once you receive a final commitment, start the process to matriculate them into your organization. And congratulations! You did it!

The Least You Need to Know

- Compare your ideal candidate with the list of traits and characteristics you've deemed requisites for the job.

- Custom design assessments with which you can do the initial applicant qualification. This will save time and money.

- Listen well during the interview, and remember that the person asking questions is always in control.

- Design specific exercises to test the applicants' skills at performing specific tasks needed in the job.

- Focus primarily on attitude and suitability of the applicant to fit with your culture. Secondarily, focus on his or her skills.

CHAPTER 12

Setting Up an Orientation Plan

I remember my first day at Merrill Lynch. When I returned from New York City after 6 months of training, my brain was full of ideas. Having passed all the tests to become a stockbroker, I arrived at the office early—6 A.M. The office manager greeted me, put his hand on my shoulder, showed me my desk with a phone and phone book on it, and said, "Here you go, Dave. Good luck."

At home I had a pregnant wife. We lived in a small rental, and I was excited and scared. Would I make it? What do I do next? What are they thinking about me, the new guy? Everyone was busy working on the phone. The name of the game was "dial for dollars."

Well, I made it, and actually did very well. However, over the years, I've learned a lot about people and business. In this chapter, I want to share some ideas on how you might welcome new people, help them assimilate into your company, and train them to be powerful contributors. It'll be good for you and good for them, and your company will profit.

In This Chapter

- Making a great first impression
- Organizing the orientation process
- Establishing effective training
- Orientation mistakes to avoid

The First Impression

It's essential that you have a written, well-organized orientation plan to bring new people into your company. Your plan should include the necessary events, the people who are responsible for those events, the sequence of what needs to be learned and completed, and the when and why of each element. I recommend you structure the plan so it's a celebration to welcome the new employee, establish relationships, help him or her learn all about the company and your group, and make the new team member feel as if they're a vital part of the company.

Paperwork, documentation, and legal requirements must be completed, but that shouldn't be the main focus of your plan. Yes, you must have all that done in a timely manner; however, remember that people will remember how you made them feel on their first day much longer than all the smaller details and paperwork.

> **LEADING THOUGHT**
>
> In the same way that I tend to make up my mind about people within thirty seconds of meeting them, I also make up my mind about whether a business proposal excites me within about thirty seconds of looking at it. I rely far more on gut instinct than researching huge amounts of statistics.
>
> —Richard Branson

Meeting the Mentor

One of the very first things you should do is introduce the new person to their buddy or mentor. This is a person who knows the company, your group, or your team and has experience for a considerable amount of time. The mentor has the big-picture perspective, and they enjoy working with people. Do not assign a grumpy or negative person to help the new person.

The buddy should have a copy of the orientation plan and basically be available to answer any questions the newbie has and anticipate areas that might be problems. He or she should be able to tell the new report everything from where a good place to grab a quick lunch is to the history of the company and who the real people of influence are within the company and why.

Making Introductions

After you introduce the mentor, the three of you should make the basic rounds of who's who, what they do, and why the new person might want to talk to or get to know these key people.

For example, introduce team members with something like, "Joe this is Mary, our payroll and accounts payable supervisor. You want to know her because she prints and distributes your paycheck every two weeks." Then explain to Mary why you're so excited to have Joe in the company.

When you tell others about the new person, you're setting expectations for the new person as well as your current people. Don't just say a bunch of platitudes. Instead, make your description of the new hire specific and relevant to the real qualifications and future responsibility you expect the new person to fulfill.

It's an excellent idea to have some kind of event—be it a coffee break, team meeting, or formal announcement—to introduce the new recruit to everyone in the company. This is an ideal time to brag a bit about why he or she is such a good find and why you're looking forward to his or her contribution to the group. Note this is different from what you put in the company newsletter. This is more personal and emotional, and it's expressed on the new hire's very first day. Make it a time to celebrate the new person.

More First-Day To-Dos

As part of the orientation plan, have a two or three people be prepared to speak to the new hire and ask them out to lunch on their first day. Be sure these folks are excited about the opportunity to get to know the new team member, and give them some ideas of what to cover during the lunch. Share with them the concept of how important it is to ask questions and listen to the new person's responses. There's nothing more beautiful than the sound of your own name and an opportunity to talk about yourself. Also, have the company pay for this lunch if possible.

Near the end of the first day, be sure you personally check in with the new hire to see how their day went, if they need anything, want to ask you anything, and what their impression of the company and your people is. During this time, you can brag about the company and your team a bit. But be sure to let the new staff member know how glad you are he or she decided to join you.

Do you see how different this kind of a first day is compared to my own, "Here you go Dave. Good luck," first day?

Your Orientation Plan

One day does not a career make. It's wonderful that your new hire have a dynamic first day, but your orientation plan that starts on day 1 needs to be the beginning of a long-term process. I suggest your orientation process be at least 90 days and preferably up to 6 months.

The elements of a good orientation plan include welcoming, administrative requirements, company policies, employee handbook, training program, and progress monitoring. The tone of the entire plan should be congruent with the culture of your organization. If they differ, be sure you modify the previously suggested ideas for the first day to be consistent with your company's culture.

Company Policies

Your new hire should have a copy of all critical company policies. Ideally, this will be in the form of an employee handbook. Seek professional counsel when putting this together if your company doesn't already have one. You want to ensure you cover everything, plus there are many legal issues to consider.

Be sure you include the vacation policies, the definition of a sick day, and how many sick and vacation days are authorized. Also include safety rules and concerns as well as the schedule for safety meetings and other required briefings such as sexual harassment and substance abuse training. It should cover all employee benefits, pay schedules, and security restrictions, too. Another section should cover termination policies and any other conditions that affect employees.

Training

If you're a learning organization, you'll have a program of continual learning both inside and outside the company through seminars, schools, and external training programs. Outline these in the material you furnish a new employee.

> **LEADING THOUGHT**
>
> Starbucks is not an advertiser; people think we are a great marketing company, but in fact we spend very little money on marketing and more money on training our people than advertising.
>
> —Howard Schultz, chairman and CEO of Starbucks

Also include a review of the company's education policy, training requirements for various positions, and what's necessary to earn promotions. The military is a good example of this. Many young people join the military because of the benefit of the special schools and training it provides.

It's smart to invest in training your people so they have more knowledge and expertise. This, in turn, makes them a more valuable asset for your company. But you must be sure you have such a good company and take such good care of your people they don't want to leave. Make it a win-win situation.

In the financial services industry, certain firms are known for quality training. Often people will seek to join those firms specifically for the training offered. Then the firm has the option of keeping the best-educated employees and letting others move on to other firms.

Monitoring

Staying in touch with your new recruit and ensuring continual follow-up will make or break your orientation program. In your written orientation plan, have a clear schedule of who is responsible and what the checkpoints are along the way. The mentor is a part of this program, but it's not the only part. As manager, you are ultimately responsible. On a regular basis, you need to check in with your new employee to see how they're doing. Don't only get feedback from their supervisor, if there is one. Also periodically talk directly with the employee.

The orientation theme should include a team approach. That team involves you, the employee, the mentor, his or her coworkers, his or her supervisors, and upper management. You need to be continually monitoring all your people to see how they're doing. The new employee is just another of your key people now.

The same manager who patted me on the shoulder the first day at Merrill Lynch came by my desk my second or third month and asked me out to lunch. I still remember it. He did it because I was doing well and bringing in nice commissions, but it still was a kind gesture.

You cannot underestimate the power and impact of an act of kindness to a new employee. When people perform well, reward them with unexpected acts of kindness. You and the new worker will both benefit and appreciate it.

Effective Training

Training is done to affect a result that invariably causes a change in behavior. The only way people will change is if they see a reason to change that creates a benefit for them or avoids a loss. The decision is usually made because of a significant emotional event or a person realizes they must make a change to get what they want. With either option, for the change to be most effective, it takes commitment, repetition, and time.

As a manager, you first need to define what results you want to achieve and then determine what behaviors in you and your people are required to achieve those results. One way to learn and ensure those changes take place is by implementing a well-structured training program.

> **LEADING THOUGHT**
>
> Tell me and I may forget. Show me and I may remember. But involve me and I will understand.
>
> —Chinese proverb

People learn by being immersed in a process that requires participation. Effective training includes the following elements:

Spaced repetition Forming a habit takes multiple repetitions over a period of time. Some say at least 30 days.

Sensory involvement Talking is the least effective way to share information. People need tactile, auditory, visual, and interpersonal dialogue and involvement to learn.

Relevance Everyone wants to know "what's in it for me?" Unless there's a personal benefit and a clear connection to that benefit, the training will be ignored.

Foundation The basis of all learning is what the individual has already experienced and learned in his or her past. Growing from that foundation is critical and must be clearly understood.

Impact Memory is emotion-specific. Science has proven that without emotional involvement, the memory is not strong.

Because of these fundamental realities, the one-day seminar or all-day speech isn't very effective. For lasting change, a commitment and investment of time and money is required. The seminar or speech is a great way to introduce a subject or course, but if you want to achieve a long-term benefit, you need involvement, repetition, a clear reason the participant understands, and emotional impact. I also recommended you establish a system of feedback and follow-up to help reinforce the learning.

Many companies have, what we call in the seminar business, "smile sheets." These are close to useless. It's good to get instant feedback to see if people enjoyed themselves—and they will if the presenter uses humor, stays on schedule, is relatively knowledgeable, and is charming. However, that's not enough to warrant paying money for a presentation, in my opinion.

Just like companies hire people because of their technical skills and fire people because of their lack of communication skills, they also hire speakers and presenters because of their celebrity draw and get frustrated after the event because of the lack of content or value delivered. People might enjoy the moment, but there's little or no tangible benefit for the money spent.

You have to decide if you're trying to simply entertain your people or if you're designing and implementing a program to help shape their behavior, increase their knowledge, and change the future of the company for the better.

Mistakes to Avoid

I've seen managers make five common mistakes with new employees. If you can avoid these, the probability of your new employee being successful within your organization dramatically improves.

Unclear Expectations

Be sure the new person understands what's expected of them. This is best done by writing down exactly what's expected and having precise measurements to show how well they're doing. It might be necessary to adjust your expectations up or down from time to time. To determine if an adjustment is necessary, you need to personally communicate with the employee.

At the beginning, keep your communication mostly task focused, and be very direct and specific. As they develop some ability and confidence, you can reduce the focus on the task and start to include some relationship communication. All the while, the basis of your relationship must include specific and tangible measurement.

SKILL BUILDER

You must present opportunity and rewards for your people as they improve and grow. If they perceive your company as a dead-end street or someplace that lacks exciting options in the future, they'll either leave or not try to grow in any way. Your employees need to help your company grow, and your company needs to give your employees room to grow, develop, and personally profit from their growth and contribution.

Old Habits

The majority of all human behavior is habitual. This goes for you, the new person you just hired, and everyone in between. Be aware of this, and monitor your behavior and theirs.

Periodically—at least a few times each year—review your habits and ask yourself if each behavior is helping advance your goals or holding you back. Get feedback from others as well. They'll be aware of things you do, perhaps unconsciously, that might be destructive or hindering your progress.

Let your new hire know they'll be monitored for their habits and you have a system in place to continually evaluate and improve habits. Be sure they know this system applies to everyone and they'll not only be expected to work on themselves but also help others improve. This can be a positive team initiative if you deliberately set it up that way.

As you identify each habit, in yourself or in your staff, list it as either having a plus, minus, or neutral impact on getting the results you want and need. Virtually all the habits you and your people have developed over time will relate to four basic categories when in the work environment: plan, communicate, manage, and execute.

As a manager, you'll spend most of your time planning and communicating, followed by managing, and finally some execution. The front-line worker spends most of his or her time in execution and some time in the other three areas. Continually evaluate how you and your people are spending time.

When you have habits that don't directly relate to accomplishing one of these primary activities, it's time to implement a program to change habits. A few examples of nonproductive habits you might observe in your organization are arriving late for work, spending inordinate amounts of time having coffee breaks, and too often participating in idle chitchat or gossip.

In each of the four areas, certain habits advance your goals and some hinder them. The following table outlines a few ideas to stimulate your thinking.

Positive Habits	Negative Habits
Planning:	
Scheduling set times to plan every day	Erratic or sporadic morning and evening planning time
Getting feedback and input from team members	Impulsively deciding to change things
Referring to written plan often and using it to guide others	Getting too busy to plan how to inspect what you expect
Communicating:	
Listening well to understand how people feel	Interrupting others when they're speaking
Scheduling one-to-one time with all direct reports	Ignoring others or focusing on tasks over people
Taking notes of ideas and concerns people express and following up	Humoring people and brushing off complaints

Positive Habits	Negative Habits
Managing:	
Establishing agreed metrics of performance	Evaluating people for likability versus results
Asking questions to help workers discover their own solutions	Telling people how to solve problems rather than helping them figure it out
Holding people accountable even when it's uncomfortable	Giving people too much slack and seeking favor
Executing:	
Doing what you say you'll do	Using excuses or blaming a scapegoat
Being timely, considerate, and accurate	Being casual and laid-back
Admitting and apologizing for mistakes	Using the word *I* a lot

Training is the best way to help people change the way they allocate their time so they become more effective and efficient. Stay on top of this concept so you can avoid having to change in reaction to a significant emotional event.

 MANAGER MINEFIELD

Some of my clients have tried to have anonymous computerized reporting systems as part of employee evaluations. It's very easy for this system to turn negative and create fear and animosity between workers. I don't recommend them. There's no substitute for two people meeting face to face to work out issues of disagreement as well as positive issues designed to help each person improve. Communication is an art form, that's why it's not uncommon for people to be misunderstood, especially when using email or other forms of sterile communication.

Low Emotional Intelligence

Emotional intelligence is a combination of several abilities. First and foremost, you must be aware of your own emotions and have the ability to control them. In addition, you need to develop the ability to read, understand, influence, and lead other people's emotional states. This is most important because as I mentioned earlier in the book, decisions are made based on a trigger that's primarily emotional in nature. Decisions are not based on rational facts and figures alone. The final and determining factor is emotional.

Becoming sensitive to your own emotions as well as others' is a skill most people can learn, and you'll be able to improve with training. The process of increasing your emotional awareness takes significant effort, understanding, and possibly even coaching. The same is true for learning how to control your emotions and influence others. You've spent a lifetime becoming who you are right now. To change in any meaningful way requires time and effort, sometimes with skilled guidance as well.

Notice the role emotion plays in both your own decisions and your staff's. When combined with improved emotional intelligence, the DISC model (discussed in Chapter 4) will make you a powerful, influential, and dynamic manager when it comes to dealing with people.

I recently received an email from a coaching client who has decided to change companies after being constantly frustrated with his employer. He's analytical and good with numbers yet has highly developed interpersonal skills. Over time, he has evaluated lots of data composed of facts and figures. He decided to leave his current company after much analysis and anguish. The trigger that caused him to consider leaving was pure emotion.

My client didn't get what he wanted, emotionally, from his current employer. He received a significant raise, but his employer didn't understand what he really wanted. It wasn't just more money; he had his heart set on certain achievement benchmarks. The company didn't communicate their intentions with him about career development because they thought the main factor was money. My client perceived this as a lack of respect, honesty, and fair play.

They say depression is when reality doesn't meet expectations. Understanding people isn't easy. It takes hard work and highly developed perception.

Inadequate Feedback

Feedback must be frequent and fair. The orientation plan you create and use should have a structured method of obtaining feedback often. That feedback should be objective as well as subjective. You need to know what the performance numbers are and, most importantly, how those numbers make your employees feel.

Here's how you could approach this:

> Joe, you are ahead of our scheduled production. I am very proud of you and your effort. Looks like we made a good decision hiring you. How do you feel about it?

Or:

> Joe, it looks like you are a bit behind in production. I'm really glad to have you with us, so how can we ensure you master this part of the job? What do you need?

Then you need to deliberately work with the employee to define what comes next. If they're below the predetermined standards, design a plan to provide more training or coaching to get them up to speed. Then check in with the employee periodically to find out how things are going. Do you need to make any adjustments? Are there any personality conflicts? Is progress on track? And if so, what's the next step?

When you have an employee who's achieving ahead of schedule, you still need to be involved. How can you continue the great progress? Is the job too easy for them? Are they still excited and motivated? What else should you provide for them to accelerate their progress even more?

Never lose sight of how valuable recognition is, even if that feedback is a simple "Thank you." People need to be noticed, talked to, and given positive and negative feedback. In their book, *The One Minute Manager,* Kenneth Blanchard, PhD, and Spencer Johnson, MD, recommend 1-minute praisings with 1-minute reprimands and 1-minute goal-setting. It's good advice.

Lack of Caring

Everyone is busy. If you're too busy to stay in touch with your people, especially the new ones, chances are they'll leave.

Examine your reason for being in your current position. Be sure you want to be there, and if you do, get involved with your team members. Let them know you care, but know that the only way they'll believe you care is if they see it in your behavior. How are you spending your time?

> **LEADING THOUGHT**
>
> I may have made my reputation as a general in the Army, and I'm very proud of that. But I've always felt that I was more than one-dimensional. I'd like to think I'm a caring human being.
>
> —Norman Schwarzkopf

You show how much you care by the consistency and quality of your interactions with your people. Many frequent check-ins with your group make much more of an impact than the rare long meeting. It might help to set up a checklist upon which you list all your people and each time you spend a few minutes with someone, put a check mark next to their name. It's very easy to get into routines and just see and talk to the same few people often while you hardly interact with others. Believe me, they notice.

It's just like brushing your teeth or dusting your house. You have to do it consistently and often. Otherwise, small problems continue to build up and gradually turn into crises. A good manager is always reviewing, checking in, and dialoguing with his or her people.

The Least You Need to Know

- The first impression a new employee has of your company will last, so plan for it well and be sure it's organized and efficient.
- Structure a comprehensive orientation plan that ideally lasts at least 6 months.
- Be sure each new employee has a handbook and that company policies are well documented and explained.
- Training is vital and should be part of a continual learning process that starts with orientation.
- Avoid mistakes by being involved, having clear expectations for new hires, and providing frequent feedback and clear communication.

Your Management Toolkit

Any job is easier when you have the right tools and you know how to use them. In Part 4, I give you myriad proven as well as new ideas of ways you can perform your job better.

First up is communication. This is probably the most important task you must master as a manager because nothing can make or break your career faster, and with more impact, than the quality of your communication. Related to communication are meetings. In Part 4, you learn why you should have meetings, why you should minimize their number and length, and how to conduct them so they're relevant, productive, and yield results.

It's not always easy, but you must learn to delegate. The single most important way for you to increase the impact and effect you have on your organization is by delegating. I share tips on using delegation to help your people grow, encouraging them to focus on their strengths, and at the same time expand your influence throughout your company.

Your last set of tools relates to systems, operations, and technology. You learn how to build in accountability, efficiency, and a focus on what's important. All systems need to be congruent and focused, so I share principles you can employ to be sure you do just that.

CHAPTER 13

Communication Is Key

The common denominator of everything you do as a manager is communication. The better you learn how to communicate, the better everything you do will be. It's as simple as that.

I'm constantly amazed, as I work with CEOs and organizations, at how often very intelligent people have such a poor ability to communicate. You don't have to be one of them. You can become an effective communicator if you choose to work on it. In this chapter, I give you key information on all the dimensions of communication you need as a manager. Take it to heart, and realize that it takes effort in the form of learning, training, and lots of practice to become really good at communicating.

A graduate student I'm mentoring is struggling with his habit of referring to everyone as "guys." This doesn't put forth a professional image, and it's not who he wants to be. I really admire his effort and desire to correct this problem. With hard work and a clear focus, you, too, can learn to become a great communicator. Every word you say, and how you say it, does matter.

In This Chapter

- Make-or-break communication
- Communicating clearly and concisely
- Composing professional emails
- Presenting like a pro

What Matters Most

Certain principles will guide you as you strive to become a great communicator. First and foremost, you need to realize that communication is a two-way process made of broadcasting and receiving. You broadcast in many ways—letters, memos, emails, texts, as well as by using your words, tone, emotions, and body language. You receive communications in many forms, too, and process them through your eyes and your ears. Given this limitation, of just the two sources of receiving, it's essential that you really tune in and pay attention while listening.

Listening

The more perceptive you become with what you see and hear, the better you are as a listener and the more you'll understand. Recent studies have found that when people multitask, they compromise their ability to listen, remember, and focus.

Can you imagine driving your car at high speed in heavy traffic with music blaring, kids screaming, and cars in front of you driving erratically? When you try to listen to multiple things or listen to one thing while watching another, you're inhibiting the quality of your listening. If your goal is to listen to someone, you must focus on them with your eyes, with your ears, and with your concentrated attention. That means you deliberately allow no distractions.

Some managers think multitasking is almost a badge of honor—they're so much in demand, they talk on the phone while reading a note from someone standing at their desk and then wave or nod to someone passing in the hall. These folks are totally out of control, not fully focusing on anything they're doing, and not showing respect for others. They fundamentally don't know how to effectively communicate.

SKILL BUILDER

Listening is the most important part of communicating. You need to listen with your entire mind and body to really be effective.

So what are you listening for? The easy part is words and information. The person you are talking with may be sharing some facts and figures in the business environment. The best way to be sure you understand and remember lots of facts and figures is to ask for the numbers in writing or take notes.

Most people can easily remember roughly seven digits. For example, phone numbers are seven digits without the three-digit area code. When people approach old age or show signs of dementia, one of the tests often administered is to tell them three words: *tree, book, pear,* for example. After a while, the interviewer goes back and asks them if they remember the three words. If they don't remember, it's assumed they've shown one sign they might have some form of dementia. Of course, it takes several different signs to indicate someone actually might have a problem.

Another interesting fact is when a person is under great stress, is emotionally excited, or hasn't had enough sleep, they typically won't remember or listen well. The way your brain is wired makes it difficult to do several things at once, especially if you're stressed, tired, or distracted.

As an Air Force pilot, I was trained to always have a good "cross-check," which meant I always keep my eyes moving on the instruments, outside, inside, back to the instruments, etc. It's easy to get fixated on one thing and become oblivious to what else is going on around you. As a manager, you need to have a good cross-check to stay abreast of all the moving parts on your team and in your department.

When you're communicating with someone, be sure you can concentrate on them and not get distracted by other stimuli. Have you seen people fixated on their smartphones and be unaware of what's going on around them? Have you been trying to talk to someone like this and felt you weren't being listened to? It's not a good feeling, is it?

The point of these examples is to help you become more aware of yourself. What are you doing, feeling, and projecting to others? What are they doing, feeling, projecting, and saying? As a listener, you want to cross-check all the ways a person communicates—eyes, tone, body language, words, etc. It's best if you focus only on them. By doing all this, you'll soon realize that the most important part of listening is often to hear what's *not* being said.

Have you ever known someone who never talks about certain members of their family? There's likely a reason for that. Maybe they're estranged, maybe the child or spouse have mental or physical issues, or maybe it's just that they're not comfortable enough to share that with you or others for some simple but unknown reason. My point is, there's always a reason. When you're a good listener, you become sensitive to this type of issue. You also learn how to gently open doors or probe to discover what's really going on and how you might be able to help.

LEADING THOUGHT

The key to success is to get out into the store and listen to what the associates have to say. It's terribly important for everyone to get involved. Our best ideas come from clerks and stockboys.

—Sam Walton

Practice being quiet and curious while using gentle questions. Don't be the manager who's always loud and pushy and barking out orders. By deliberately striving to be understanding, you'll dramatically improve your ability to listen and, therefore, become a better communicator and a better manager.

Clarity

Without clarity, your communication is just a lot of noise. Several factors are key to ensure you're communicating clearly. As with listening, it's really your responsibility to adjust and take into consideration the other person or group of people you're communicating with.

In verbal communication, it's critical you learn how to enunciate clearly and articulately. Articulation is all about saying each syllable in a distinct, precise, and fluid manner that's easy to understand. Be sure you have excellent pronunciation, your diction is clean and sharp, and your words are well balanced and spaced. Don't mumble, run words together, or be sloppy with your speech patterns. The more you practice, the better you'll get at expressing yourself clearly.

When I was in school, no management professor ever even approached the subject of how a manager should speak. They just taught theory, models, and different ways to approach issues and problems. I'm here to tell you that in the real world, if you learn how to speak really well, you'll have fewer problems, people will respect and follow you better, and the results will be altogether greater for you and your company.

The one thing you can never hide is the way you speak. This is especially true if English isn't your first language. Invest time and energy in perfecting your ability to speak clearly, articulately, and with proper grammar.

Once you consider *how* to speak, it's important to know *what* to say and *how* to say it. I highly recommend you get in the habit of saying what's important first. Naturally, you want to be sure to provide the appropriate greetings, protocols, and a bit of self-disclosure before you jump right in, but keep all of that brief.

SKILL BUILDER

Strive to be precise, specific, and focused when communicating. Take into consideration the other person's culture, gender, and experience. Avoid jargon and irrelevant technical expressions as you speak.

During a conversation, there can be a lot going on between two people. One person is trying to share an idea, feeling, or thought with the other. The thing to be shared is affected by the speaker's past experience, culture, education, gender, and personal interests. The sender must translate the shared thing into words that are effectively "code words."

The person receiving the message will interpret the sent code words into meaning based on their own past experience, culture, education, gender, and personal interests. Then there's a process of translating the code words into new code words to communicate back to the original sender. It takes time and effort to learn how to effectively communicate.

As a manager, you'll have to give feedback, encourage your employees, and tell your staff what to do. Sometimes confrontation is difficult; feelings aren't always easy to share; and as a new manager, you might be questioning your self-worth or confidence. At times, it's almost easier to ignore a situation rather than get involved in a lengthy discussion. But you need to.

There's a helpful model to use in this process. It's really very simple, but I guarantee it's effective. It is called *being assertive*. When you observe a situation that you need to respond to, try using this three-step model:

1. I think ….

2. I feel ….

3. I want ….

For example, let's assume you have a worker who is underperforming. Here's what you could say to him:

1. Joe, I think you are behind schedule.

2. I feel you're really a very valuable part of our team, and I'm hoping you feel that way, too.

3. I want you to improve your production rate and get back on schedule by the end of the day.

Here's another example. This time, let's look at how you'd approach your assistant who isn't following up on meetings for the team:

1. Bill, I think we have a problem with follow-up from the team meeting. I haven't gotten any reports back this week.

2. You know how much I rely on you to help me keep this team working well together; without you regularly staying in touch with each team member, I don't know where we are and that causes me real stress. We can't let that happen. There's too much at stake for you and me both. Our goal is to be number one.

3. I want you to check with each team member every Tuesday morning, and give me a written report of the results by noon that day.

Being clear, articulate, and assertive doesn't come easy to everyone, so take some time to practice these simple techniques.

SKILL BUILDER

It's also important to review the behavioral style information I covered in Chapter 4. Each person is a unique individual, so you need to be continually adjusting and refining the way you communicate.

Self-Disclosure

Talking about yourself might not be the easiest thing for you to do, but it's a necessary part of effective communication. The amount of self-disclosure you share and the way you do it is worth considering.

You need to be able to share honestly about yourself with others to have authentic communication. Most of what you might share can be categorized into four areas:

- Information
- Feelings
- Needs
- Thoughts

The easiest to share is typically information. That might include your name, where you went to school, and an explanation of your work experience. When it comes to feelings, needs, and thoughts, many people feel a normal level of reservation and hesitation before they disclose this type of information.

As a manager, you might share what you need for people to do to help you accomplish your job. Imagine if you also shared how you feel about needing the work done or another form of support. Building a team requires an emotional involvement by both you and your team members. It's good to gradually share your thoughts and feelings.

When you first meet someone, it's appropriate to share a small amount of personal information before you ask them any questions. Earlier, I shared how powerful it is to ask questions and how the person asking questions is always in control. By sharing some information about yourself, before you get into any questions, you help build rapport with the other person.

Remember, communication is like dancing. You need to be in rhythm, flexible, and maintain a balance of give and take.

Communicating via Written Word

Writing is easy to do, but not always easy to do *well*. It's also a way to create a more permanent record of what you say, think, or do. When you write, you advertise to the world the quality of your thinking, your education, and your ability to express yourself. Therefore, it's essential that you write well.

Keys to Writing Well

Years ago, "father of management" Peter Drucker was my teacher at Claremont Graduate University. On the first day of class, he made a special point to assign a paper in which we summarized our thinking on a topic covered in class. Keep in mind that Drucker has written for the *Wall Street Journal, Harvard Business Review,* and countless other publications and has authored 39 books. In class, he explained how he writes, edits, rewrites, edits, and rewrites again. Vividly I remember him saying, "When you have finally gotten the paper written and rewritten so it's ready to hand in … you are ready to begin. If I have to write and rewrite, so do you."

> **LEADING THOUGHT**
>
> I have yet to see a piece of writing, political or non-political, that doesn't have a slant. All writing slants the way the writer leans, and no man is born perpendicular, although many are born upright.
>
> —E. B. White

Writing is hard work. As a manager, you need to approach writing as the sometimes-difficult task it can be as well as and a vital part of your job.

Here are a few principles I suggest you honor:

1. Clearly define your purpose. What do you hope to accomplish in this piece of writing? Be specific.

2. Start with what's most important.

3. Be brief, eliminate any unnecessary words, and use short sentences.

4. Make it conversational. Don't get too formal or technical or go off on irrelevant tangents.

5. Edit, review, edit, and review. Always use spell check.

6. If at all possible, sleep on it and review your work again the next day.

7. Have someone you respect read and edit your work before you use or send it.

MANAGER MINEFIELD

Because you don't have the advantage of being able to use your tone of voice, body language, and observation of the other person's immediate reactions, seek others' opinions on what you've written and how they might react to your communication. It's very easy to send the wrong message in writing, not knowing how the recipient might perceive your communiqué.

Email Essentials

These same principles apply to email. You might want to be clever and use abbreviations, symbols, and avatars as you do in your personal email, but I caution you to be professional and consider the recipient of your email. Do they know what LOL, AWC, BRB, OTL, or WBS mean? How would you feel if you received any of these in an email from your manager? When in doubt, keep it professional and spell it out.

Keep your emails short and to the point. You might use email for sending files and transmitting large amounts of data, but email isn't the best or most effective way to engage in significant conversations. Email is quick and easy but it's not always the best medium for time-sensitive communication. If you really need an answer or a fast confirmation, picking up the phone, walking to someone else's office, instant messaging, or even text messaging might be faster. (Stay tuned though because technology preferences change like the weather and people are always innovating and creating new technologies.)

Many busy executives I've worked with only read the first three lines of an email. That's why you want to put the important information up front. Also, be sure you use an appropriate and informative subject line. Many people only read the subject line or sender's name and then make a decision to read or delete the email. I use MailChimp to send out notices, and according to the reports I receive, the industry average of "opens" (or the number of times an email I send is opened and read) is 18.8 percent. Fortunately, my open rate varies between 35 percent to more than 50 percent.

The advantage of written communication is its ease, low cost, and flexibility. But a big disadvantage is that you're not face to face with your recipient, so you miss out on the personal connection of looking someone in the eye, watching their body language, and relating to him or her on an emotional level.

> ### 💡 SKILL BUILDER
>
> If you want to communicate in person but are across the country—or across the world—from the person you need to speak to, why not take advantage of today's technology and set up a live or video conference using Skype, FaceTime, or one of the many online meeting tools? With these resources, you at least can see the other person as you chat with them. This will greatly improve your ability to communicate effectively.

Public Speaking

There's amazing power in being able to stand up and give a presentation with confidence. But if you have a fear of or are uncomfortable speaking in front of a group, you're not alone. Some studies have indicated that public speaking is more feared than death! Even television and movie stars, who are often in front of the camera or groups of people, fear public speaking.

I've been active in professional speaking for many years and a member of the National Speakers Association for more than 20 years. I've taught college courses on speaking, coached professional speakers and executives on presentation skills, and even been coached myself. Based on my experience, I want to share with you what I believe is most important for you to know as a manager about giving presentations.

Fear Is Normal

First and foremost, realize that any fear you have about public speaking is normal. It's really all about your self-concept, so if you want to minimize your fear, work on your self-concept and especially your self-concept as it relates to speaking. What you believe and think about yourself is based on your past experiences. To have confidence, you have to have accomplished something and believe you're worthy. To be worthy is a value judgment you must make about yourself. False self-confidence or self-worth can relate to narcissism and self-absorption.

Try new things and keep track of how you do. As you get better and better, you'll develop more self-confidence. This isn't about being better than other people; rather, it's being good at what you do, knowing you're good, and not having the need to brag about it. As you develop more and more skills, your confidence will grow. When you're really good, you don't need to tell others. It'll be obvious, and they'll know by simply watching your behavior.

It might help you to join a chapter of Toastmasters International near you to gain confidence in your speaking ability and to get more comfortable in front of a group. Toastmasters chapters meet all over the world, and membership is very inexpensive.

The best advice I can give you is, to quote Nike, "Just do it." Simply make the decision that you're going to get up and speak with confidence. It helps to speak at every opportunity you can find. The more you try and practice, the better you'll get and the more confidence you'll develop.

LEADING THOUGHT

We worry about appearing awkward in a presentation. But up to a point, most people seem to feel more comfortable with less-than-perfect speaking abilities. It makes the speaker more human and more vulnerable.

—John P. Kotter

Perfect Your Presentation

How you give your presentation is about as important as what you say. Don't read your speech. It's very difficult to create and share emotion when you read. Your objective needs to be clearly defined—it will probably relate to sharing information, education, persuasion, or entertainment and above all, to get people to take action. Decide exactly *why* you're speaking.

Also, rather than writing out word for word what you want to say (which increases your likeliness to read your speech), design an outline of what you're going to say. You should do this even if you are merely doing brief introductions at a meeting. Have a beginning, body, and ending. Ideally, also tie in a call to action at the end. Here's a short example:

> Good evening. Coaching executives to create a masterpiece personally and professionally is my passion. I am a best-selling author, former CEO, and U.S. Air Force fighter pilot. If you would like a copy of my book, *The CEO Code,* please come by and say hello. My name is David Rohlander.

Notice this example starts with a focus on the audience and how they might benefit from knowing me. Then I give three facts about my credibility, and follow with a call to action. I wrap up with my name so people will remember it.

When you're giving a presentation, think about your opening and closing because you want both to be memorable. I suggest you actually memorize your first and last sentence so you can deliver them more powerfully and authentically.

Also have an idea for the introduction that will be engaging and really grab your audience. Keep in mind who your audience is and what their interests are. And try opening with one of these techniques:

- Three quotes

- A poem

- A startling statement

- An unusual or shocking fact

Your goal is to engage and get your audience's attention immediately.

Notice that when you listen to the news on television or read the newspaper, the headline is designed to hook the audience. As a manager with integrity, be sure your statements are true and grounded in reality. Don't play fast and loose with the truth just to create an interesting hook.

The body of your presentation can be long or short, but ideally you'll have three points and have emotion embedded in your message. People tend to remember things that are connected to emotion. Without emotion, they'll soon forget what you said. That's why stories are the best way to share information and teach.

Use handouts for facts and data. If you use PowerPoint, keep it simple and follow the 6×6 rule: each slide should have a maximum of six lines and six words per line. Pictures and jokes are a great use for PowerPoint. But never read from or look at the screen. Always look at your audience instead.

Finally, always be well prepared. Be sure your presentation or meeting has a theme. Create a clear and concise outline of your presentation to use as a reference, but remember not to read it or your slides. Practice your speech beforehand, and arrive early to the venue so you can get comfortable in the room. If you're using audiovisuals or a microphone, be sure to test them before anyone else arrives.

Making Your Delivery Dynamic

A few words on delivery. While you're standing in front of your audience but before you utter a single word, take a slow, deep breath and survey the room by making eye contact slowly with several people. This helps establish rapport, confidence, and curiosity for the people in attendance.

When you do speak, project your voice to the person in the back of the room. Don't shout, but do speak from your diaphragm.

And don't rush. There's a power in speaking slowly and using artful pauses and moments of silence. People who speak very rapidly often are doing so because they're nervous. Relax, take your time, connect, engage, and use pauses throughout your speech to make it understandable.

Finally, minimize the use of the first person pronoun, *I*. Tell stories, but don't share your life story or spill all your emotions in the form of a confessional. Speak with dignity and poise, and relate to your people from their frame of reference. It's really all about them.

The Least You Need to Know

- Listening is the most important part of effective communication.
- When communicating, be sure to check the other person's eyes, body language, and tone of voice in addition to the words they use.
- Listen for what the other person *isn't* saying. That's often the most revealing part of their communication.
- Communicating has give and take. Talk a little and then listen a lot; then talk a little and listen a lot.

- When you write, be sure to edit, have someone else read what you've written, and edit some more.

- When giving a presentation, make it an easygoing conversation with the audience, one person at a time. Breathe slowly and deeply, and relax.

CHAPTER 14

Making the Most of Meetings

Sure, meetings can be fun, but sometimes (more often?) they can be long and boring. And whether you enjoy meetings or not, it's probably safe to say you have far too many to go to, if you're like most managers. If you must have meetings, it's essential that you plan them well and preferably do so as far in advance as you can.

Meetings come in all types. The most productive meetings are the quality, one-to-one meetings you have with your direct reports. You also might have meetings to make announcements; celebrate events; or introduce new people, ideas, or programs. And then there are the meetings held because "that's what we've always done."

In this chapter, I give you the critical guidelines for holding productive meetings. I start at the very beginning—why have a meeting?—and then take you through the whole process of conducting great meetings and share tips for following up afterward.

In This Chapter

- Know why you're meeting
- Elements of a worthwhile meeting
- Setting useful agendas
- Following meeting fundamentals

Why Are You Meeting?

The best reason to have a meeting is to create a memorable encounter during which people can share ideas, bond, solve a problem, create a solution, or build the future. As a manager, you'll have many meetings that you'll be required to attend. You'll also find it necessary to have numerous meetings with your people for training, to release new or special information, and for a host of other reasons.

When you consider the cost of a meeting, it becomes apparent that the meeting better be very important to be worth its while. Imagine the total cost of a meeting—the preparation time, the number of people who have to be involved in the prep, and how many hours each of them has to invest. Then think of the time of all the people invited—their commuting/transportation time, waiting time, attendance time, and then more commuting/transportation time. Plus what's the loss of productivity while all these people are involved in commuting and attending the meeting? When you stop to think about it, the total expense can easily become huge.

Before you schedule a meeting, be sure to evaluate all the other ways you might accomplish your objective. Can you get by with a phone conference call, memo, letter, Skype conversation, or internet meeting? Many of these options are free or close to it and could be more effective than a meeting.

The one thing that *is* best handled in a meeting is something that requires an intense exchange of ideas, give-and-take, or a progression of decisions that require interpersonal negotiating.

If you have a choice, seek any possible way to minimize holding meetings, and if you do have to conduct a meeting, keep it short.

SKILL BUILDER

One trick to ensure short, productive meetings is to have people stand during meetings. Some managers go so far as to remove all the chairs from the room before the meeting. When people have to stand, they'll be glad to have a short meeting, cover the necessary material, and get back to their work station.

Elements of Successful Meetings

A meeting needs to include several primary elements if you want it to be a worthwhile use of both your time and others' and also produce a significant result for you and the company. Those elements are: planning, gathering, engaging, and follow-up.

Planning

You need to plan for your meeting well in advance. If any special guests are to be in attendance, you need to contact them and be sure the meeting fits their schedule before you can do much else.

Also, your meeting should have a theme. Even a short meeting with only a few people benefits from having a theme in addition to a clearly defined purpose. Themes can relate to a company initiative; a special holiday or season; or basic concepts like quality, safety, or production. When you clearly define your purpose and establish a compatible theme, your meeting has cohesion. Plus you increase the emotion and memory of the meeting for the participants. That, in turn, improves results. For example, you might be able to refer to a meeting again by saying something like, "Remember the Thanksgiving meeting last November on quality? I had a real breakthrough on how to use gratitude to my direct reports as a way to reinforce quality."

Plan in advance the topics and events of the meeting, timeframes for each part (start and stop), and who will attend. What process of notification, confirmation, and attendance check-in will you use? Give serious consideration to why you invite the various people and ask yourself why you're inviting each person.

Determine the venue for the meeting, any necessary audio visual requirements, the seating arrangement, food and beverage necessity, and all the same details you'd have to consider if you were going to host a reception in your home, for example. What are you going to do or give out that will help make the meeting more meaningful and memorable? Do you want notepads, pens, computer terminals, water glasses or bottled water in the room ahead of time? Pretend you're hosting a party, and think about what you need to arrange so people will be comfortable and willing to share.

Some companies schedule a series of meetings. For example, do you have weekly or monthly sales, operation, or quality meetings? Such routine meetings can become big time-wasters. Measure the results of these meetings, and by reviewing the metrics, you can determine if the meetings are contributing to progress or growth. If they aren't helping you or your department improve, you should cease meeting and determine another way to get the results you need and want.

 MANAGER MINEFIELD

A meeting is a waste of time if it doesn't have a positive impact on the future results you and your group produce.

Agenda

Part of your premeeting planning includes creating your agenda for the meeting. Plot your agenda well enough in advance so you can get input from those who will attend the meeting as well as any of your colleagues or superiors who need to review the content ahead of time.

Start your written agenda with the meeting's purpose and your objective and outcomes. List the start time, topics to be covered with names of people involved in each part, a brief description of each part, time frames to indicate when you'll start and finish each part, and the projected end time of the meeting. Also list the location of the meeting (with the full address if necessary) and all attendees or the group who will attend.

Be sure to tackle the difficult and important items first. Make them the first items of business on the agenda. If you're going to discuss any items containing research or complexity, send out the facts, data, and details before the meeting and instruct everyone to review and study the information before arriving. It's often a good idea to check in with people a few days ahead of the meeting and impress upon them how important it is that they be familiar with the material before the meeting time.

When you ask specific people to present a brief review of a section of the material, you increase the odds that they'll study the material well. You also might find it helpful to arbitrarily call on people during the meeting and ask detailed or probing questions about the material to help enliven the discussion.

Each person is different in the way they prepare for a meeting. D's and I's are quick to get ready and are happy to arrive and improvise. The S's and C's will want extra time before the meeting to prepare and think about the part they'll play in the meeting. If they don't have time to prepare, they'll be very quiet during the meeting because these personality styles prefer to be precise and thorough when they contribute. Ensure they have time to reflect on the agenda before the meeting.

 LEADING THOUGHT

When planning for a year, plant corn. When planning for a decade, plant trees. When planning for life, train and educate people.

—Chinese proverb

During the Meeting

It's meeting time. First things first, be sure you begin the meeting on time. If some attendees haven't arrived by start time, don't wait for them. Begin anyway. You must establish your culture and rules of engagement, and honor your principles.

If you don't start on time, people will assume it's not important to be prompt. Waiting invites sloppiness and often results in continued casualness with time commitments. Don't allow this to happen to you.

Be Positive and Enthusiastic

We all know meetings can be dull and boring, but not yours. Right? Right. Be upbeat and excited as you begin and run your meeting, and your people will follow your lead and reflect your attitude and energy. Have a positive point of view and upbeat attitude, and you demonstrate that the meeting is going to be productive.

When you select the first person to contribute or speak, remember that they, too, help set the tone for the meeting. If you're energetic but then call on a very dull, low-key, and dry person to contribute, you'll essentially let all the air out of the room.

You are the orchestra leader, so start off with high energy and call on people to set and keep the positive energy going. In the middle of the meeting, you can call on the lower-key people. But then, near the end of the meeting, return to those upbeat folks to wrap up your time together on a high note.

> **SKILL BUILDER**
>
> Consider having lively music in the room before and after the meeting. This can be a good mood-booster.

Stand up in front of the group to commence the meeting even if you have a small group. Deliver a brief welcome (you prepared ahead of time) and then jump right into the agenda. Explain the agenda with a special focus on the purpose of the meeting and a review of the desired outcomes.

Involve Everyone

Each person at the meeting should have an opportunity to contribute. After all, if they're not providing input and ideas, why are they there? Having attendees participate shows that you trust and respect them, you want their feedback, and you value their opinion. Just be sure you treat everyone equally when you ask for input.

Also, you need to be keenly aware of how you relate to each person during the meeting. Avoid playing favorites, cutting people off, and showing disregard or annoyance by your tone of voice, hand gestures, or eye patterns. If you embarrass or slight someone in front of the others, it will take a major effort to bring them back into the group emotionally and for them to consider you trustworthy again.

If this is your first meeting with this particular group, use the first few minutes to agree on "rules of engagement" for the meeting. If you have an established group, make a point to have your rules of engagement posted and remind those in attendance by pointing out the rules.

DEFINITION

Rules of engagement are the agreed way you as a group will behave and interact during a meeting.

Ideally, you'll have time to get everyone to suggest and participate in establishing these rules, but if time is too short, you can outline how you want everyone to behave. Be sure to ask for acceptance after you share; otherwise, someone could get upset or choose not to participate. Remember, you are the servant to the group, not a dictator.

Here are some sample rules of engagement you might want to use:

> We will respect each other and all opinions and contributions at this meeting by honoring the following behaviors:
>
> > Only one person will speak at a time.
> >
> > We will listen and pay attention to others.
> >
> > Suggestions will be stated in positive terms.
> >
> > We will take notes and complete agreed follow-up.
> >
> > We will honor the time schedule from start to finish.

This gives you a starting point, but please change and adjust this definition to fit your values and needs. The best set of guidelines will be composed when you have everyone create, select, and agree to your own rules of engagement. These rules are important to establish, but don't let this exercise eat up too much time during the meeting.

As the leader, you are bound to the rules of engagement, too. The easiest way to compromise your authority and respect is to disregard the agreed time commitments. To avoid this, you might want to appoint one person to be the meeting timekeeper and remind you when you're approaching scheduled breaks. It's also useful to assign one person to take minutes, or notes of who said what and any agreed commitments set at the meeting.

The best meeting is one in which everyone has an opportunity to make a contribution. Call on the low-key, reserved people first. If they got a copy of the agenda well enough in advance, they likely have planned out what they want to say.

The extroverts will be happy to contribute anytime. However, you'd be wise to bridle them at the beginning of the meeting. Once they sound off with all their opinions, the S's and C's tend to remain quiet. You want to hear from the S's and C's, though, because they have a special point of view that's usually more thought out than what the D's or I's might present. (If you need to, review Chapter 4 on behavioral styles again.)

Always repeat any question asked during a meeting. That way, everyone can hear the question and you can ensure you understand what the question is about. It's easy to be confused when people don't explain themselves well or use a verbal shorthand to suggest an idea or ask a question. Encourage people to speak clearly and explain their views and questions well. This will demand your patience and empathy.

When people come up with ideas or suggestions that aren't closely related to the topic or purpose of the meeting, you need to acknowledge and respect their idea first and then gently say that although it's a valuable comment, it doesn't directly relate to today's meeting's topic. Instead, suggest that you place the topic on another flip chart, in a notebook, or someplace on the white board in a special area you might call the *parking lot* so you can come back to that topic at a later time.

 **DEFINITION**

> The **parking lot** is a written list of ideas, topics, and agenda items that are mentioned in a meeting and deemed worthy to discuss but are not directly related to the current meeting. They're written down and addressed at the end of the meeting or some other time.

Add Variety

Add variety to your meetings by changing the participation format. Use group discussions to focus and brainstorm on specific topics. Then have each small group report to the entire group the ideas and suggestions they've come up with.

If appropriate, bring in a guest speaker to explore a particular discipline or topic. Or have upper management join the meeting to share company updates and hear firsthand the concerns of your people.

Best of all, have your meeting participants give mini-presentations about business topics and procedures. This will build their self-confidence, make them more engaged with the meeting, and help them develop new skills. If they're hesitant or just want to improve their presentation skills, you can recommend they join Toastmasters International.

Circle Back

If you have extra time at the end of the meeting, you might come back to the parking lot items; otherwise, agree at the end of the meeting when you'll revisit those topics. It could be in a separate meeting, at a private appointment, or at the next regular meeting of the group.

Strive to keep your meetings as short as possible and still get your work done. During the meeting, it's a good idea to take a break and ask how it's going. Are we on track? Do we need to adjust the time for a particular item? Shall we set up a few people to do some research on a particular topic and cover the subject at a future meeting?

Remember, you are being paid to produce results. Stay focused on the purpose of your meeting, and accomplish the goals you established for the meeting. Always remember the person asking questions is in control, and you as the leader are primarily the servant of the group.

At the end of the meeting, review what's been accomplished, who has made commitments, and what the deadlines are. Also seek feedback in the form of a plus-*delta* chart, where + = positive things and Δ = things to change for the next meeting. Use a flip chart or white board make your chart. In one column, list what was best (the +'s of the meeting), and in another column, list those things that might be changed (Δ) for the improvement of future meetings, as shown in the following example.

+	Δ
Started on time	Have coffee and water
Good prep	No one leaves early
Open sharing	Fruit instead of donuts
Good ideas discussed	
Enjoyed the humor	

Finally, be sure you thank everyone for attending the meeting and announce when the next meeting will be.

 **DEFINITION**

Delta (Δ) is a Greek letter that's also used as a mathematical symbol to represent change or difference.

Meetings can be a very positive experience and produce great results when properly conducted. Be sure you plan and organize your meeting ahead of time, intelligently select the right people to attend, respectfully include everyone in the discussion, and stick closely to your agenda and time schedule.

Follow Up

After the meeting, type up the meeting minutes. You can do this simply by composing a memo to all concerned parties. Note who attended and who was late, and review what was covered in the meeting. List each item covered separately, and specifically recount the action plan determined in the meeting. Be sure to specify the who, what, and when for each person who has a commitment to perform after the meeting so they'll remember.

Then, in your calendar, add a reminder to yourself to check in with each person to see how their assignment is developing. The purpose of this check in is to see if anyone needs help, to reward your employees if they're making good progress, and to take preventative action if for some reason progress isn't being made. Inspect what you expect. Do this early enough so that if any problems develop, you have time to take action and correct the issue.

Fundamental Meeting Guidelines

No matter what kind of meeting you're holding, keep these fundamental guidelines in mind:

1. Always have a predetermined goal or objective, or have or request an agenda. Ask, "What is the purpose of this meeting? How will we determine if it's successful?"

2. Before you agree to a meeting, assign a priority relative to the other things on your to-do list. Meetings are not your number-one priority. You should fit them into your week based on your priorities.

3. Clearly define and honor the start and end times of every meeting, whether you're the one holding the meeting or you're an attendee.

4. Remember, you learn when you listen, not when you talk. Only one person should talk at a time.

5. Develop the art of asking good questions.

6. Always have a notepad and pen or pencil handy, and take notes. Be prepared to use paper, a white board, or your computer to illustrate ideas and major points.

7. Stay focused and on topic, and eliminate possible interruptions from phones, email, etc. It's simply a matter of respect and adequate planning.

8. Always end with feedback and the agreed action to be taken by each person. Then set the time and place of the next encounter. Be sure this is all written down.

SKILL BUILDER

To save time, schedule your next get-together at the end of your original meeting while everyone is present and hopefully has their schedule handy. If you don't, you could waste a lot of time trying to find a good time later. This applies to all appointments, not just meetings.

9. Ask participants to bring their computers, tablets, smartphones, or a notepad and pen or pencil.

10. Deliberately plan the venue to accommodate people's special needs, comfort, and confidence.

11. Be flexible, and adjust to the needs of the people in the meeting.

12. Remember, the leader is the servant of the group or of the other individual if it's just you and another person one to one.

Your consistent preparedness, for meetings and otherwise, is the hallmark of a professional. Approach every meeting or situation with or without other people as a test of your own philosophy and self-discipline to prove you are a manager of the highest integrity.

The Least You Need to Know

- Clearly define why you're having a meeting. If at all possible, use some other means of communicating.
- Always have an agenda for your meeting, and give people ample time to review and prepare.
- During the meeting, call on the shy people first. Let them know ahead of time they'll be asked to contribute so they can plan ahead.
- Together with everyone present, establish rules of engagement for the meeting and post them on the wall.
- Send out a review of the meeting afterward with specific tasks highlighted along with who is responsible for each task. Set target due dates as well.

CHAPTER 15

Deciding, Delegating, and Deciding to Delegate

If making a prioritized to-do list is your best time-saver in the short term, then delegation is the absolute best way to increase your effectiveness in the long term. The better you get at delegating tasks, the more productive you and your group will be. Your impact on your group will be greater, too.

Delegation is a powerful way to groom and develop your people. When you delegate properly, you empower your people, teach them, and build their self-esteem. In addition, delegation helps you measure your peoples' progress and skills.

In this chapter, you learn a matrix approach to measuring and managing delegation that helps you accelerate the growth of your team. I'm not talking about dumping unpleasant tasks on the unsuspecting new employee. Instead, I show you how people will learn to anticipate, willingly accept, and actually crave for you to delegate duties to them. Delegation is a powerful tool for you and your people, so let's learn how to do it artfully, with integrity, and in everyone's best interests.

In This Chapter

- The four D's of delegation
- Decisions you'll face
- Making decisions by the numbers
- Decision-making from your gut
- Delegating to accelerate growth
- Taking responsibility

Do, Defer, Delegate, or Destroy?

The quality of your ability to make good decisions greatly affects your success in business. According to Woody Allen, 80 percent of success is showing up, but even that requires a decision to get out of bed in the morning and show up.

As a manager, every day you're bombarded with decisions big and small only you can make. Will you answer that phone call? Read your email? Check your social media accounts? Attend a meeting? Walk around the shop and survey production? Call a customer? The list goes on and on.

Throughout this book, I've encouraged you to base your decision-making on your values. However, there are many things—so many bits of *stuff* that just have to be done—that don't necessarily directly correlate with a value discussion. If you're not careful, your life will become filled with this *stuff* and you won't have time to do what's really important.

I mentioned the four D's first in Chapter 2, but it's time to revisit them. The four D's stand for *do, defer, delegate,* or *destroy,* and they provide an action plan for each item on your to-do list.

Should You Do or Defer?

Earlier I mentioned that the most important thing you must do as a manager is plan. After that, in order of priority, come communicate, manage, and finally execute. When you first started with the company, or if you were a front-line worker, the majority of your time probably was spent on execution. The execution types of work are the easiest kind of tasks to delegate.

But before you do, take a step back and ask yourself a simple question:

> Should I do it now or defer it to a later time?

Apply this simple question to virtually everything that comes up on your radar. Whether you're considering opening the mail, calling a customer, sorting papers, reviewing budgets—whatever task you face, ask yourself this simple question.

SKILL BUILDER

If you defer the item, decide on a specific time to either complete or revisit the task, and write it down on that date in your calendar or file it in a specific file for the time period you deferred it to.

Should You Delegate?

Once you've done this a few times, you'll start to notice patterns. For example, you'll be able to group certain things together, such as making calls to customers about problem orders, reviewing contact information for your customers, or scanning the production and delivery records for glitches and hot spots in the system. These are all important things to do, but maybe they're not the most important things for *you* to do.

This is where delegation comes to your aid. Each of these items lends itself to delegation. The good thing about this type of delegation is that the task is important, and if someone else does it, they'll become more knowledgeable about the way the business works. It's an opportunity to train someone in a new area and at the same time thin your task list.

The time the typical manager sits doing nothing productive while trying to decide what to do is unbelievable. Don't let it happen to you. Develop a habit of only touching a piece of paper once. Either do it—which might mean filling out a form, answering some questions, or making a decision—or defer it to a specific date. If that's not an option, delegate it. (I talk more about delegation later in this chapter.)

Should You Destroy?

The last option of the four D's is maybe the biggest time-saver. Destroy it! Yes, throw it in the trash or recycling bin and don't think anything more about it.

Hoarding every piece of paper, each memo, and all kinds of miscellaneous papers is a waste of time and space. Some things you need to keep for legal reasons, but most of what the average manager keeps is useless. If you have trouble throwing things away, find an organizational coach who can come in and help you establish a simple filing system and identify what items you can throw away.

If you have an issue with establishing a filing system or maintaining it, get a coach or, if you can, hire an assistant who is gifted in this area. Being unorganized can cause you additional, unnecessary, problems and could adversely affect your productivity. Basic organizational skills are critical for you to master as a manager. Take a course, go to a seminar, and read books about how to get organized. Organization skills are mandatory.

Making Decisions

How do you make decisions? Do you have a system in place, or do you just wing it? Or do you procrastinate until the problem resolves itself? I recommend you have a system in place, even a simple one.

In U.S. Air Force pilot training, I was taught how to make decisions in an emergency, whether it be an engine on fire, hydraulic failure, loss of radio or navigation systems, or any number of things. Any time I faced an emergency, I learned to activate the universal emergency procedure:

1. Maintain aircraft control.

2. Analyze the situation.

3. Take appropriate corrective action.

This simple set of rules helped me keep a clear and cool head when I faced problems in my plane, and it can help you make decisions as a manager, too.

Maintaining Control

Maintaining aircraft control is essential because under emergency conditions, it's easy to get excited and confused. It reminds me of the old saying: fly the airplane, not the radio. This came about because many student pilots got so excited when cast into an emergency situation, they started talking on the radio and sometimes even yelling for help. While doing so, they forgot about flying the airplane and, ultimately, crashed.

The best way to maintain aircraft control in the F-4 Phantom, which is what I flew in combat, was to focus on the large, circular instrument in the center of the console called the attitude directional indicator (ADI). The ADI quickly told you if you were climbing, diving, or turning. This is important to know, especially if you're in heavy clouds, flying at night, or in turbulent weather and can't clearly see the horizon.

When you're making any decision, facing an emergency situation, or under great pressure, it's important for you, as a manager, to maintain attitude control. This is number one, the most important thing to do. Stay calm and positive.

SKILL BUILDER

When flying fighters, it's important to monitor your breathing. In an emergency and at high altitude, it's easy to become unconscious and even knock yourself out with shallow and rapid breathing. As a manager, when things get rough—and they will— monitor your breathing if you find yourself having trouble staying calm. Breathe slowly and deeply to feed your brain oxygen. You'll think more clearly and make better decisions.

Analyzing the Situation

The next step in making a decision is to analyze the situation. Be very deliberate in accumulating as much information as possible. Ask lots of questions; listen to people from various points of view; and talk to your coworkers, other managers, customers, vendors, or even outside experts. Don't try to be a noble, solitary, all-knowing manager. That's either a sign of insecurity or uncontrolled hunger for power, and neither is a wise course to follow. You need to consider other points of view to make a wise, informed decision.

Take all the information you accumulate, and put it into a graphic or numeric array. You might use a T chart with + and − columns (see Chapter 5 for a review of T charts) or organize and sort lots of facts and figures on a spreadsheet. Clusters of ideas and similar items visually grouped together sometimes gives you a fresh way to see all the information in front of you. Or try mind-mapping: draw pictures and connect items based on their relationship to each other so you can see how your decision might play out as you try various potential outcomes.

As you work, take into consideration how each decision will affect the various constituents involved. Realize that some decisions can cause unintended consequences.

And give yourself some time to think about your decision. Ideally, wait until you've at least had time to sleep on it before taking action.

Taking Appropriate Action

If, when all is said and done with your analysis, you've done a thorough job mulling over all the information available to you, you probably feel in your gut what the right decision is.

Go with your gut.

Science has proven that our memory is more than just in our brain. Our whole body and all its parts seem to have the capacity to remember things. Scientists believe that's why we feel anxiety in our gut when we get in uncomfortable situations. That muscle memory is reminding us of a past unpleasant experience.

Once your mind is made up, you must *execute*. Execution is easiest when you're implementing a written plan of action. Write down exactly what you're going to do, when you're going to do it, and have a space where you can check off each step as you complete it.

The Best Way to Delegate

A good system of delegation empowers your employees, gives them enthusiasm for their job, and builds teamwork. When a person is given the responsibility for making a contribution to the organization, he has an opportunity to increase his stature and improve his career potential within the organization. As each individual within the organization is able to handle increasingly more significant responsibility, the power of the total team increases.

 MANAGER MINEFIELD

Before you decide to pass a task on to someone else, take a moment to verify that it is, in fact, a worthwhile task. Don't just pass off something to pass it. And remember, there's a significant difference between delegation and dumping menial, unpleasant tasks on others.

How to Do It

As with most management functions, your first concern is to plan properly. What task are you going to delegate? Who are you going to delegate the work to? Define how much authority will be required to complete the task. What is the desired outcome or result? Be sure to tell everyone involved about the new role of the delegatee and how other people will relate to that person.

Next, you must design a way to train the person how to do the new task. Take into consideration the delegatee's strengths and weaknesses, as well as his or her personal style (DISC). Try to focus more on the results you want than on the method the delegatee might use to get there. When you delegate something, you get a guarantee: the delegatee won't do it exactly the way you'd do it—hopefully they'll do it better.

Timing is also very important. Be sure you choose the right time to do the training and the delegation. It won't do any good to overload another person. The manner you use to notify, train, and monitor the person you've chosen to delegate to helps establish trust between the two of you. The art of delegation is really a sharing of responsibility and authority. Each of you must have a benefit to gain for this sharing to be successful.

The last step is to develop a simple way to track and receive feedback on the delegatee's performance. Write down the specific results you're looking for, and develop a simple system, such as a chart, to monitor those results. Get input from the delegatee for the design of this system.

Use this checklist to help you remember the essentials of delegating:

- Identify the **goal.**
- Define the **benefit** to the delegatee.
- Consider the delegatee's **DISC** style.
- Is now the right **time** to do it?
- Do you have a positive **attitude?**
- What's your **follow-up** plan?

Levels of Delegation

There are five commonly used levels of delegation, divided into progressive levels of responsibility and authority:

Level 1   Stand by for instruction.

Level 2   Look into it, provide information on possible action, and wait for instruction.

Level 3   Look into it, provide information and recommend specific action, and wait for approval.

Level 4   Look into it, take appropriate action, and provide frequent and immediate feedback.

Level 5   Look into it, take appropriate action, and provide planned periodic feedback.

As an individual gradually demonstrates more knowledge, competence, ability, and value to the organization, he or she moves higher on the scale.

By charting the various tasks that need to be learned in a particular job function and relating those tasks to the levels of delegation, you can assess a person's contribution to the organization. Using a chart with tasks on one axis and levels of delegation on the other, you can develop a simple evaluation and communication tool that's very objective. (More on this in the "Rewards and Responsibility" section later in this chapter.)

The Results of Delegation

Effective delegation increases your contribution to the organization. You will be helping others increase their abilities as well as developing new skills of your own. All managers need to constantly be seeking people who are able to be pushed up within the organization. This develops a positive attitude throughout the group and breeds achievers. It also emphasizes personal growth, encourages creativity, and rewards initiative.

It takes practice to learn to let go and delegate well. Be patient with yourself and the delegatee. Be sure you praise the person who has accepted a delegated task and done a good job with the added work and responsibility. If corrections are necessary, do it in private.

> **LEADING THOUGHT**
>
> It is one of the most beautiful compensations of this life that no man can sincerely try to help another without helping himself.
>
> —Ralph Waldo Emerson

Authority and Responsibility

Authority and responsibility go together. One of the most frustrating situations in any person's life is when there's confusion between authority and responsibility. This can be a very subtle problem, yet sometimes it's blatant.

The beginning of a solution to this issue is realizing the complexity of effective communication. As discussed earlier, it's not good enough to think communication is just transmitting on the one hand and reception on the other. Communication only takes place when you, the manager, and a worker are able to share an experience. This is especially true when you want to delegate something to another worker.

You can't just tell a worker what to do. Instead, it's better to ask the worker what has to be done to reach a desired result. You know and are the expert on what the goals and vision of the company are. The worker is the expert on how a particular job needs to be done. When the two of you share this information, you have the beginning of communication.

Now you have the authority and responsibility to set the company goals and establish the vision. The worker has the authority and responsibility to produce a specific amount of work, product, or service. Only when the two of you have shared your experience, expectation, and needs will you both be able to establish realistic goals.

Beware the Risks

There are risks in this kind of an exchange in that both parties are vulnerable to the other. In reality, however, you cannot achieve the desired results unless you're relying on each other. For this reason, it's imperative that you clearly define the guidelines for the worker's behavior as well as what he or she will produce.

Workers can and sometimes do sabotage managers, and managers have the means to terminate workers. When you and your delegatee learn to share goals and expectations, you start to make the necessary adjustments and develop understanding of each other. Hopefully, then, this reduces the risks to both of you.

Giving and Receiving Feedback

Feedback is a two-way street. It should flow down the organization from management to staff as well as up the organization from staff to management.

You need to be giving feedback to your group in the form of praise and reprimand as well as formal performance reviews. Frequent, informal feedback is required for everyone, managers and workers alike. You can apply the slogan, "inspect what you expect" to praise and catch people doing something right just as well as to find exceptions. Ideally, you should periodically be doing this as your worker becomes more and more competent in the delegated task.

Your direct report needs to inform you about what works and what isn't working. If this is going to happen, it's necessary for you to listen to your team member and address his or her concerns by making adjustments where needed or at least explaining why a situation has to stay the way it is.

One of the easiest ways to tell if these communication lines are open is to ask yourself, *When was the last time a worker came up with an idea to improve a system or product?*

> **SKILL BUILDER**
>
> People repeat behavior that's rewarded.

Rewards and Responsibility

Clearly defined responsibility and authority are not attained by having rigid rules. You'll only have the proper balance between authority and responsibility when mutual respect exists for each other's areas of expertise and you have open lines of communication because of the sharing of experience, expectations, and goals.

Everyone in the organization will be part of your team. People will start to help each other produce and also give gentle warnings when a person is stepping out of line. It will be in the best interest of everyone to keep clear lines of authority and responsibility. This type of attitude will make your place a great place to work.

Ultimately, the responsibility and authority are yours, and you share both of these attributes with the people to whom you delegate. It's still up to you to know what's going on, and it's up to you to assess how your people are doing. It's essential that you continually evaluate as well as encourage them.

A very useful way to stay up to speed on a person's progress, and also encourage them systematically, is by using a simple chart. In the left column, list the delegated tasks, or elements of the task. Across the top, list the five levels of delegation discussed in the earlier "Levels of Delegation" section.

	Level 1	**Level 2**	**Level 3**	**Level 4**	**Level 5**
Review report	May 1 ✓	June 16 ✓	September 1	October 15	December 1
Summarize					
Edit					
Rewrite					

This example shows how you might keep track of an employee's progress in learning how to understand, summarize, edit, and then become capable of developing and using production reports for a manufacturing or administrative function. As the two of you meet periodically and you discuss their progress, you can enter a date of completion and a checkmark as they reach each level.

Create this chart when you first give your employee a copy of an established report (Level 1) and ask them to read and review it. The next time you meet, you'll expect them to advance to Level 2, look into the report and what it means so they can recommend future action necessary. By the time they get to Level 5, take action and provide feedback to you, they have taken over the report and are managing the people and activities covered in it while keeping you in the loop with periodic feedback.

After your worker has mastered all five levels in the "Review report" category, they're ready to start working on the "Summarize" category. That might mean they present the findings to your boss or other workers. Next they learn to adjust and edit the report and procedures in a partic-ular production area. Finally, they create and write reports and evaluation processes for other departments. They have become the resident expert on how to formulate, write, evaluate, and use reports to keep management informed on any number of tasks. As with the first category, when they complete each task, add a date of completion and a checkmark.

You can see how this simple process gives you a written development plan for a worker to focus on specific tasks they must learn for any number of jobs. As your team member learns new tasks and responsibilities and is able to handle more authority, he or she becomes more valuable to the organization and might even warrant getting a raise.

This is also a great tool to use during your one-to-one meetings with your direct reports. It shows them how they're developing as well as gives you an opportunity to share how well they're doing from your point of view. This will be very motivational for them and also gives you the confidence to know how they're doing.

Everyone wants to know if they're winning or losing, and this type of matrix is a continual score card of progress.

The Least You Need to Know

- Use delegation to help your people grow and develop new skills, not to move unpleasant tasks off your desk.
- Establish a standard formula for how you make decisions. Remember, maintain control, analyze the situation, and take appropriate action.
- Ultimately, as manager, you are responsible for everything in your department.
- Use a chart of tasks and levels of delegation to help your people grow as you monitor their progress.

CHAPTER 16

Operations Management

People are clearly the most important aspect to becoming a great manager. You have to understand them, relate to them, inspire them, and hold them accountable. People like to know what they're doing, understand why they're doing it, and have a system or framework in which to operate at work.

In his book, *The Game of Work*, Charles Coonradt recommends you make work more like a game. The reasoning is that people try harder at games than they do at work because it's fun, they know the rules, they know when they make a foul, and they know when they're winning or losing. It's only common sense to incorporate the good elements of games and how we play them into the work environment.

In this chapter, I share the principles that help you create effective and efficient systems and procedures along with the keys to planning and execution. Based on my MBA in finance, experience teaching college accounting and economics, and work in the investment area, I share what I feel are the most important fundamentals of money and cash flow and offer guidance on how to use financial statements to help you manage and grow your business.

In This Chapter

- Management: more than the people
- Putting systems and processes in place
- Planning and executing projects
- Becoming a financial whiz

People Plus

People are the lifeblood of any organization. And although this chapter is about all the things *beyond* people, it's important to remember that people create and run the systems that make a business function. People also enable the processes that allow work to get done. Planning wouldn't happen without the input and effort of intelligent and diligent people, and execution doesn't even start until a person makes a decision, throws a switch, or exerts the effort to make something happen.

What's more, all these people are working for many different reasons, yet they all expect to be paid money for their efforts. Business is all about creating ways for people to use resources, systems, processes, and effort to serve a customer and receive money in return for the goods and services provided. Money is not the objective; it's simply the way we can measure if the objective of serving a customer is being accomplished. The better that objective is met, the more potential there is to earn money.

The Importance of Leverage

In a very real sense, this chapter is all about leverage. By *leverage,* I mean the use of a tool, system, or process to increase the return based on a given output. If you use a tractor to move dirt, for example, you can move many times more dirt than a man with a shovel, and with a lot less effort. That's leverage. And this chapter is all about the many ways you can accomplish more with less effort by using leverage.

The most basic example of leverage is a crowbar. If you have one of these steel bars, you can put the point under a very large rock; pry up the rock with the rod while leaning the rod against another rock (the fulcrum); and with not a whole lot of effort, you can push on the long end of the rod and move the large rock. Leverage is a way to get great results with a reduced amount of effort. That might be with a rod, money, other people, or a system.

Delegation (discussed in Chapter 15) is a form of leverage. When you train others to do things for you, you increase your influence, which causes a greater long-term result. At the same time, you can actually reduce your personal effort. Leverage is an amazing concept.

 MANAGER MINEFIELD

Leverage is a double-edged sword, so be careful! If you lose control of the money, people, or system, the damage can increase exponentially and destroy you.

The Importance of the Knowledge Worker

In 1941, before the United States was even involved in World War II, the U.S. government asked auto manufacturer Henry Ford to build an airplane factory. The Willow Run plant, located just east of Ypsilanti, Michigan, became the largest building under one roof ever constructed up until that time, measuring a mile long and a quarter mile wide. Charlie Sorenson, a long-time Ford employee, was asked to bring all his knowledge of building cars using Ford assembly lines to the new factory designed for airplane construction. Sorenson sketched out the process and manufacturing layout in one long night in his hotel room. It was approved the next day, and $200,000,000 was committed to build the Willow Run plant. By the end of the war, Willow Run was producing a new B-24 bomber every hour.

In the last several years, I have had the opportunity to tour a few European auto manufacturer factories. The buildings are exceptionally clean and spotless, and the cars are built almost entirely with precision robots while workers watch and monitor the machines. People design these systems and processes that produce remarkable precision, require little human labor involvement, and work at great cost savings.

What can we learn from this evolution of manufacturing? The Ford plant was the precursor to what later became known as just-in-time or lean manufacturing. Modern automation in auto, medical, or aerospace manufacturing, and even nanotechnology, has been advanced by technology over the last several decades, and we've been witness to continuous innovation and improvement. Now whether it's the semiconductor industry, medical technology, aerospace research and development, or custom-made auto parts, the speed of technological and manufacturing advancement is mind-boggling.

This trend gives new emphasis to what Peter Drucker called the knowledge worker (see Chapter 8). As a manager, one of your main concerns has to be getting people who know how to create, design, and operate advanced systems and procedures.

One of my current clients designs and manufactures subsea pumps, controls, and robots used all over the world in deep-sea exploration for the oil industry. The majority of the management and production teams are highly educated and trained engineers, scientists, and researchers. They truly are brilliant knowledge workers.

LEADING THOUGHT

I cannot teach anybody anything. I can only make them think.

—Socrates

Knowledge, when applied well, is power. You need to be always encouraging your people to continually improve their knowledge. The high unemployment among low-skilled workers is a travesty, but the only solution is to teach and train people to be able to compete by seeking improved knowledge and skills. You and your organization will be well served if you are continually reinforcing this concept with your people.

Systems and Processes

A system or process helps you avoid total confusion and disorganization. When you have no established system to do things, people are naturally encouraged to improvise and behave any way they see fit. There's an old adage used by many successful companies that I recommend you employ with your new people: "For the first six months on the job, please spare us your genius and just do what you're told."

If you use this concept, your intention is not to stifle creativity, initiative, or enthusiasm. After people grasp the way things are done, why they're done that way, and what the long-term objectives are, then they can contribute their original ideas on how to improve your systems and processes.

Established Systems and Processes

A system is a compilation of parts, separate units, and processes that, when grouped together, complete a whole or unified end result. When you consider the big picture, companies have accounting systems, computer systems, and often manufacturing systems. A process is a subset or part of a larger system. It's the sequence of events or tasks that create a result. Take the accounting system, for instance. It has many processes as part of the larger system. Balancing the checkbook, collecting receivables, and paying bills all need a process to enable them to work well as part of the overall accounting system.

By having established definitions, guidelines, and procedures, you're able to be productive, accurate, and efficient with a system. In accounting, for example, there are generally accepted accounting principles (GAAP) that focus on basic principles and guidelines; the rules and standards issued by the Financial Accounting Standards Board; and finally, generally accepted industry practices. These guidelines facilitate the use of standards and regulated accounting definitions, assumptions, and methods. This enables accountants to maintain consistency from year to year with the methods they use to prepare a company's financial statements. It also provides an accurate understanding of the current status of a company or department as it relates to the past and future forecasts are created.

This highly regulated system is an interesting contrast to computer systems and protocols. I'm sure you know the difference between PC and Mac computers. Many years ago, when I was in graduate school, we accessed the computer with punch cards. The operating languages were COBOL, Fortran, and later, DOS.

This all led to competition between Apple, IBM, Microsoft, and many others—a rivalry that's been going on for several decades. Developing new products and systems to capture the world of computing is intense, and the competition has developed into two camps: PCs and Macs. Because of the thirst for dominance—as well as the greed and egos involved—it's still difficult to intermingle information, programs, and utilities easily between the two opposing systems. The consumer is forced to choose between PCs or Macs, adapt, or compromise. Many of the IT consultants I've coached in Fortune 500 companies use PCs at work and Apple products for their personal computers and smartphones.

The same thing happens within companies when you have one department trying to outshine another, attempting to build a power base, or is just being stubborn or arrogant. This isolationist attitude, in which people are only concerned about themselves and their own issues, is commonly called the silo effect. This outlook does not breed a quality, dynamic, and profitable company. Rather, it causes waste, confusion, and animosity.

The most common example of this type of conflict is when the accounting department has issues with the sales and marketing departments. The system the accounting people want is totally different from the system the sales and marketing departments prefer, for example. As a manager, always seek to coordinate and blend the efforts of your department with other departments. The systems must be designed to be beneficial for all parties involved.

 MANAGER MINEFIELD

It's almost comical, or maybe sad, when you see a company that designs its systems primarily to make it easy for its employees to do their job. You'll damage your company's reputation and profits when you do this at the expense, discomfort, or mandatory extra effort of your customer. Always have your customer's needs at the forefront of your thinking and planning.

Manufacturing is another area that's focused on creating systems. A classic example of a manufacturing system is enterprise resource planning (ERP), a computerized system that provides an integrated picture of several business processes. ERP can monitor cash, materials, production rates, order completion, delivery, and even payroll and share all this information among departments and even with entities outside the company. The larger the company, the more sense these complex systems make.

Your Systems and Processes

These examples of big systems indicate some of the reasons why systems are used and the benefits to be gained. But what about you and your team? If you're a new manager, what should you be concerned with in designing systems? What's the goal?

It really boils down to honoring a few critical principles. First and foremost, be sure you've clearly defined exactly what the system is being designed to accomplish. This must ultimately directly relate to a positive financial result. Therefore, you must take into consideration the cost to create, install, learn, operate, and maintain the system and analyze that cost with real numbers, not just estimates or wild guesses.

The simpler the system, the better. By having clearly defined goals and implementing focused, measurable participation, you'll get things done with higher quality, at less cost, and in a more timely manner. Continually ask your people, "How can we do this simpler? How can we save time and money?"

> **LEADING THOUGHT**
>
> Everything should be made as simple as possible, but not simpler.
>
> —Albert Einstein

Several years ago, I was teaching management skills to a major accounting firm. One of the assigned exercises was to review all the forms, reports, and procedures the partners used on a regular basis. The office's administrative officer queried headquarters about a particular required report two of his people spent three days a month to generate and sent to regional headquarters. To his amazement, when asked the simple question, "Why?" headquarters said, "Roy, why do you keep sending us that report? We haven't used it for more than two years."

Now that you're a manager, please develop the habit of asking the simple question, "Why?"

How Do You Measure Results?

In business, everything is measured by how it improves the bottom line—money. Any system or process has the ultimate goal to improve profits. If the system or procedures don't improve profits, they're a drain or roadblock to helping the business improve.

A good system should make work easier for your people; improve the process of creating, making, delivering, or administering your business; and always improve profit. Superior customer service and satisfaction are the best ways to grow long-term profits.

Inspect What You Expect

No system runs by itself and stays useful if it isn't continually evaluated, measured, and monitored. It's dangerous to assume everything is running smoothly just because you're not getting complaints. You need to be continually checking to ensure the results are accurate, timely, and useful. As things change—and they always do—you need to update your systems.

As a manager, you should be checking on a few fundamental elements continually:

- Quality

- Responsiveness

- Delivery

- Price

These four qualities are the cornerstones of a successful business, and you must always be aware of how you and your people are doing in each area. By this I mean timely measurement of each element.

The best source of feedback to accurately measure these qualities is your customer. Do you have a system to get customer feedback on these four qualities?

Project Planning

As you design and implement systems or focus on other aspects of your business, you'll want to create projects. A project is a formalized process to solve a problem, create a new initiative, or fulfill a need, either internal to the business or external to satisfy customers. Projects typically have a finite start and completion dates.

As in all business endeavors, you start by clearly defining the goal and developing a plan. Then comes the execution. With a project, you also have a close or completion date.

 MANAGER MINEFIELD

A badly-planned project takes three times longer than expected. A well-planned project takes only twice as long as expected.

When planning a project, be sure to consider the impact of external conditions on your project. These could include current economic conditions, the business environment, organizational culture, objectives and finances, your people and other constituents' interests and abilities, and unforeseen risks.

Remember, too, that only what's written down exists. You must have a written plan—a formalized chart, graph, or diagram of the process you'll follow; budgets; cost control procedures; and a review and inspection process.

The most common area of problems in projects relates to communication. It's better to over-communicate than let things slide or operate based on assumptions. Continually seek feedback and clarification at each step of the project. This includes but is not limited to setting the goal, planning, selecting people, establishing guidelines, administering details, monitoring the process, identifying and handling changes, and performing quality inspections.

There's a huge difference between changing the goal and changing the deadline. You need to be flexible but really firm on the critical things that cannot be compromised. Knowing the difference is your responsibility as the manager. The best way to define the difference is to look at the dollar cost of each alternative.

Financial Essentials

Accounting is the language of business. It's the way we record, monitor, and forecast the monetary aspects of the business. Finance is the way we plan, manipulate, and use accounting information to develop and advance the business. Some consider accounting record-keeping and finance planning and implementing. As a manager, you need to understand how money works, how you monitor money, and how you use money to grow the business.

Money is a tool that must be used effectively. If you don't use it productively, it'll gradually dissolve or lose value. The wise use of money is how business grows.

The Value of Your Company and Your People

Think of the value of your company. It might be $5,000 and you just started your journey of becoming an entrepreneur, or it might be $5 billion and listed on the New York Stock Exchange. Apple, Exxon, and Google are three of the largest companies based on net worth, and each is approaching a net worth of $500 billion.

Now try to imagine how many people work at each of these top three companies. How much do you think each company has invested in plants and equipment? How much revenue do you think each produces per employee? If you just divide total revenue by the total number of employees, you'll find that Apple produces an astonishing amount of revenue per employee—well over $2 million per person.

Virtually every company on the planet would love to be even close to Apple's revenue per employee number. In general, you can assume the more people in a company, the lower the revenue per employee. Restaurant, hospitality, and retail businesses typically have low revenue per employee. Labor cost is usually the largest part of any company's expenses.

As a manager, you need to realize that your people are the most expensive part of your business, so it's important to get the maximum possible production or revenue per employee. Equipment, systems, and innovation are the keys to making that happen. However, also remember it's your people who figure out how to make this really work. Therefore, a person who is dedicated, innovative, and able to lead others is invaluable—hopefully that's you.

The Cost of Money

For a company to grow, it must invest money in plants, equipment, and of course its people. The best way to invest is by using profits. Some companies need to bring in more money by selling stock or ownership in the company. This is the most expensive way to raise money, as the owner is giving away part of himself, his equity or ownership, by selling stock or ownership in his company.

The least expensive way to raise money is to borrow it. Then you keep the ownership totally to yourself and just pay the bank or lender a small interest payment. The problem with this approach, called financial leverage, is that if you miss a payment, the lender can take control of the company or you might lose the company completely. Remember earlier the warning that leverage is a double-edged sword? Borrowing is easy and cheap to do, but if you get out of control, you could lose everything.

Interest is simply the "cost" of money. If you want to borrow money, you pay for it with interest. The stronger your company is financially, the better the terms you can negotiate, and the less you have to pay to a lender. Banks raise the rates if you miss a payment. Interest and fees are how they reap huge profits and at the same time insure against people or companies not repaying their loans.

Accounting for Depreciation

In accounting jargon, *depreciation* is a non-cash expense. That means you don't write a check or pay anyone for depreciation. Rather, it's a way to gradually account for the theoretical wearing out use of a thing you paid money for.

If you buy equipment for $1,000 today, for example, you might depreciate it over a 5-year period at the rate of $200 per year. Then, after 5 years, it's $0 on your accounting books because you've "expensed" it over the 5 years at $200 per year.

The Problem with Cash Flow

Cash flow is the amount of money you have coming in plus depreciation, versus the amount of money you have going out. When people or customers owe you money, it's not considered positive cash flow until you've collected it.

Executives often talk about having "cash flow problems." They sometimes like to think everything is fine, except they're having some "cash flow problems." Sometimes this is meant to imply the problem isn't their fault. Rather, it's because their customers aren't paying on time.

I would suggest that many people who complain about cash flow are ignoring a much bigger problem. The real problem is that they're either not controlling expenses, not driving sales, or not managing their business well—especially managing collections.

Cash flow is merely an indicator, and negative cash flow is usually a sign of more serious problems.

Accounting Fundamentals

Now that we've looked at the primary concepts—and ones often misunderstood by new managers—let's briefly review a few accounting fundamentals.

Accounting must be designed and managed in a way that ensures reliability, verifiability, objectivity, consistency, and comparability. When there's doubt, such as when current values of specific assets are being estimated, an accountant relies on the actual cost because it's clearly known. This points out the difference between accounting and finance. The simple accounting need is based on cost, and the finance approach is more focused on current value or how to manage the asset in the accounting realm given its cost relative to options such as replacing or keeping an old asset.

The *balance sheet* is one of the key financial statements you'll need to understand. A balance sheet shows the current assets, liabilities, and equity, at one point in time—it's like a snapshot of the company's condition. You should use the balance sheet as a comparative report from year to year.

Assets on the balance sheet are shown based on the cost of the assets. If the assets have appreciated in value, they're still listed at cost. Assets might include cash, accounts receivable, supplies, equipment, and land. *Liabilities* might include accounts payable, wages payable, and unearned revenue. The owner's *equity* is the difference between assets and liabilities, or what's owned minus what's owed yields what the business is worth (liabilities + equity = assets).

The *income statement* is a representation of what has happened over a period of time, be it monthly, quarterly, or annually. It shows the company's revenue minus expenses (income = revenue − expenses).

Accounting is based on a matching principle. Expenses are matched either with revenues or with a time period when they were expensed or used. As assets such as cash are used, they're subtracted from the asset section of the balance sheet and added to the expense section of the income statement. This causes the owner's equity or prepaid expenses to go down. The matching principle keeps the two columns balanced (assets = liabilities and equity).

Income and *expenses* are the two categories for funds coming into or leaving the business in the normal course of business. This is typically from sales of goods and services. *Gains* and *losses* are how funds are recorded that come or go from transactions not in the normal course of business. This might be from the sale of land the company owns.

SKILL BUILDER

You also might work with budgets, journal entries, and other financial statements that may be project oriented or department focused. The principles outlined here apply to all these different formats.

As a manager, your primary concern should be the trends you see in the various statements. Ideally, you want expenses to go down, revenues to go up, and equity to increase. I recommend that you get in the habit of using charts and graphs to monitor and manage the various financial statements you have. It's great to use spreadsheets and computers to calculate the plethora of numbers you must manage. However, with a chart, you can quickly see the trends—where you're coming from, where you are right now, and where you plan to go. Your objective is to get the trends going in the right direction, quickly notice deviations from the norm, and clearly see the progress you're making—or if you're falling short.

When each department, each project, and all of your key people are all using charts to personally monitor their progress on a daily basis, your job as a manager becomes much easier. You'll be able to stay on top of multiple issues and know where the most valuable and valuable use of your time and effort is.

The Least You Need to Know

- Leverage is a double-edged sword; be careful how you use it with people, finances, and all applications.
- Encourage your people to go to school, learn, and be perpetual students. The work environment is requiring more and more knowledge and skill than ever before.
- Designing good systems and processes is critical to making a business grow and creating profits.
- Cash flow is king; however, it's an indicator of other problems within the business. Look into expenses and revenue, reduce costs, and increase sales.
- Get your financial performance off the spreadsheets and up on the wall in the form of charts so you can more easily see trends.

CHAPTER 17

The Technology Advantage

Technology is advancing at the speed of light, and it can be difficult to stay on top of all the latest gadgets and gizmos and not get distracted by what they can do. However, you must remember that these are merely tools for you to use to manage well. You need to balance the use of such items with all your other responsibilities.

It's to your advantage to use technology to help you manage. You need not fear technology because you don't fully understand it. An abundance of books and online tutorials are available if you want or need to learn something new. Technology is the foreseeable future, and it's incumbent upon you to become proficient with computers and how to maximize their use.

This chapter can be your starting point. In it, I show you how to learn, manage, and utilize the power of technology without getting a degree in computer science. The tools are powerful and waiting for you to use them to your advantage.

In This Chapter

- The best ways to use email
- Web meetings and video conferences
- Making the most of social networks
- It pays to listen
- Tips for staying current

The Best (and Worst) of Email

The convenience, speed, and low cost of email make it a remarkable and important part of communication for any manager.

To maximize the use of email, I highly recommend you have access to it on your smartphone as well as your desktop or laptop computer and/or tablet. This gives you access 24 hours a day, 7 days a week—which can be both a blessing and a curse. You'll need self-discipline to manage the amount of time you spend on email and avoid the distraction when you have such easy access.

Email Time Management

To keep from getting bogged down with constantly checking and answering email, it helps to set specific times of the day to address it. If you go this route, be sure your employees and coworkers know that's what you're doing. People expect to get a response to email in a timely manner, so give them an idea when they can expect to hear from you. For example, you can formally let everyone know they'll receive a response to their email within 24 hours, but you decide what works best for you.

Once people receive immediate email responses from you, they'll expect to always hear from you immediately, so be careful. People are creatures of habit, and they learn based on how you relate to them. Your employees will be most secure, comfortable, and dependable when they know what to expect. As a manager, it's important that you're consistent and reliable.

Email Best Practices

When you send an email, there's a high probability that even when the recipient receives it, they won't read it, or read all of it, or read it carefully. Studies have shown that many people only read the subject line and skim the first few lines of an email before moving on to the next email or hit delete. I caution you to not rely *only* on email for important messages. This medium is a great way to touch base with people any time of the day or night, but you don't know when or if they'll read your message.

Take care that all the names in the To: field as well as those you type in your message are correct. When you use mail servers that automatically fill in names and addresses, it can be very easy to overlook such details. Few things are more precious to a person than his or her own name so get it right. Also, when at all possible, be sure to use a person's first name in your message.

Short and specific subject lines get the best responses. Experts estimate that 50 percent of emails are opened on smartphones, so be sure your subject lines are short, concise, and to the point.

You increase the likelihood of your email being read completely rather than skimmed if you keep the body of your message short, too. Using bullets for your main points is a good idea for this reason. Email is not a good way to share a large amount of data or ideas that are complex or convoluted. Keep it short, direct, and to the point.

Also, keep business email about business. Only put in writing in an email (or anywhere else, for that matter) what you're ready to see on the front page of your local newspaper—or you're prepared to defend in court. Attorneys are fond of saying "if it's not written down, it didn't happen." By the same token, if it *is* written down, it did. You better be proud of everything you write and ready to defend it in court as being moral, ethical, and truthful if it comes to that.

When you use email to communicate, the recipient does not hear your tone of voice or see any of your body language, which can lead to misinterpretation of your tone. Emotion is a key part of communication, and with email, picking up on the sender's emotional mood can be difficult. Therefore, do not use email to transmit emotionally charged messages. This is best done in person or possibly on the phone.

LEADING THOUGHT

As a writer I've learned certain lessons. One of them is to be careful about how you put a view, and to bear in mind how easily and readily you'll be misinterpreted.

—Alexander McCall Smith

Along the same lines, never send an email complaining about another person. Remember, there's no such thing as a private email. Your note might be read by an administrator or coworker or even forwarded to your boss, human resources, or your local newspaper.

Also, do not use a lot of bold type or capital letters in your emails. Both are considered rude and can come across as shouting.

Before you hit send, be sure you reread your email and correct any grammar and spelling errors. Just because email is a quick and easy means of communication doesn't mean you should be lax in your writing. Save smiley face symbols and internet acronyms for your personal email. (The same applies to text messaging if you use that for business use.)

Be careful, too, how you use carbon copy (CC) and blind carbon copy (BCC). It's best to use CC to openly share your correspondence with all your recipients and use BCC when you send to a large distribution list or when you want to keep recipient addresses private.

Avoid sending strings of emails when you're involved in an email discussion with someone. Instead, cut and paste or summarize the details rather sending the complete string back and forth. If you need to remind the other person about something you discussed in a previous email, you can simply forward that email again rather than keep the long back-and-forth string going.

> **SKILL BUILDER**
>
> Computer programs can help you stay in touch with your customers and key employees. Customer relationship management (CRM) is useful for monitoring your contact information; frequency of contact; and many other things depending on the product you use such as mailing campaigns, project management, and appointments. Several options are available. Clearly define what you want to accomplish, how important it is, and what the options are. Weigh each alternative, measuring the pros and cons, and talk to others who use such programs to find out what their experience has been.

As a manager, you need to remember that just because technology can do marvelous things, your ability to make good decisions and find and grow good people is still most important.

Web Conferencing

Thanks to the internet, keeping in touch with clients all over the world has never been easier. With web conferencing services such as Skype, you can set up free audio or video conferences with another person anywhere in the world. I use it to talk to my Swedish relatives as well as clients in India, Hong Kong, Australia, and all over South America. A similar service, Apple's FaceTime also provides video and audio calling.

Several other options are available for holding meetings online with one or several locations all at once. Search the internet to evaluate the latest offerings and see what might work best for you.

The biggest advantage of such web conferencing options is the cost savings. Traveling to meetings is becoming less and less desirable, and thanks to this technology, you no longer have to leave your office for several days, spend money on airline tickets, and rent expensive hotel rooms. Think about the savings for not only you, but for all the other people you bring together for a meeting. Now you can teleconference or use the internet to conduct a meeting at a much lower cost, and each person can stay at his or her work location or home, wherever around the globe that might be.

The only potential problem is coordinating a convenient time for everybody involved in the meeting. Use email in advance to arrange the details and find a suitable time. When you're faced with participants in different time zones, utilize one of the many world clocks online to calculate the time in any time zone. If a person has to miss the meeting, he or she can view the recorded file many web conferencing services offer at a later time or date.

Advances in technology are happening so fast that before this book is printed, internet meetings and hosts of other computer applications likely will have dramatically advanced. The field of technology is in a continuous state of flux and change. Your real dilemma is keeping up with all the changes.

Social Networking

Online social networking is everywhere and available in so many different mediums. But before you log on, it's important that you ask yourself some questions: Who do you want to socialize with on the internet? And are you doing it for business, pleasure, or another reason?

> **LEADING THOUGHT**
>
> Sometimes, idealistic people are put off the whole business of networking as something tainted by flattery and the pursuit of selfish advantage. But virtue in obscurity is rewarded only in Heaven. To succeed in this world you have to be known to people.
>
> —Sonia Sotomayor, associate justice of the Supreme Court of the United States

Understanding Your Audience

Your target markets for social networking are largely younger generations who are primarily consumer-oriented. These folks are the heart and soul of internet social marketing.

Members of older generations who are in executive suites are not necessarily the key social networking audience. (Although there are always exceptions to the rule.) Very few of the executives I work with in my coaching and mentoring business have much, if any, exposure to social networking. Many of them have delegated those functions to younger people in their organizations and tasked them with using social outlets for marketing purposes. When you think about how you use your time as a manager, it can be very difficult to justify logging a lot of hours on Facebook, Instagram, Twitter, etc. if you don't have a specific purpose to do so.

That said, one of my clients who spent more than 30 years with a medical devices company, and worked his way up to a senior executive level, retired a couple years ago. Now he's traveling, consulting, and having the time of his life taking advantage of what the internet has to offer, especially LinkedIn, Instagram, and Facebook.

Baby boomers such as my client aren't your typical consumers, but they are out there. Those who are have money to spend and are a great target market you can reach via the internet and social networking.

Now for the exception that proves the rule: if your target audience is younger consumers, you need to be involved enough to understand what they're interested in, how they think, and what motivates them to take action. Remember, your first-line customers are your workers, and if they're in synch with you, the next level of customers are your company's customers. You and your people need to walk in your customers' shoes so you can relate to their interests and concerns. It's important to relate with them the way they prefer to relate.

Do or Delegate?

The key is to know your market and really be honest with yourself about what the best use of your time is. As a manager, spending excessive time on social networking is not a primary or wise way to advance your career.

Yes, you absolutely need to use online social networking enough so you understand the how, what, and why of the products and markets. However, that doesn't mean you should spend hours every day using these tools. The actual work should be delegated or automated.

Your success as a manager depends more on developing your people than becoming a technology whiz.

Making and Keeping Connections

The one area of social networking I encourage you to work at keeping up to date is LinkedIn (linkedin.com). What started as a tool to help people find jobs is now so much more than a job board. It's the best social networking platform for managers and other executives.

Historical evidence indicates you probably won't stay with your current company for 30 or 40 years like your parents or grandparents might have done. Odds are, you'll have an opportunity to move to another company. When you do, be sure you stay connected with the outside world.

It's very sad to see someone lose their job and join the ranks of the unemployed. Too often they were so focused on their job, they allowed all their outside relationships to evaporate. You need to socially nurture your outside connections in other industries and at other companies. I encourage you to have your employees stay connected with the outside world as well. This is helpful to them if they are ever in need of another job, and it's also a great way for you to find people who might be the perfect fit for you and your company.

Another form of social networking—this time offline—is through trade associations and industry groups. I encourage you to join these groups. You'll get to know your competition and be able to assess the effectiveness of other companies and managers. You also will develop friendships outside your own company that might prove very useful in the future when you need to change jobs, look for sharp people to hire, or want to enhance your view of the market by conferring with knowledgeable friends.

Before you join any groups, be sure they're involved in things that interest you. Don't join a group just to belong to a group. For you to get any significant benefits from a group, you have to start by giving. People will watch and evaluate you when you join, so it's in your best interest to have high integrity, volunteer to help with running the group, and make a serious and worthwhile contribution.

LEADING THOUGHT

I don't know what your destiny will be, but one thing I know: the only ones among you who will be really happy are those who have sought and found how to serve.

–Albert Schweitzer

Outside groups and associations are a great place to practice your leadership, presentation, and team-building skills. Give, give, give, and at the appropriate time, you'll reap your reward or benefit.

I was in Rotary for many years. One of Rotary's mottos is, "Service above self." Use that motto as your guide for any group or association in which you participate, be patient, and you'll find the personal rewards are plentiful.

Social networking online isn't much different. The key to building a loyal social network online is to give away value. It's not a place to advertise and only talk about yourself. If you want people to like or share your name, ideas, or posts, you have to share true value. It also helps to add a bit of humor from time to time.

Listen and Learn

It's difficult to learn when you're doing all the talking. When you ask questions and then listen, you learn as well as maintain control of the direction of the conversation. In whatever your venture, continually seek feedback from the end user or customer.

When building the platform for the technology and marketing company I founded, I held biweekly dinner meetings with 20+ industry executives. During these dinners, I showed them the latest technology developments, and they gave me great feedback. Their original ideas included everything from unique concepts to formatting and desired functionality. The end result was fantastic. As you might imagine, it turned out completely different from anything I or any of my tech people ever imagined at the beginning. It pays to ask and then listen, with your mouth shut, to the answers.

> **LEADING THOUGHT**
>
> If A equals success, then the formula is A = X + Y + Z, with X being work, Y play, and Z keeping your mouth shut.
>
> —Albert Einstein

I've found that it's wise to guide technology people closely. They might be absolutely brilliant at writing code, but they typically don't think the way the average consumer or businessperson thinks. The real mark of a genius is a person who can take something very complex and make it simple.

The best example of a practical genius is Albert Einstein. He invested most of his life working with ideas, formulas, and other scientists to define relativity and eventually came up with his simple formula, $E = mc^2$. Einstein's theories revolutionized physics, and the impact of his work still influences our daily lives in a very practical way. Without the application of his theories, we could not do so many things we often take for granted today.

Consistently strive to make all your technology efforts practical. Listen and learn as much as you can about those special theories, ideas, and computer programs, but always remember that making it simple and practical is the most important thing.

Dealing with Change

Change is inevitable, and it will continue to occur despite anything you try to do to stop it. In fact, the more you try, the more frustrated you become.

Embracing Change

So why not just embrace change? Decide to enjoy change and actually encourage it. Strive to anticipate how and where the change will occur so you can be a leader through the changing situations and not a stubborn obstructer of the future.

The best place to start is inside your own head by changing your way of thinking. Are you able to be positive when things don't go the way you want them to go? Can you easily see the bright side of the future?

The past is gone, and you have this present moment and opportunity to shape the future. It's difficult to do so if you're dwelling on the past. Don't focus on what's behind you unless you intend to go that way.

Becoming an Agent of Change

Develop a plan outlining how you're going to become a change leader. Think about how you could help your company improve. What changes in behavior need to take place?

Start this process by evaluating yourself. Make a list, write it down, prioritize each item, and block out a specific time to work on each one at a time.

Push yourself to be creative. Creativity starts with your imagination and an idea and then you explore every possible article, blog, news report, seminar, book, and course you can find on the topic or related topics. This is the accumulation phase. Fill your brain with ideas, possible solutions, and new visions.

Recently, I logged on to CNN's live updates from the Apple Worldwide Developers Conference. As the meeting went on, I learned what Apple's future plans are as well as what new products are available and how I might use them. I wanted to know because I use Apple products, but more importantly, my client is the audit firm for Apple. I need to know the news from Apple so I can give my client timely advice.

Similarly, you need to pinpoint your areas of special interest based on your job and scour news feeds, articles, and other sources for information essential to you. You can easily request email notifications for select topics on various websites. Or you can bookmark or download articles or blog entries for future reading. If you don't have time to read these, you can convert them to podcasts and play them in your car while you commute, on your smartphone or MP3 player while you exercise, etc.

> **LEADING THOUGHT**
>
> If a man empties his purse into his head, no man can take it away from him. An investment in knowledge always pays the best interest.
>
> —Benjamin Franklin

A number of websites and apps can help you cull such information. Rather than recommend any specific ones, I'd rather give you a simple yet elegant way for you to find them all easily. Plugging in a search term or keyword into Google, Bing, Yahoo!, or any other search engine yields a multitude of different results you can start with. But I encourage you to dig deeper, with long-tail searches. Expand your search criteria by adding more words. For example, let's say you don't know what a podcast is. To perform a long-tail search, you might type in the search engine: "What is a podcast and how do you use it?" With this type of search, you'll get numerous articles and sources for learning exactly what you need to know about podcasting as well as services offering to help you create a podcast. You can perform similar searches on topics that interest you.

The real trick is blocking out time in your day, every day, to work on learning new things. If you aren't continually learning new things, you're quickly becoming obsolete, just like yesterday's technology. Make learning a high priority, and commit to it if you want to become a great manager or successful in any endeavor. Say it with me: "I am a continual learner, and I love change." Now that didn't hurt, did it?

The Least You Need to Know

- Design a study program for yourself so you can keep up with the latest advances in technology.
- Be cautious because everything you write, email, or say could be recorded and used against you at some point.
- Technology enables you to conference from your office with anyone around the world, but there's no technological replacement for meeting one-to-one in person with another human being.

- Marketing is becoming more and more the process of giving away value in order to establish a relationship.
- You need to become a change agent. Don't wait for change to happen to you.

PART 5

Management Challenges

As a manager, you will deal with challenges. It's just part of the job.

One such challenge is change. Change is a reality, so you need to be prepared to deal with it—especially change you didn't see coming. I offer several suggestions on how you can anticipate and get ahead of the change cycle. You'll also need to manage conflict, tension, and crisis in the workplace. There are ways to best handle these situations, and I cover each one.

With today's opportunities for remote workers easier than ever before, you might manage employees in and out of the office. Each comes with its own challenges.

As you're building your group, you must remember that your team is only as strong as its weakest link. Repairing and, when necessary replacing, weak or damaged links is part of your job now, so Part 5 ends with recommendations and perspectives on firing employees and dealing with layoffs. These situations are difficult in the best of circumstances. It's key to stay close to your people and to mitigate the trauma created when team members aren't able to fulfill their expectations.

CHAPTER 18

Managing Change

Given that change is constant, in this chapter, I explain how you can adapt, improvise, and overcome the reality of change and talk more about how you can develop the qualities of a change agent or leader within your company. Your ability and willingness to change will determine in large measure how fast and well you advance in your career. You need to manage change just like you manage anything else.

You'll find that if you attempt to avoid change, you'll see a natural disintegration of equipment, facilities, and people if they're all not continually worked on, reconditioned, and improved. As manager, your job is to evaluate the current condition, assess where and how things need to be improved, and lead the implementation of that improvement and change.

Innovation is the highest form of change. You will want to fully utilize the resources you currently have—material, systems, and people—and be innovative in the way you nurture and develop each. Your goal is not only to stay current but actually to lead the way to remarkable progress.

In This Chapter

- Your ever-evolving role
- Playing musical chairs with your people
- Shifting geographies and territories
- Restructuring within your organization
- Business climate change

Change Starts with You

A lawyer by trade, Mahatma Gandhi changed the world in a very positive way as the leader of India's struggle against British rule. His bias toward nonviolent civil disobedience was a positive catalyst for millions and still influences people today. Gandhi also is famous for saying, "Be the change you wish to see in the world." You need to live, breathe, and demonstrate the change you want to see in your department and company.

Dwight Eisenhower became the thirty-fourth president of the United States after a successful military career and leading the United States' allies through World War II—a rather impressive résumé. Eisenhower often used this example to teach leadership: you have to be the first person of your group to charge, lead, or just be productive. You have to be a living example of the ideal manager to lead change.

Leading Change

Imagine a piece of string setting on the table in front of you. Now grab one end of it. If you pull it, the string will follow where your fingers go. If you try to push it, the string will bunch up around your fingers and end up in a tangled mess.

Like that string, your attitude toward change, innovation, and adapting to the unexpected makes the difference. If you lead the change, you'll be more successful than if you push back against it.

And that doesn't apply to only you. Your mind-set, good or bad, will be reflected by your people as well.

MANAGER MINEFIELD

The way you treat people can help or haunt you. Remember to "be nice on your way up the organization because you never know who you might meet on the way back down," as the saying goes.

Helping Others Deal with Change

Realize that change is one of the hardest things for many people to do. As a manager, you need to be empathetic toward those who are struggling to adapt to new situations. In fact, for some, experiencing change is similar to the cycle of emotion after a close friend or relative passes away.

When a person is expecting a certain thing to happen and it doesn't, there's a natural tendency to become depressed. When a person experiences a change, at first there's a loss, removal, or absence of what they were expecting or what their current situation is. This might cause negative emotions that relate to resentment and doubt. That could manifest in numerous ways, including resistance, cynicism, lethargy, and various forms of fear.

Gradually, they start to process the situation, and as they do, they often experience anxiety, confusion, and more fear. This evolves into an attempt to understand themselves, what happened, and why. During this period, they often have self-doubt or possibly even consider leaving their current job. As a manager, you need to be on the lookout for these signs and get together with your people to help them process their feelings.

The last phase of processing change, just like the last phase in mourning, is when they start to behave in a practical manner. What has happened is done; it's a part of history. The time has come to move forward.

People will gradually become more productive again and rebuild their self-confidence. They'll have more positive emotions that are obvious, such as joking, sharing stories, and having a bit of fun. Soon they'll gradually become an energetic member of the team again, be able to focus on being productive and reflect on what they've learned about themselves and their job.

Each person goes through this process at a different rate. Some process change very quickly while others need a few months to work through it. Your job is to be aware and sensitive to your employees' emotions, meet with them, and help them understand and process the change. Ultimately, they need to see how the change will impact them. If it's clearly derogatory, it might be necessary for them to leave and find another opportunity.

LEADING THOUGHT

> All companies of any size have to continue to push to make sure you get the right leaders, the right team, the right people to be fast acting, and fast moving in the marketplace. We've got great leaders, and we continue to attract and promote great new leaders.
>
> —Steve Ballmer, former CEO of Microsoft

It's actually positive and productive to have new people come in your company and others move on. As things change in your organization—hopefully for the better—it might be necessary to find new people who are more compatible with the new direction the company is moving.

Don't avoid progress and change because you get resistance from your current people. Look at the big picture and realize progress will only come if people are willing to change. When you encounter people who cannot or will not change, it's in everyone's best interest to help them move on to another position.

Properly Placing People

In his book, *Good to Great,* Jim Collins writes a lot about getting the right people on the bus. With the right people, you can conquer any obstacle, but without them, every obstacle seems insurmountable. Let's look closely to see how you can tell if the right person is in the right job.

Who Are the Right People?

As a manager, the big question for you is, how do you know who the right people are?

It helps if you evaluate and hire people based first and foremost on their attitude. It's difficult to change a person's attitude toward themselves and the world. Each of us has spent years and years becoming who we are based on our genetic makeup, where and how we were raised, and a lifetime of unique experiences.

You don't really have the expertise (or time or energy) to change a person's psychological and emotional character. Hire and find positive people and then train and develop them in the skills and behaviors required to be successful in your company.

But let's dig a little deeper.

Understanding Your Employees

When you think about the necessary changes you and your company will always have to make, now and in the future, you'll realize that to survive, people will have to adapt or leave. It's in your and your company's best interest if your employees are able to adapt.

The best way to orchestrate all the necessary and inevitable changes is to thoroughly understand your group, their talents, their preferred style, and their intelligence. Let's look at each of these factors one by one.

> **LEADING THOUGHT**
>
> A really great talent finds its happiness in execution.
>
> —Johann Wolfgang von Goethe

Talents are the things people do well, enjoy doing, and seem to have an edge over other people in their ability. It's difficult to make a rigid or definitive statement of exactly what talent is. Many views suggest it's intuitive, a natural ability, and something that's not learned or trained.

I think of my nephew. When he was just 3 years old, he could hit a ball with a bat and knock it across a few lawns. As he grew up, he played baseball, football, and all kinds of sports that required good hand-eye coordination. His grandfather had lettered in every sport during his high school days. Did they both have natural talent in their gene pool?

My son, who shares some of the same gene pool, is an accomplished skier and swimmer and is focused on exercise and fitness. When he was 5, he won his first-grade art contest. Now he's a professional artist, teaches art at the finest art school in the world (from which he also graduated with honors), and sells his paintings all over the globe. He paints and draws with his left hand, and he hits a ball, swings a hammer, and performs other macro skills with his right hand. There's something going on there that relates to talent.

Capitalizing on Talent

Watching your staff's behavior is going to be the biggest indicator you can use to identify who has talent and what that talent is. Some people naturally are good with people, for example. They enjoy others and seem to know how to relate without any training. Other people gravitate toward working with numbers and prefer to come up with solutions to computer problems rather than focus on the people around them.

People enjoy doing what they're good at. So if someone has talent for a particular type of work and they get rewarded for doing it well, they'll probably try to do more of that same kind of work, enjoy it, and gradually get better at it.

Imagine you have a direct report who continually excels at dealing with people, provides excellent customer service, and displays extrovert tendencies. Assume the situation at work changes and you must reassign this person, the extrovert, to a new location with a bunch of computers and little to no contact with people either inside or outside the business. I'm sure I don't have to tell you this just won't work. Either the person will leave the company or ask for a different job. He needs and loves the interface with people.

It would be totally different if you had to move people around, but this time you did it a bit differently. This time you relocated the extrovert, not to an isolated setting with only computers to interact with, but instead into a position of coordinating with the people in the new location to be sure everyone assimilated well. You also had him learn new skills that related to customer service and your company's new products.

MANAGER MINEFIELD

Focus primarily on a person's strength and talent. If you're continually finding fault and trying to correct a person, you'll destroy morale and motivation.

It's easier to train people in new skills than it is to ask them to change who they are, to create a different self-concept, and to behave like totally new or different people. It's also much better to have people focus on their strengths rather than trying to get people to correct their little flaws.

What you see is what you get when it comes to people's attitudes, emotional profiles, and character. All three can be improved, but you won't see the same type of dramatic change you can create with training and education in new job skills or business and technical knowledge.

So how do you identify the key areas for change as opposed to those areas that will always be pretty much the same?

Considering Behavior Styles

There are two distinct areas in which you can identify and categorize clear differences in people. The first is behavioral styles, which you learned about in Chapter 4. Nothing is more valuable, less inexpensive, and easier to use than the DISC assessment tool when you're identifying your employees' (and your own) strengths and weaknesses. It shows you the types of jobs each behavioral style does best and the types of jobs that will only frustrate and inhibit different styles. You need to become a master at interpreting this assessment.

When you have a high D, for example, be sure he or she has the freedom and enough power to exercise decisiveness. Also realize that you need to watch them so they don't get carried away with themselves. It's easy for high D's to make changes—in fact, they thrive on change.

High I's are also extroverts, so they typically need to be in a job where they interface with lots of people. They do especially well in roles that require meeting and greeting. A caveat with these folks, however: if you ask them to be out of the office a lot, it might be difficult to keep them accountable. They don't like rules and regulations, but change is something they do fairly well and easily.

The majority of your people will be high S's who don't like change. These folks need clear instructions and procedures if there's a new way to operate or a new job. For these workers, the considerations of providing for and dealing with family and the current status quo are important.

They'll do what they're asked to do without complaining, but throw too much change at them, especially if it's not well thought out and explained, and you'll cause them to become idle, confused, and nonproductive.

The people you can count on to do it right, the high C's, expect you to be well organized and give any change a lot of thought before you implement it. These folks are a great resource to help you with tasks that require quality, precision, and a job done correctly. Give them time and information to process change and their new responsibilities, and they make amazing allies. Botch up the planning, however, and you'll have a difficult time getting them to commit to and respect you.

Before you make any changes, you need to take into consideration the various behavioral styles of the people who will be affected. Take the time to understand the assessment, your people, and how the various total picture comes together, and use this information to help orchestrate how and when you make the necessary changes.

 LEADING THOUGHT

There is only one corner of the universe you can be certain of improving, and that's your own self.

—Aldous Huxley

Considering Types of Intelligence

The second area you should consider when faced with change is the type of intelligence each of your people have. I've discussed emotional intelligence (EQ) earlier in the book, and that's obviously important to take into consideration. However, you also need to think about the various *kinds* of intelligence.

To better understand the theory of multiple intelligences, developed by Harvard psychology professor Howard Gardner, think of the brain as a multifaceted computer that has an array of mental capabilities to solve problems, learn new tasks, and operate the human body. Gardner's idea defines the different types of intelligence—bodily-kinesthetic, interpersonal, intrapersonal, linguistic, logical-mathematical, musical, and visual-spatial—and argues that each is separate to some extent, almost like seven or eight different computers networked together for a brain rather than just one supercomputer brain. All the individual computers have varying levels of capability, so when you focus on the strongest type of intelligence for an individual, or the most capable computer, it's much easier for them to learn and function at any task, especially on the job.

Here's a quick rundown of the seven types of intelligence and the qualities of each:

Bodily-kinesthetic   Enjoys movement, dance, touching and making things, physical activity, and expressing him- or herself through body language.

Interpersonal   Understands people, enjoys discussions and interaction with others, has many friends, and is street smart.

Intrapersonal   Has a more inward focus when thinking; shies away from others; has strong opinions; and is confident, intuitive, and independent.

Linguistic   Focuses on words, talking, listening, and reading; enjoys books, computers, multimedia, games, and lectures.

Logical-mathematical   Uses numbers; enjoys calculating, reasoning, finding patterns and relationships, testing concepts, and investigating.

Musical   Notices background music, concentrates best with music, speaks rhythmically, and taps fingers to music.

Visual-spatial   Is aware of and drawn to shapes, graphics, pictures, models, videos, space, and environment.

Scientists are now also looking at a few additional types of intelligence—namely, spiritual and naturalist.

When I was tested to qualify for pilot training, I had to submit to a host of examinations to test my aptitude, intelligence, and physical condition. I remember that the area in which I had the highest score was spatial intelligence. That's the ability to see relationships and shapes and identify similarities and differences. The Air Force wants their pilots to be able to easily read maps; quickly relate the map to the ground; and be able to see and relate to multiple dimensions while spinning, flipping, and turning an airplane around in the sky, whether in clear skies, at night, or among the clouds. This takes a high level of spatial intelligence.

When my son was in junior high school, we had him tested in virtually every area possible. His mother was a teacher, so she had pull. We wanted to know how hard to push him because he wasn't getting all A's. It turns out he's gifted, but his highest score was in spatial intelligence. Today, his career as an artist requires a high level of spatial intelligence. As an artist, he has to see shapes, proportions, and relationships accurately to draw and paint.

I see two interesting takeaways in these stories:

- It gives more substance to the notion that intelligence is probably genetic.

- It's important to work in an area that capitalizes on and requires your natural intelligence if you want to be successful.

You need to consider this for yourself and for your people. Clearly identify what skills and aptitudes are going to be required for a job or new position, and thoroughly complete an assessment or evaluation of each of your employees so you can match the talents, skills, and aptitudes of each with the specific job or position for which they're best suited. And as you identify each type of intelligence in your people, also think about the types in which you're both strongest and not as strong. When you want to learn or teach another, it's important to use several different types of intelligence to enhance the learning experience and make it as comparable as possible with the individual's ability to learn.

LEADING THOUGHT

I not only use all the brains that I have, but all I can borrow.

—Woodrow Wilson

Recently I spent some time playing with my four-year-old grandson. Using plastic mats that hold a letter of the alphabet within a square, we practiced learning the ABC's by singing the jingle, "A-B-C-D-E-F-G, H-I-J-K-L-M-N-O-P, etc." In addition, I tasked Sixten with finding the next letter and placing it on the floor. As he did, he walked to each letter, sang its name, and placed it in the right place within the alphabet. As we played, we included visuals, singing, finding and putting in place, repetition, and of course, lots of praise. The bonus was then to count all the letters, 1 through 26.

You should combine learning for your people the same way, using drawings, discussions, opportunities to touch and manipulate, compliments, measurements of progress and completion, etc.

When you're making changes or trying to solve problems, think in terms of who has the required type of intelligence as well as which behavioral style will be most useful to accomplish the goal. If you want to sell to the music industry, for example, get someone with musical intelligence to help select the approach as well as someone with linguistic intelligence to explain the product or service. If dancing or video is involved, be sure to get someone who is kinesthetic and visual. And ideally, the whole team will be strong on interpersonal intelligence. Bring a high D to close the deal, a high S to carry all the equipment, a high C to be sure it's all hooked up correctly, and a high I to plan the party after the sale is successful.

We all have some of each type of intelligence, but we learn best when we can relate to the subject using our strongest type of intelligence. (And ideally, all training and instruction will include several of the modalities to include as many people as possible.) Find what works best for each of your employees, and you'll all have the most success.

Location, Location, Location

With the internet and the trend toward more global trade, people and companies are becoming more and more mobile while having a brick-and-mortar base is less important. And manufacturers are increasingly moving their operations to India, China, and other countries around the world to take advantage of low labor rates.

One of the most important indicators of the worldwide expansion of business is the desire of young people today to learn Spanish and Mandarin. They realize we live in a global marketplace. What are you doing to expose yourself to international knowledge, opportunities, and connections?

My last book, *The CEO Code,* is a best-seller on Amazon in English, but more translated books are being sold in India, Brazil, and Turkey than English versions here in the United States. You need to think in terms of a global economy and do specific things to help position yourself for the ever-expanding future. For example, your knowledge and your experiences are totally within your control, so think of what you can do to increase both. How many languages do you speak? How well do you know geography? What's your industry doing to compete globally? Are you studying economic and political trends outside your immediate locale?

Nathan, my artist son, has had work featured in museums and galleries in several countries. His paintings on the set of the TV show *Modern Family* have led to sales of prints on several continents due to the show being broadcast in many countries. He was even a featured artist on a Swedish reality show, *Swedish Hollywood Wives.* Over several episodes, he painted a family portrait for the star of the show, Gunilla Persson.

One of my favorite sayings is, "cast your bread on the water and see what comes back." Nathan has actively pursued his presence in the art world and has worked—and networked—to get his name and his art known. You have to do the same. You can't sit back and wait for such opportunities to find you. You have to strive to make yourself, and your company, more attractive to prospects both around the corner and around the world.

The future belongs to those who can adapt and change to a changing environment. How comfortable are you traveling in foreign countries? Do you use technology to expand your reach to the other side of the world? I suggest you make a list of those things you can do, those things you want to do, and those things you think might enhance your ability to compete in a global economy. Then start working on them one at a time.

Organizational Restructuring

The reasons for restructuring an organization may be the need for new ownership, a *leveraged buyout* (*LBO*), or simply because new management has taken over. Each of these circumstances can easily become very complex.

When a public company undergoes a hostile takeover, for example, the legal expenses can become onerous. In the case of a LBO, there's usually severe disruption within the company. By comparison, other things being equal, it's much easier to adjust to a new management team.

> **DEFINITION**
>
> A **leveraged buyout (LBO)** occurs when investors purchase a company and then restructure the finances, operations, and people to maximize their investment profits. They often refinance the company with debt to recapture their initial investment and have the company pay off the debt incurred.

Listen and Learn

In any of these or other such situations, you, as a manager, need to really pay attention. It's important that you be aware of the people who control the change. Why and how have they gotten the position they have? How will that affect your reporting requirements? What will the new criteria be for doing a quality job?

Next, you need to assess the new leaders' preferred method and style of communication. In a sense, you need to do intelligence work to figure out what makes them tick. In all likelihood, they're different from the last group of individuals who were in charge. Find out how different. Ask lots of questions, and listen and learn how the new person or people in charge communicate. Then review Chapter 4 and determine the best way to communicate with each person. Remember, it's always better to do a little too much communication than not enough.

Focus on the big picture, and find out how they'll be measuring people and departments. Encourage them to visit your area or department, and be sure your people know who they are.

The Importance of Power

You need to clearly understand the way power works in an organization. When any kind of restructuring takes place, there's also an evaluation of and possible adjustment to the power structure. Everyone has power, and understanding power is vital to your survival.

There's *legitimate power,* which usually derives from the assigned job function or title a person has. With the title of "manager," you automatically have some power you wouldn't have without the title and job description.

Other forms of power can be divided into two categories—personal power and position power. *Personal power* may be in a combination of three different forms—referent power, expert power, and information power. You completely control these forms of power and can develop them with hard work, awareness, and practice.

With *referent power,* people look up to you, respect you, and will follow your lead because of the quality and integrity you exhibit in your daily behavior; you are highly admired by others. This is the noblest form of power, so strive to have the character to attain this lofty status and still be good enough to be humble.

Expert power is attained by your skill, ability, and experience in your chosen field. When you take the time and effort to become an expert, you have influence and power. This isn't a bad thing, nor should you ever be ashamed of being an expert. It takes hard work. A real expert never has to tell anyone they're an expert; it's obvious without their saying so.

Information power is associated with having a special status, relationship, or inside track that gives you valuable information. Some people use information to retain power by not letting anyone else know what they know. This is a form of perversion, and unfortunately, people sometimes abuse this, using their knowledge to their advantage rather than sharing and helping others.

There are also three forms of position power—*connection, reward,* and *coercive.*

Connection power is most obvious when you have relatives working in a company. It's also obvious when a manager favors certain people because of a personal arrangement or relationship. They say it's important who you know; it's also important that you operate with integrity in your dealings with others. When you have a personal relationship or friendship with another, you automatically have a heavy burden to be fair, proper, and ethical. Be careful you don't abuse this form of power.

> **LEADING THOUGHT**
>
> Power tends to corrupt, absolute power corrupts absolutely.
>
> —Lord Acton

Reward power comes in many varieties. It may be the person who assigns special parking spots, or it may be the power to determine bonuses. Any time you control the purse strings, access to others, or the influence to control another person's future, reviews, or ability to get promoted, you have power. Again, with this power, comes an awesome responsibility to deal with integrity.

Coercive power is based on fear, intimidation, and threats of punishment or taking something away from another. Hopefully, you don't practice this, nor are you in an organization that uses it to manipulate people. Some managers believe a little bit of coercive power is a good thing. I disagree.

You and everyone else have some form of power in varying degrees. You should use it, but be sure you use it wisely. Focus on the higher forms of personal power whenever you can. These will require you to primarily work at becoming a better person, and that's a good thing.

Cycles of Change

It's important for you to stay aware of political and economic developments in your industry and geographic area so you can plan intelligently, take appropriate action, and survive. Whether it's interest rates, taxes, or environmental regulations, there's little to nothing you can do to change some things. Your primary job is to anticipate and adapt to the environment.

As a manager, you need to continually do research; listen to people outside your company and industry; and assess trends in consumer tastes, fashions, and desires. There will always be new products that make the current products obsolete. Think way back when people made buggy whips for the horse and wagon. Or more recently, the smartphone replacing public pay phones, PDAs, and soon desktop computers. When is the last time you used a fax machine, for example, or a camera that required film?

If your department was producing film or fax machines, *now* you would be out of a job. The future is changing faster and faster. You need to be continually exploring, learning, and changing.

The Least You Need to Know

- Change is with us to stay, so embrace it, learn from it, and adapt to it. Survival is only possible if you learn to change.
- Talent is highly desired, but it also requires hard work, consistency, and a positive attitude to be effective.
- Study your staff and look for their strengths. People will always do best when they're using their strengths, not by overcoming their weakness.
- Power is a natural and normal thing. Understand it, and learn how to use it artistically.
- You must always be learning, discovering, and exploring ideas and concepts beyond your workplace.

CHAPTER 19

Refereeing and Playing the Diplomat

Conflict is inevitable within any organization. And although there are many things you can do to minimize or possibly even eliminate conflict, odds are good you'll have to deal with it sooner or later, be it with your own manager, your own people, or with customers. When conflict does arise, it's important for you to have a preplanned approach for how you handle it. It's also important for you to teach your people how to handle conflict.

The sooner you intervene in heated situations, the better. Managers often tend to try to ignore conflict, but this isn't an effective way to manage. It's far better for you to be proactive when you see even the slightest stirring of trouble. A conflict-free environment is possible, and the result is a delightful place to work. It enables teamwork, high productivity, and quality feedback from customers and upper management.

In This Chapter

- Why conflicts erupt
- Elements of successful conflict resolution
- Managing conflict with your employees
- Managing your boss
- Handling organizational politics

As manager, you are in an ideal position to deal with conflict. You will be able to help people become more aware, increase their self-esteem, and learn to not only handle conflict but be able to teach others how to solve problems without resorting to conflict.

The What and Why of Conflict

Stop playing with my toys.

I want my toys.

I want your toys.

Oh, if only it were that simple. But in a sense, it is. Conflict arises when one person wants or takes something or does or doesn't do something for or with another person and they struggle, compete, or surreptitiously maneuver to get their own way. People often choose to clash because, based on their past experience, it's a way for them to get what they want. They think it works. It's the epitome of the adage, "the squeaky wheel gets the grease."

In reality, conflict causes anger, animosity, and resentment and can lead to sabotage, criticism, and even violence. Pursuing it is a sign of a person with low emotional intelligence. War is the worst form of conflict, and it's been said that war is man's grandest form of insanity. I've been there, and I agree.

So what do you do about it?

First, you have to understand what conflict really is. Conflict is a way to behave to fulfill your own agenda. People use conflict to attain their agenda because they believe it will work because it has worked for them in the past. Or maybe they don't know what else to do and choose to clash as a last resort.

It's important to admit that when people choose conflict, they know what they're doing. It's also important to realize that they're willing to put their desires above those of someone else with their "I win; you lose" philosophy. This won't build friendships nor positively influence others. The sad thing is, often the winner doesn't care. He or she just wants his or her own way.

My many years of experience in businesses focused on money—real estate, insurance, mortgages, and investments—have revealed a high percentage of people who favor winning at any cost. (That's one of the reasons I left that industry many years ago.) This illustrates behaviors that reflect values. When dealing with conflict, consider that the two clashing parties probably have different values.

You see this in politics, too. Many politicians are attorneys by trade and were taught in law school how to argue and defeat their opponent. This causes polarization of views, and you often witness the extremes—liberals versus conservatives—in conflict.

> **LEADING THOUGHT**
>
> Honest statesmanship is the wise employment of individual manners for the public good.
>
> –Abraham Lincoln

People who are inclined to embrace conflict often are driven by passion. Not the passion to create the greater good or pull people together, but rather greed, power, or fear. My experience in the investment world revealed greed as the primary motive for many in the business.

In politics, you often see narcissistic people driven by power. The remainder of people caught up in clashes comes from some form of fear, whether they're frightened, insecure, or severely disappointed with the result being nothing like their anticipated outcome.

To be fair, it's important to also realize that sometimes a person can be stonewalled, ignored, or pushed to the breaking point. When a person is in such a vulnerable position, and they see no rational way out, they may choose conflict. For example, I think the early Americans would agree that they had no other recourse than to fight the British in the American Revolution.

There's a better way to resolve disagreements than resorting to fights. This better way requires that both parties establish a modicum of civility and agree to communicate. Conflict erupts when communication fails.

Successful Conflict Resolution

Several principles can help you formulate a peaceful communication to resolve disputes.

Listen

First, it's essential that you listen. Let each party express their interests and why they see things the way they do. You should only ask a few simple and probing questions and spend the majority of your time listening attentively. Focus on facts, patterns, sequences, and emotional triggers in the responses. Your goal is to understand the situation from the other person's point of view.

Demonstratively show respect and patience as you listen. Don't be overly concerned with sharing your own point of view. Remember, the person asking questions is always in control. Don't dominate or crowd the other person; be relaxed and open.

Gently paraphrase what the other person is saying without adding judgment or opinion. Just seek to understand and summarize their words and point of view so you're sure you get it.

Then be patient, wait, and ask, "Is there anything else?"

LEADING THOUGHT

The most important thing in communication is to hear what isn't being said.

—Peter Drucker

Share

Ask permission to share your point of view or what you see as the situation.

When you've received the okay, express your view in a calm and friendly voice, focusing on what you think has happened or what the factors are that need to be considered. For example, "I know this is a tough time; however, we have been informed that budgets have to be cut," or "Several people have expressed concern about your habit of coming to work late." Concentrate on the behaviors and the situation, not the person.

Also remember the "I understand how you feel" approach. You're trying to connect with the other person and relate information, so avoid inflammatory, emotional, and sarcastic words and phrases. Discuss the situation, period. Don't attack the person nor use a broad brush to accuse or criticize them or their personality.

Build Bridges

Strive to reach an agreement on exactly what the problem really is. Do this with questions, not by telling them harshly your view of reality. They need to discover it themselves. You need to guide the other person to the reality, get the problem on the table, and have all parties involved on the same page.

Get agreement on those facts and details that are understood to both sides of the discussion. Look for common ground, but also define issues that are definitely different for each party. Ask about and get into the open any unsaid, hidden, or sensitive factors such has gender, age, or cultural differences.

Seek to define the greater good, the best possible outcome for all concerned. "We all agree we want to do what's best for the company, right?"

Explore Possibilities

Use brainstorming to explore possible solutions because no idea is, on the surface, a bad idea. Get creative and look for all kinds of solutions. Don't worry about agreeing or not, just explore ideas.

Find out what the limits are. Determine what's absolutely a "no go" and what will and won't work with each idea broached.

Negotiate a Win-Win

Agree that you all want a win-win outcome. No matter what each party's opinion or viewpoint is, a win-win should be everyone's desire.

> **LEADING THOUGHT**
>
> One of the hardest things in this world is to admit you are wrong. And nothing is more helpful in resolving a situation than its frank admission.
>
> —Benjamin Disraeli

Be willing to let the discussion incubate until another day if necessary. If you take this course, be sure you have notes and are able to review and agree on the progress you've made next time you meet.

Explore possible solutions and an agreement. Keep in mind that neither party should be forced to be unreasonable or suffer a major loss. Find a common ground. It might be that you have to get approval of any decisions made.

As you talk, strive to make your discussion as positive and respectful as possible. Agree to learn from the experience. It's possible, and preferred, that an impassioned discussion will actually build a better relationship and reach deeper understanding.

Handling Conflict with Employees

Conflict can erupt between you and your employees in various ways. It might be precipitated by behavior problems, production issues, personality conflicts, or an array of other things. When a clash occurs, you have several actions you need to take.

Your first goal should be to be absolutely clear on your company's rules, standards of performance, and expected behavior so you can quickly identify if someone is out of line. Next, you need to be walking around, chatting with people, and always observing so you can spot trouble immediately. Finally, when you do see a problem, you should act quickly, establish open and transparent communication, and be decisive. This is why it's so important that you "hire slowly and fire rapidly." Each state has its own laws, so connect with your human resources department to be sure you're clear on the rules, laws, and guidelines your company honors and abides by.

There are some issues for which you'll have little, if any, tolerance. If an employee steals, comes to work under the influence, is guilty of sexual harassment, or is flagrantly insubordinate or violent, they need to be fired. If only the law would allow that, however, life would be easy.

It's important that you write down everything that relates to disciplining employees. Remember that it doesn't happen unless it's written down. At least, that will probably be the legal view. If you have to reprimand an employee, record the incident, what you said, and what the employee said and agreed to and then have the employee sign the report as acknowledgement.

By the same token, be careful what you write down. During the hiring process especially, anything you write down, any email you send, and any conversation you or someone else records on their smartphone or any other recording device might be brought into a court of law or find its way into the media.

Attorneys I know recommend that notes and memos be focused, limited, and only contain minimal information. Minutes from meetings and board discussions and resolutions should be designed with the realization that all of it could be used against you or the company at some time in the future. This is a very sad state of affairs, but it's the reality of our current society.

Friends of mine who are still in the security investment business moan about the burden of heavy restrictions and the persnickety rules they must follow about what they can say and write down. Many companies won't even allow their employees to have access to the internet because of the potential liability.

Several of my clients are major Fortune 500 companies and are very limited as to what they say or do without first running it by their legal department. That's probably a good idea for you, too.

 MANAGER MINEFIELD

Caveat emptor means "let the buyer beware." Anytime you're going to fire someone, you need to get legal advice from an attorney before you act. Wrongful termination is a very sensitive area of the law, and to make matters worse, the law seems to change every day. Nothing in this book should be considered as any form of legal advice or legal opinion, nor are there any opinions or recommendations on any legal matters or anything relative to state, federal, or EDD laws. Please consult your attorney for legal advice on hiring, firing, and disciplining your employees.

You already have a means for resolving conflict, especially as it relates to communication issues. Now let's focus on situations in which people are out of bounds, underperforming, or basically being troublemakers.

Dealing with an Out-of-Bounds Employee

Every organization has established rules, traditions, and mores. When someone is unaware of or deliberately chooses to violate or break those boundaries, it might or might not be cause for alarm. Some things are either old or outdated ways of doing things, and when that's recognized and improved, it can be cause for celebration. Unfortunately, depending on how it's done and how people react to it, conflict might arise.

If you see someone doing or asking to do something differently than what's traditional, try to be open-minded. As you ask questions and evaluate the situation, you might discover the change is, indeed, progress. If you decide to implement this change, apply what you learned in Chapter 18 as you go about it to help you mitigate any potential conflict.

On the other hand, if the new action or behavior is detrimental or harmful for the greater good of your group, you need to have a meeting with the person involved and seriously and sincerely discuss the problem behavior. Again, apply what you learned earlier in this chapter about handling conflict.

If the action wasn't deliberate, approach it as a learning opportunity. Don't get negative. Rather, strive to understand the employee's thinking and action; explain how you would prefer he or she learn; and monitor their future behavior, taking into consideration the greater good. Help the individual understand the correct or preferred way to do things. Maybe also have the employee partner up with a more experienced team member and develop a coaching relationship.

For deliberate actions that contradict the norms of your group, you need to put an edge on the discussion. By asking questions, get to the core of why the employee did what they did, and help them understand that there are certain rules of the road they must follow. For example, if they went over your head and made a decision to refund money or changed an order without having the complete picture and approval, this might not be a major deal, but it shows that you need to spend more time training your people.

When things go really well, give the credit to your people and praise them. When a mistake is made, it's probably partly your fault either directly or because you didn't train and prepare your team well enough. Take responsibility, and fix it.

Dealing with Performance Problems

When an employee is underperforming, they probably know it, and the people around them probably know it, too. In fact, sometimes the manager is the last to find out. But this won't be the case with you because you'll have already established good measurement criteria, status charts, and a policy and consistent practice of "inspecting what you expect."

The ramifications of someone underperforming are complex. Some of the issues include the employee develops low self-esteem, other workers see them get paid the same for doing less, morale suffers, the slowdown may spread if not addressed promptly, quality will usually be lower, production will be delayed, pride of quality craftsmanship will suffer for everyone, organizational income and profit will suffer, high producers will get frustrated and may leave, complaints will develop for unfair labor and management practices, and the list goes on.

One of the biggest mistakes I've seen in organizations is management spending an inordinate amount of time trying to fix people and neglecting to work with the high achievers and develop positive growth strategies. They focus too much on putting their finger in the dike. If a worker isn't helping make your job easier, you should consider a replacement.

Winners love to be measured; losers don't, so as manager, you need to establish a culture of high achievement as the norm. Create an environment in which people are continually striving to win and compete with their own last best effort.

If a worker isn't learning and able to improve, they might belong in a different place or doing a different job. Your responsibility is to provide the necessary training, encouragement, and a positive environment. As the sign on my old manager's desk said, "Produce or perish." The truth is, compensation has to relate to contribution. If you're paying someone a wage, they must produce or move on.

LEADING THOUGHT

Good leadership involves responsibility to the welfare of the group, which means that some people will get angry at your actions and decisions. It is inevitable, if you're honorable. Trying to get everyone to like you is a sign of mediocrity: you'll avoid the tough decisions, you'll avoid confronting the people who need to be confronted, and you'll avoid offering differential rewards based on differential performance because some people might get upset. Ironically, by procrastinating on the difficult choices, by trying not to get anyone mad, and by treating everyone equally "nicely" regardless of their contributions, you'll simply ensure that the only people you'll wind up angering are the most creative and productive people in the organization.

—Colin Powell

Dealing with Troublemakers

Some people just don't get it—or they do, but they just don't care to follow the rules. This could be due to a rough childhood, bad parenting, or being raised in a bad neighborhood. Your job is not to be a social worker, psychologist, or counselor. You are being paid to lead and manage a group of winners to produce.

When a person in your group perpetually causes problems, you need to take action. First, really look into the situation, and listen to the individual's perspective, concerns, and emotional makeup. It could be that they need help and you can refer them to a professional. Or your firm might provide assistance to get them counseling or care that will help.

While you're looking and listening, pay special attention to the rest of your team and the people the person works with on a regular basis. It's possible that the group or another individual is causing the problems, harassing, or abusing the individual. I've seen situations in which a very clever coworker figured out how to sabotage another worker and deliberately set them up for failure. Your best way to determine if this is occurring in your organization is by getting feedback from numerous people who interface with the individual. Look for behavior among everyone.

Once you have all the information you think you need, consider having your human resources representative, an outside psychologist, or a coach evaluate the situation. It's also advisable to have an attorney involved.

With their guidance, take notes and build the necessary documentation. I would highly recommend you have another person with you for all meetings with the individual. Your HR rep is the ideal candidate.

If the decision is made to terminate the individual, do it with the guidance of human resources. Be sure you aren't alone with the individual when the termination occurs. Make the meeting as focused on behavior and work results, or lack of results, as possible. Don't attack, criticize, or belittle the individual in any personal way. It's all about job performance, the good of the company, and an opportunity for the individual to find something more appropriate and fulfilling. Stand up at the end of the meeting, wish them well, and say good-bye.

Avoiding Conflict with Your Boss

Conflict doesn't occur only between your employees. Sometimes you'll clash with your own boss. To avoid this situation, you can learn how to manage up.

Obviously, you manage your employees, your direct reports. But believe it or not, you can—and should—manage your boss as well. This doesn't mean you tell her what to do, nor does it mean you try to pull a fast one or do something behind her back. Rather, it means you influence her. You also do everything you can to help her be successful and look good.

There are two very specific strategies you can use to influence your boss. The first is to remember that the only way you influence another person is by your own behavior. Also, it's key that you work on your own referent power.

Maintain Professionalism

How do you act around your boss? Are you casual, always joking or telling personal stories, or are you professional? The more professional and appropriate you are with your boss, the better.

When you have a scheduled meeting with your boss, be early, come prepared to ask good-quality questions, and take notes. Ask enough questions so you know exactly what your boss's goals and objectives are. How will they be measured, and what can you do to help her achieve them? Then, factor in your boss's goals and objectives as appropriate into your own goals and objectives.

Let her know ahead of time how you're doing on projects, before she has to ask you or call to remind you that something is due. Always give her respect, listen attentively, and strive to make her look good in front of your people. When in doubt, give a little extra, whether it's a quality issue, a production target, or a presentation you give in the office or in public.

If she has an assistant or secretary, get to know that person well. Help him do his job by thinking ahead, anticipating his needs, and giving him the same respect you give your boss.

Both of these folks are worthy and deserving of your respect. Remember the earlier discussion of power? Your boss and her assistant both have power, so honor it.

Work on Your Own Referent Power

Your referent power, if you remember from Chapter 18, is derived from others as they respect and admire you. Think of the relationship between a parent and a child. My son manages me because I know I can trust him, I can rely on him doing what he says, and I know he would do anything to help me. I often ask him for advice, and he tells me the truth but in a way that demonstrates his love and desire to be helpful.

There's no reason not to treat your boss the same way. Don't go out of your way to tell them what to do, but when they ask your opinion, tell the truth in a way that helps build them up and improve. Never give faint praise, and absolutely don't even think about being a *sycophant*.

> **DEFINITION**
>
> A **sycophant** is a person who compliments, flatters, or praises an important person to win his or her approval or gain an advantage for themselves.

Fighter pilots often use the expression, "Check your six." This refers to the 6 o'clock position on an aircraft where 12 o'clock is straight ahead and 6 is behind you. One of the main reasons fighters fly in formation is so they can cover for each other. Your wingman is your insurance policy, your comrade in arms, and a trusted teammate. You need to watch out for your boss's 6 o'clock vulnerability. Hopefully, your boss will also watch out for yours.

If you follow all these recommendations, you probably won't have any conflict with your boss. The key is to keep open and transparent communication going, even when you're embarrassed, behind schedule, or have made a mistake. If you do get in a conflict with your boss, I encourage you to use the same strategy described earlier in this chapter to resolve it.

The Inevitable Office Politics

Politics is a reality in every organization. In the broadest sense, it's the system of rules and behaviors agreed to by a group of people who work together. All people are different and have diverse wants and needs; politics is how the people discuss and try to resolve these wants and needs given the available resources.

Both businesses and governments use politics to organize, allocate, and decide what will be done. In business, the primary power is held by the owners of the business. In the case of the government, at least in the United States, the ultimate power is with the people who choose to delegate that power to representatives in congress, the executive branch, and the judiciary.

The goal is to have a civil and functioning society, whether it's a business or a government. The way various people get to influence the whole and acquire what they want is by using their power. You might take a minute to review the types of power discussed in Chapter 18. Ideally, people will use their power artfully and be open to concessions and dialogue.

When governments give up on politics, they go to war. When business owners or employees give up on politics, they force their will on the other or file a lawsuit.

Ideally, you'll choose to master the art of politics by using your new tools in effective communication, understanding power, and developing your people to seek the greater good for all.

The Least You Need to Know

- Be a peacemaker, and reward people who get along well with others. Eliminate anyone who does not make your job easier.

- Always seek a win-win outcome. Avoid zero-sum games, or those with a "I win; you lose" outcome. Those are only destructive.

- Inspect what you expect! Do it often, and do it to catch people doing things right.

- As a manager, your job is to sincerely strive to make your boss look good and be successful.

- Politics are a necessary part of working together. Seek to be a statesman and not a politician. Say what you mean, and mean what you say.

CHAPTER 20

Handling Firings and Layoffs

The days of spending a lifelong career in one company and getting an engraved gold watch at retirement are long gone. Several studies reveal the average CEO of a major company holds his or her position for less than 10 years, and many CEOs only make it a couple years. The same is true with all levels of employees, not just CEOs. Change is everywhere, and this has helped create an environment in which people move around to new positions and companies quite often.

If this is the new normal, what do you need to know and do to make the most of it? Any time there's a problem, there's also an opportunity to find a solution and figure out how to benefit from the situation. As manager, you are in a position to lead and show initiative in finding good solutions to what many consider to be a travesty, disaster, or the end of the road—a firing or a layoff.

In This Chapter

- The promise of job insecurity
- Firing for cause
- The ins and outs of layoffs
- Letting go of good people
- Looking out for those who leave and those left behind
- Learning from adversity

You have a clear opportunity to make a simple choice, and you can come from a place of scarcity or abundance. In this chapter, I review the many ways to mitigate the reality of firing, layoffs, and people thinking their dreams have been shattered. The fundamental truth is that life is continually in a state of flux, and victory goes to those who are best able to adapt.

Attaining Success and Significance— or Falling Short

Where there's no job security, how do you continually move forward and stabilize your career? Do you really want stability? What are the alternatives?

My dentist was a U.S. Navy corpsman, medical assistant, in the Korean War. His rescue helicopter broke down over enemy territory, and he was captured by the North Koreans and interned for almost 3 years as a prisoner of war.

Because of his medical training, he was appointed to be the camp doctor. When new prisoners arrived in the camp, one of the first things they did was get a physical exam, and Norm, the corpsman, would clean their wounds, set any broken bones, and at times, even perform operations. But the conditions in which he had to work and live were dirty, primitive, and cruel.

Over time, Norm made a profound but sad observation. Consistently, about 10 to 12 percent of the new prisoners would die with no physical injuries, ailments, or punishments. They just rolled up in the fetal position, gave up, and in a matter of weeks they were gone. His conclusion, based on his experience personally trying to help them, was that they had nothing to live for, nothing to rely on, and they weren't grounded in any faith.

There's a difference between being successful and having significance. Money is often considered a mark of success for some, while success is a promotion or a corner office. For others, success is simply surviving. You can approach significance when you realize the value of giving and helping others. One of the real joys you have as a manager is the ability to help others.

LEADING THOUGHT

Success breeds complacency. Complacency breeds failure. Only the paranoid survive.

—Andy Grove

Everybody wants to be a winner in their heart. You can help them convert that intangible desire into specific behavior on the job so they can be productive, feel good about themselves, and provide for their family.

Helping others sometimes requires you to share the truth with them—what some call "tough love." If they're going to be successful and, some day significant, they must take personal responsibility for the way they live their lives and the results they do or don't get. As manager, you must let people know when they're winning and when they're losing. It's also incumbent upon you to share with your people what they must do, specifically, to change their behavior from loser to winner.

Another responsibility you have as manager is to place the right person in the right place. I shared several ways you can identify the differences in people, so please seek to move a person, provide him or her additional training, or terminate them when they're not making progress.

When you don't let people know they aren't cutting it, you do them a disservice, you do the company a disservice, and you really are shirking your responsibility. There's no reason people should be *surprised* when they get fired if it relates to poor performance.

The four primary management functions—planning, communicating, managing, and executing—are broad. Managing includes training, performance evaluation, and measurement. Communicating includes frequent feedback, coaching, and counseling. When you perform these duties properly, your employees will know when they're in jeopardy.

"You're Fired"

Those words are tough to say—and maybe even tougher to hear. Have you ever been fired? If you haven't, can you imagine what it feels like? In this book, *Fired Up! How the Best of the Best Survived and Thrived After Getting the Boot,* author Harvey MacKay tells the story of Larry King, Donald Trump, and even Harvey himself plus many more who learned and grew from the process of being fired.

Hopefully, the final result will be a learning experience, but for now, I want to focus on how you do it to cause the least amount of pain, save a person's self esteem, and help them learn from the experience.

 LEADING THOUGHT

The moment you feel the need to tightly manage someone, you've made a hiring mistake. The best people don't need to be managed. Guided, taught, led—yes. But not tightly managed.

—Jim Collins

Building Your Case

The process of firing a worker needs to be well orchestrated whenever possible. Sometime an emergency, crisis, or event makes it mandatory for you to take action quickly, but in the majority of cases, I've seen managers spend days and even weeks agonizing over how and when to fire someone.

It's important to know federal and state laws as well as union agreements and any Employment Development Department (EDD) rules that apply to you. Your human resources representative will give you guidance on the process, and you also probably should develop a working relationship with a labor attorney.

From a management point of view, you need to maintain a lot of documentation in the normal course of business. It's also important that the documentation is accurate and kept up to date. Part of this documentation includes past performance reviews. It's not rational to fire someone suddenly for no reason—that will be the attorney's argument if you have a worker with several outstanding reviews and then you decide to fire them. You must build a case in writing and document poor performance.

Giving a Warning

When you have someone who isn't performing up to standard, the first thing you need to do is give them a warning. The warning is a formal process you need to prepare that includes the reason for the warning, details of what's wrong, and a target date to correct the shortcoming.

Then meet with the worker, go over the warning, and have them sign the receipt of the warning. I suggest that any time you have a meeting where it concerns unsatisfactory performance, you always have another person in the room with you. All three of you then should sign the document.

You need to not only list and detail the problems, but also be very clear and explain in person and in writing the behavior and performance you expect and by when. Again, this all needs to be written as well as spoken to the worker with someone else present as a witness.

Keep your discussion professional and focused on their job performance. This isn't the time or place to get into counseling, discussing personal matters, or participate in any kind of argument. Keep the meeting short, to the point, and very precise.

Firing an Employee

If, after the warning period, you, with the potential assistance of human resources, determine the person must be fired, be prepared. Have your documentation along with a list of any equipment or materials like keys, files, computers, or tools that need to be turned in before the person leaves the building. Again, have someone else in the meeting with you. Your human resources representative might also need to be there.

Be sure you've discussed with your labor attorney any release documents and how and why you might want to use them. This is especially important and sensitive if the worker is part of a special or minority group.

The termination meeting should be brief, to the point, and well documented, similar to the warning meeting. Many professionals suggest you perform terminations early in the week so you have an opportunity to get things back on track with your other people and disrupt their routines as little as possible.

Be very precise as to when the worker will be terminated and expected to leave the office. I recommend it be immediately, and at least the same day you give them the news. If it's "for cause," which it will be if they haven't performed sufficiently, simply state their employment with the company is being terminated effective immediately (or whenever you have decided) because they have not met their performance requirements and leave it at that. Do not get into an argument or share a lot of details. You have decided, and that's that.

In some organizations, this is all you need to do, and you can leave the meeting and let the human resources rep take over. If you need to continue with the process yourself, next explain how much they'll receive for severance pay, how much vacation pay they have coming to them, and any other benefits, plus information on how long these things will last. (Because you've already spoken to human resources and an attorney, you have this data.) It's best to have this in writing to give the terminated employee. Be sure you have a copy to keep, too.

Once this has been done, you or your human resources rep should be sure the terminated employee does not go back to his or her workstation without an escort. Make the process of them gathering their personal belongings expedited, and be polite and courteous but firm with them if they try to stop and talk to someone or go somewhere beyond their own workstation. You never know when someone will lose their cool and react emotionally, so be prepared and make it as efficient as possible.

Then you or your human resources rep will escort the terminated employee out of the building, and be sure you have requested and received any keys or security cards they might have so they can't get back into the building later.

> **LEADING THOUGHT**
>
> Good people are found not changed. They can change themselves, but you can't change them. You want good people, you have to find them. If you want motivated people, you have to find them, not motivate them.
>
> —Jim Rohn

Once the terminated worker is gone, meet with all the people who worked with the affected former employee. Explain that worker X is no longer working here, but do not go into any further details. If you want to reassure your remaining employees, you could mention that this was a one-time firing and not the beginning of layoffs. People sometimes fear for their own jobs after learning of a coworker's firing.

Be sure you reassign all the duties that employee had, and let the receptionist, security guard, mailroom staff, and the IT department know the person no longer works there. Also, instruct all your people, including the receptionist, how to handle phone calls for the terminated worker. You might want to discuss this with your attorney in advance, too.

You might get sued, and you might not. You might have to pay increased unemployment insurance, and you might not. The one thing you can know for sure is that the only thing worse than firing a worker is *not* firing a worker who isn't meeting his or her set performance standards or isn't making a positive contribution to your team and the company.

Removing a nonperforming employee is like cutting out a cancer. It must be done, and the sooner, the better.

Conducting a Layoff

A layoff is similar to a firing but also different. Whereas a firing is often based on performance, a layoff tends to be based on less personal reasons and is more company-focused. For example, if your company needs to save money, you might be forced to lay off a staff member. The choice of who might be the employee with the least amount of seniority, or the one with the highest salary, depending on your situation. Layoffs are less about performance and more about numbers, especially money.

Before a layoff can be executed, a lot of preparation is required. Be sure to analyze all positions, how they fit together, and which ones can be combined if you have a reduction in your workforce as the result of a layoff.

 MANAGER MINEFIELD

> Deliberately plan any layoff so you can keep the best and eliminate the weak or nonperformers. Some people need to be fired but you can't let them go because of the union or other restrictions. Often layoffs are a way to purge the deadwood. Strategize with your human resources and legal departments so this is optimized.

Under the best of conditions, layoffs are traumatic and hard on everyone. Invest time with your human resources and legal advisers to be sure you clearly understand all the ramifications of severance, unemployment benefits, insurance, and health-care packages for the laid-off employees. You'll need to explain these in the employee meetings.

Schedule private meetings with all the employees affected by the layoff. Prepare a packet of information so they can look through and process what you've told them after they settle down, are home with their family, and are able to think clearly.

Keep the meetings short and to the point, and clearly explain the decision and why certain groups of people were picked. Don't let it get personal, and try to avoid emotional words and explanations.

Have a personal meeting with each affected person before you make any announcements to the rest of your employees, and have empathy for each person you speak with. Do not use mail or email to notify people. If a person is geographically restricted from coming to the office, at least make a phone call to tell them the news. Design your schedule so you can do all the necessary layoffs at once. Do not drag it out over a few days.

If you can, offer a recommendation, a positive reference, and any assistance finding another job that you can facilitate.

After the last appointment, meet with your remaining employees as soon as possible. Explain the why and how of the layoffs, and assure them there won't be more, that it's finished. Also share with them what they can expect of any job or duty changes they might face because of the layoffs.

When in doubt, be open and honest, and don't play games or try to be clever. Be sincere and strive to understand how your people feel, having just maybe lost several friends, worrying there might be more layoffs, and wondering how they'd pay their bills and feed their families if the situation had happened to them. Reassure your staff as much as possible, but don't make promises you know you might have difficulty keeping later.

When You Have to Fire Good People

When you find quality people, it's in your best interest—and ultimately your company's—to develop a relationship with them, whether they're in your employ or not. People attract people like themselves, and if you know good people, they'll know other good people.

Some of the best people will have to leave your company, not because they can't perform, but perhaps because although they perform well, there simply isn't room or sufficient opportunity for them to advance or achieve their own goals at your company. You want to help these people find new opportunities and ensure they know you care. The best way to do this is to encourage and support them and help them do what's in their best interest.

One of my favorite clients is Ernst and Young (EY), a high-quality worldwide accounting and professional services firm—one of the global "big four" accounting firms. EY has a very active alumni organization composed of people who no longer work for EY but did at one time. Although these folks are no longer EY employees, they all stay in touch with each other.

EY holds seminars, hosts open houses, and regularly communicates with its alumni group. I have had the privilege of giving a presentation to this group, and I was impressed with the quality of the attendees and the good rapport the current partners have with past EY employees.

This relationship makes good business sense. Many managers and partners leave EY for management roles in other companies. Staying connected is a way to stay current with business trends, maintain a positive image in the marketplace, and in time, lots of business comes in because of these still-connected relationships. The EY partners also make a very deliberate and positive effort to help former EY folks who may be in transition find good jobs with their clients and other companies.

Are you connecting with your company's alumni in a similar way?

 MANAGER MINEFIELD

In most industries, people know people in competing companies and in the industry. If you burn a relationship, word will get out and the damage could come back to haunt you years later. New people in an industry will ask others about companies and specific people in those companies. "What's he like to work for?" "Are they fair to their people?" "Would you want to work for them?" The truth will always come out, so it's best to live a life with integrity.

Keeping the Keepers Happy

Have you ever noticed an ad campaign by a bank, car dealer, or a retail business that offered a special discount to new customers? Sometimes the "new" discount is better than what "old" customers are paying for exactly the same service or product.

How does that make you feel if you're one of the "old" customers, knowing the new guys get special incentives? Do you still feel valued as a customer? Have you ever had a twinge of envy or anger when you found out this happens? Have you ever taken your business elsewhere, where you're one of the "new guys"?

As a manager, it's essential that you make your people feel valued and "new." You can take several approaches to accomplish this, but the most important is your attitude toward them. Do you pay attention to them with your eyes, your mental focus, and your total demeanor when you talk with them? When a person is distracted or multitasking, the other person often can feel reduced or at least insignificant. Focus on one goal at a time. If you are with an employee, lock on them and give them your total attention.

Be accessible to your people. An open-door policy is an excellent policy to have. Remember, this means your door is open and so is your attention span.

The most powerful habit you can have to build rapport and quality relationships with your people is to hold one-to-one meetings. Be sure you teach your direct reports how to have one-to-one meetings with their key people as well.

Make a deliberate effort to catch your people doing things right. Giving a simple "Thank you" or a word of praise to an individual whose behavior is exemplary is an easy way to express appreciation. Don't hesitate to do this in public, either. When you notice good work and let everyone know you're paying attention and making note of it, people will start to up their game.

Don't be a hermit. Remember to get out on the shop floor, visit other offices, and travel to the various locations where your people work. Get involved with them and their jobs. Ask how it's going, what issues they might be facing, and how you can help. People will sense when you're sincere and you mean your concern.

 LEADING THOUGHT

Nobody cares how much you know, until they know how much you care.

—Theodore Roosevelt

If you try to do this in a perfunctory way, it will backfire on you. It's essential that you be sincere and honestly work on building trust, respect, and understanding with your remaining employees.

Learning from This Experience

With every adversity, you have a chance to learn something. In this section, let's look at some of the lessons you might learn from having to fire or lay off people.

Identifying Mistakes Made

Anytime you have to fire an employee, it can be financially expensive for the company, emotionally taxing for all people involved, and a sign that a mistake has been made. You want to learn from all mistakes so you hopefully won't have to endure a repeat of the same mistakes. And anyone can make mistakes; it's part of life and of being human. The main issue is not to point fingers or accuse people but rather to learn from mistakes so the future is better.

The place to start your research is the hiring process. Were the people involved in the hiring well informed and fully trained in how to interview? What were the desired requirements, and was there a good system used for how to evaluate candidates? Basically, you want to review all the procedures and processes used and look for areas that might need to be improved.

What were the final criteria, and how was the decision made to hire the person? Often, I have seen situations in which staff members are in a hurry or are overloaded when the hiring process is underway so they carelessly let someone else get involved. They often don't take time to do reference checks or just send the message that they don't have time for this, and the other person should "just hire someone." This rarely works out well.

Here are some other common hiring mistakes:

- Hiring a relative or friend without using an objective process.

- Not using assessments to evaluate the compatibility of the candidate to the job, department, or culture.

- Not checking references, credit, public records, and other information readily available online.

- Making a decision without having at least three different people interview the candidate and compare perspectives.

- Making the decision based on skills, education, past clients, or years of experience and ignoring or downplaying a cultural and emotional fit with your company or your staff.

- Assuming they can do the job and not training or managing them closely at the beginning.

- Having a mismatch between actual ability and desires versus the specific job requirements and potential.

- Hiring for the wrong reasons: candidate's relatives, connections, or looks rather than job specific qualities.

- Not listening well to what a candidate says and being *unaware* of what's not said during an interview.

LEADING THOUGHT

Recently, I was asked if I was going to fire an employee who made a mistake that cost the company $600,000. No, I replied, I just spent $600,000 training him. Why would I want somebody to hire his experience?

—Thomas John Watson Sr., founder and CEO of IBM

Interviewing Better

The most effective way to really get an understanding of who a candidate is, ways they might solve problems, and how they handle stress is via behavioral interviewing. Behavioral interviewing is a process of asking candidates to talk you through a process or solution to a problem directly related to business and see where they go with it, how they make decisions, and ways they handle stress.

Time and time again, I have seen companies hire for technical skills, education, or length of experience in an industry and ignore the emotional intelligence or communication side of a person's character. By using behavioral interviewing, you get to experience the candidate and witness how they think, handle stress, and adapt to unusual situations.

Here are a few examples of behavioral interview questions:

- What is the most stressful situation you had on your last job? Why was it stressful, and how did you handle it?

- What is your favorite app on your smartphone? Why? How would you make it better?

- If you noticed a coworker stealing something from the company, what would you do or say? Why?

- What was the most enjoyable part of your last job? Why?

- Why did you decide to leave your last position?

With all these questions, you're primarily looking for the way the applicant thinks, how they solve problems, and what their preference is for handling stress.

Have other people also interview new candidates and use the same concept but different questions. Then be sure to compare your notes and those of the other interviewers against the characteristics you created of your ideal candidate.

Once you determine what was missing or overlooked in the process of hiring the person you recently fired, share your research with human resources and a few trusted coworkers and then refine your hiring process so you'll have success next time.

The Least You Need to Know

- Significance is more important than success. Your legacy is what you do for others and what you leave behind.
- Hire very slowly and fire rapidly. Do not tolerate the wrong person in a job.
- Always seek legal advice before you fire or discipline an employee.
- A positive attitude is indispensable—for you and for your staff.
- Insist on using a thorough hiring process; have more than one person interview each candidate; and when in doubt, say no and move on.

CHAPTER 21

Managing Remotely

The future looks to be very exciting. Every week I find a new dynamic program to use on my computer or an app for my phone that makes my job easier. The joy and cost savings of not having to travel to the office are now real. My business is all virtual, and yours probably will be more and more virtual as time goes by.

In this chapter, I cover several ideas you can consider to ensure you stay well organized, communicating, and producing even if some or maybe most of your workers aren't in the same office building, city, or even state where you work. The internet, cloud services, and other technological advances mean you don't have to work in person as much as we once did.

But that doesn't mean you don't have to manage. You still have to relate to your people, stay connected with them, and train them. Remember, your people want to feel valuable, wanted, and needed. So do you. And so do I.

In This Chapter

- Going virtual and using the cloud
- Combining brick-and-mortar with remote employees
- Working with employees scattered hither and yon
- Keeping everyone on the same virtual page
- If you can't measure it, you can't manage it

Up in the Cloud

The "cloud" is really a simple concept. Instead of having a computer with lots of information stored on a hard drive, you connect to the internet and keep your information "out there" on servers, or storage units, that are maintained by major companies. A physical hard drive is still involved, but it's not in your office or your living room. It's elsewhere. And cloud-based services aren't limited to workplace applications. That's really what's happening when you use Google, Facebook, or Amazon, too. All the information about you, as well as their products and services, is housed on their servers and not on your computer's hard drive.

There are several advantages to this and also some distinct disadvantages.

Advantages and Disadvantages of the Cloud

The biggest advantage of working with the cloud is that you can access the information anywhere in the world you have an internet connection.

It also means you can share the information with anyone, and they can modify or work on it with you. This is great for having teams work on the same files or set of data.

Another advantage is the ability to increase or add to your data as much as you need to. You aren't limited to a finite size based on the hardware in your computer. Because the information and the applications are on the cloud, it's easy for the developers to update the program for everyone at once. This eliminates the need for you to have to sit for long periods of time while your hardware is updated. It's all done on the servers, and for you, the user, it is seamless.

I use Apple products, and Apple has its own Apple iCloud; Microsoft does the same thing. With Apple, all my devices are synched immediately, 24/7. That means all my contacts, email, messages, notes, web browser bookmarks, push notifications, news, pictures—you name it— everything is always up to date on all my devices, iPhone, iPad, and desktop computer.

The potential disadvantages of cloud computing are that the servers are owned by telephone companies (AT&T, Verizon, Sprint, etc.), media companies, and ISPs who can raise rates, go offline in the event of a glitch, or conceivably compromise your sensitive or proprietary information.

Is the Cloud for You?

Some experts predict that the capability of cloud-based services is going to continue to increase in line with *Moore's law,* and pricing is going to go down almost as fast.

Several of my clients have gone virtual already. One, a household goods company, is owned by a European company; has a small management office in southern California; contracts with designers spread across the United States, many of whom work from their homes; manufactures in Asia using an *as-needed* contract arrangement; and minimizes storage because of *just-in-time production*.

DEFINITION

Moore's law states that over the history of computing hardware, the number of transistors in a dense integrated circuit doubles approximately every 2 years. **As-needed** means you only order and receive the goods you require for a limited time, and you avoid having to buy in bulk or large quantities. **Just-in-time production** is used to minimize inventory or parts and goods. You get the parts or goods precisely when you need them in the manufacturing process and eliminate the need to inventory large quantities of parts.

Another company has contractors in several countries, very small offices in each country with people working onsite for end users, with accounting done in the Philippines, and the management working from their home offices.

Some major Fortune 500 companies have their accounting done offshore, usually in the Philippines, and many have their smallest brick-and-mortar facilities in the United States. They don't buy or build overseas; instead, they lease buildings so they're able to change countries for production as labor rates fluctuate. Several have moved, or are in the process of moving, their headquarters offshore to mitigate tax penalties.

With all this, is the cloud for you? That's something only you and your company can answer. But you need to be anticipating and actively working on your own personal development and planning for the things like this that might be in your future.

To that end, learn all you can about technology and how to communicate with computers. Explore other cultures and offshore capabilities. Learn another language, preferably Spanish or Mandarin. Study global business and economics, too. And finally, prepare yourself and your family to be flexible.

Managing Out-of-House Employees

To effectively manage a workforce that's located in an office building or factory and also working from home takes some work. The organization, efficiency, and consistency are always a challenge. Let's explore some guidelines to make it work for you as you strive to manage your people well.

Your first concern needs to be planning. I suggest you get a white board or a big sheet of paper (about 24 by 36 inches), and map your department, your group's goals, and all the people involved. This task, called mind-mapping, is a great way to visualize and arrange various things so they're organized in a congruent and comprehensive way.

> **LEADING THOUGHT**
>
> All Mind Maps have some things in common. They have a natural organizational structure that radiates from the center and use lines, symbols, words, color and images according to simple, brain-friendly concepts. Mind mapping converts a long list of monotonous information into a colorful, memorable and highly organized diagram that works in line with your brain's natural way of doing things.
>
> —MindMapping.com

Be sure you include regular phone contact, email schedules, meetings, and appointments in your map. You need to be in touch with each person on your team on a consistent basis, and you need to be proactive in ensuring they clearly know what their goals are. One of your biggest challenges is planning your time well so you don't have any team members fall through the cracks and not hear from you on a regular basis.

Another major concern should be a convenient and consistent way to monitor each team member's activities. The use of charts is a great way to do this. You might want to have each team member send in a weekly activity report at an agreed date and time. This is a way for the person to keep track of his or her own activities as well as for you to keep tabs on what they're doing.

The easiest performance metric to measure is activities. That can be phone calls and appointments for salespeople; deliveries, repairs, or new customer contacts; or units produced. Based on each person's goals, break down the critical activities required to accomplish those goals to get a list of their ideal activities. When you measure their activities, you can then assess which and how much of each activity is optimum. This enables you to quickly see when one area or another is slipping so you can make an adjustment.

You'll need to invest in the latest and quality equipment when you ask someone to work virtually, and be sure everyone is using the same or compatible technology. It's probably a good idea to provide the equipment rather than have them use their own if possible. This helps ensure security and also means that because the company owns the equipment, the company can reclaim it when the employee moves on. Plus, workers tend to focus on primarily business usage with the equipment if he or she knows the company could reclaim it at any time. I encourage you to spend some time and money to be sure your people know how to use the equipment and are familiar with any systems you intend to use for reporting, developing, or communicating with the company and with each other.

So far, you have workers working in a specific location, some working remotely, and a plan written down of how you intend to communicate with and monitor activity of all your people. This should be applied to those staff members in-house as well as in the field. It's also important to pay special attention and give extra effort to educate and embrace your virtual workers in the company mission, values, and procedures. It can be easy for them to emotionally slip away if they're not consistently included.

People do best when they're accountable. That's why having a coach can be so valuable. Your team will improve if you're able to have a few folks work together, form teams, or organize based on a specific project or region. This design adds accountability and also provides some social pressure because people like to share, show off, and be rewarded when they do good work.

The random phone call, email, or written note of appreciation; thank you note; or holiday greeting card can help you make and keep a personal connection with your team. This is very important and valuable, but it doesn't replace the absolute requirement that occasionally you have to see your people face to face. This can be done electronically, but even that isn't a substitute for the valuable one-to-one meeting you should hold with each of your direct reports.

Never forget that your employees are real people with real emotions and needs. When you rely solely on technology and reports to build relationships you're going to fall far short. To build a committed, purpose-driven team takes some emotional involvement, too. Trust and rapport are difficult without personal connection. When you do have occasion to bring your team together, include some social and fun time in addition to the work. When you relax and play games together, you often get to see a different and sometimes deeper side of people. Plus, it helps build group cohesion.

Several of my clients have included flex time and a reduced work week so they could keep valuable workers during temporary family situations. Family illness, pregnancy, or special needs children are just a few of the reasons people might need flex time. If your company isn't flexible, the employee might be forced to find another position in a company that is. If the job lends itself to flexible hours, that can be a big advantage to keeping high-value people as they work through the normal issues of living.

You also must be responsive to the cultural, religious, and social differences of a diverse workforce. As companies hire or have workers from different countries, they must honor the differences and adjust the job requirements to accommodate those unique cultures. There are distinct advantages to having a diverse work force—it increases creativity, enhances the company's worldview, and has the potential to expand the market potential because of the customization of product and services. You need to spend time with your people so you fully understand these differences and learn how to blend them all together in a cohesive team.

Finally, you need to pay special attention to clarity, consideration, and consistency when working with virtual team members:

Clarity   Be very precise when defining goals, deadlines, and reporting procedures and then reinforce this precision by phone, email, and in-person follow-up. Inspect what you expect.

Consideration   Because of unique time zones, scheduling needs to be planned well ahead of any obligations, appointments, or deadlines. You should establish a clearly defined expectation and commitment among all team members about how long they have to give research or information responses, feedback, or follow-up data and simple callbacks.

Consistency   I've said it already, but it's worth repeating: as the manager, you need to set the example in your behavior. You drive the culture and style of the team; therefore, you must honor and demand courtesy, punctuality, and accuracy from all team members and their dealings with each other.

If you have workers in your same facility, it's sometimes easy to share ideas, responsibilities, and functions with them because you can just walk over to them and share some information. With a virtual team, each team member is probably working alone, and this situation can cause a gap in communication relative to clarity, consideration, and consistency. Be sure you treat all team members equally.

LEADING THOUGHT

Strength lies in differences, not in similarities

—Stephen R. Covey

Back at your desk, be sure to factor in those activities you're going to do with your remote workers—phone calls, emails, meetings, etc.—to your personal schedule, too. Looking at one week at a time, design your ideal work week by evaluating the blocks you use to plan, communicate, manage, and execute your goals. Don't forget to include your personal time, exercise, family, and other important areas of your life. When you create your ideal week, you effectively create a picture of your life and what you're doing with it. If you don't like what you've created, it's up to you to change it to include family time, exercise, etc.

For those things you must do on a regular basis or that require periodic updates, use a simple checklist to keep track. Across the top of a page, put the days of the month, 1 through 30 or 31. Down the left margin, list the items you want to do on a consistent basis. Then, when you complete a task, you can check off the item. If you review the list at least once a day, you can easily see what you have yet to do. This helps you remember to do those more monotonous things that are actually critical even if they're a bit rote. Plus, you'll feel good when you check things off your list.

Playing Beautiful Music Together

You are the maestro of your orchestra. Your people are your hand-selected performers, and together, your objective is to play beautiful music. This metaphor fits business well. Making beautiful music is to produce results, or profits.

Orchestra leaders use and follow a sheet of music they call the *score*. You also have a score—your strategic plan that includes your mission, values, purpose, objectives, goals, etc. With a virtual team, it's imperative that everyone is reading the same score and that they know the mission, values, purpose, and objectives.

Musical scores are very precise. The key is defined; the time to rest is preplanned and set; the volume is defined by *p* for piano, which means "soft," and *f* for "forte," which means loud; and the pace and rhythm are also defined. All this and much more are detailed on a score of music.

How detailed and refined is your business plan? Have you defined the rate of activity you expect from your people? Do you have a clear and precise outline of what they'll say and do? Are your people emotionally involved in the business plan because they see what's in it for them? Does that excite them and make them jump out of bed in the morning ready to play beautiful music?

A musical score also has the precise point and time for a musician to improvise. Have you ever heard of Wynton Marsalis? He's a trumpeter, composer, teacher, music educator, and artistic director of jazz at Lincoln Center in New York City, and he loves to improvise. Marsalis has been playing the trumpet since he was a small child, and he even went to the Juilliard School of music. One could say he's earned the right to improvise.

When you have virtual workers, you'll have many opportunities for them to improvise and do their own thing. Please be sure they're well prepared, trained, and disciplined before you allow or ask them to do so. It's your responsibility to prepare your people to become experts in their chosen field and in the disciplines of good business.

If you have well-trained and disciplined workers, they'll be able to manage themselves. Then, when they're out in the business world, they'll know how to behave, have the requisite discipline, and work together to get a good result—profits.

> **LEADING THOUGHT**
>
> You will never have a greater or lesser dominion than that over yourself ... the height of a man's success is gauged by his self-mastery; the depth of his failure by his self-abandonment. ... And this law is the expression of eternal justice. He who cannot establish dominion over himself will have no dominion over others.
>
> —Leonardo da Vinci

The Continuing Importance of Measurement

It's virtually impossible to manage without measurement. The real question is how and what do you measure in a virtual organization?

The mechanics of *how* are easy. You can do it with a simple email or design a chart for specific activities and have each remote employee submit it to you once a week. Alternatively, numerous internet applications and programs enable you to measure how.

The more challenging part is getting people to consistently measure themselves and send in the information on a timely and consistent basis. This is a behavioral issue. The culture you establish determines how well people comply with this request for information. I suggest you start with a firm approach. Tell your staff this is required, and that no report means no paycheck. Granted, that's probably the harshest extreme, and you might be able to soften it by cajoling, requesting, asking, and, if you are so inclined, begging. Yes, I'm joking with that last sentence.

You'll find that winners love to be measured, and people who are struggling will have a tendency to resist, "forget," or simply not stay on top of their measurement task. This is the first sign they're not fit for what you're asking them to do. (For more information on helping those who aren't a good fit in your company move on to hopefully find a better fit elsewhere, see Chapter 20.)

You can be very nice and courteous with your people, and in fact, I recommend you do so. However, if you allow people to become laid-back, *laissez-faire*, and void of performance measurement, you might get fired yourself. Don't let this happen.

> **DEFINITION**
>
> Under a **laissez-faire** leadership style, all the rights and power to make decisions is fully given to the worker.

In Chapter 7, I discussed appraisal reviews. The way you get a perspective on what rating you'll give your people on their appraisal review is based on the measurements derived from their behavior and results. Time is the least important thing you want to use as a criteria for achieving results and performance.

When you hear someone complaining about the amount of time they're working or how long it takes to get something done, have a heart-to-heart meeting with them. They either don't understand what they're getting paid for and how to do their job, or they're incompetent. It might be a training issue, and if so, that's simple to fix.

If they have a legitimate gripe against the bureaucratic roadblocks within the organization, it's your job to fix it. Otherwise, it's the worker's job to figure out how to do things in a timely manner while working around those roadblocks. As the manager, you could suggest a good book or seminar or send them to a course on time management.

The single most popular seminar I've done over the years is all about time management. Many people have no concept of how to manage their time. You know what? There is no such thing as time management. Time just marches on, and the earth continues to spin, and you can't manage time. You can only manage *yourself* and how you use your time. It's really all about self-discipline.

One of the best ways to measure your people is to monitor the positive or negative feedback they receive from customers, clients, or coworkers. The really productive and conscientious worker will get a positive buzz going about themselves without even trying. The most important time for you to be concerned is when there's no information coming back, either positive or negative. The absolute best form of feedback is a referral.

What you should measure relates to your established key function indicators (KFIs), which are unique to each company, department, and individual. However, there are patterns that might be helpful as you design your measurement matrix. Here are some KFIs to consider:

- Income

- Appointments

- Phone calls

- Units produced or delivered

- Market share

- Product quality

- Customer complaints, retention rate, or referrals

- Reports, filings, or projects completed

- Number of phone rings or wait time

- Payables or receivables turnover, period, or late

- Return on investment

- Profit per employee

Summarize measurements on a consistent and frequent basis—ideally, the more frequent, the better. Ease and simplicity are necessary to maintain participation of workers.

Be sure to have both internal and external measurements. To manage intelligently, you must stay in tune with current economic trends, industry developments, and consumer/customer preferences. All these things need to be measured, charted, and assessed on a regular basis.

The Least You Need to Know

- Going away from brick-and-mortar shops and in-house employees is a continuing trend. Learn all you can about technology and how to use computers and the internet to stay in touch and productive.

- Change is constant and rapid, and it doesn't stop. You must continually be learning and anticipating the future.

- Accountability and measurement are absolutely necessary to manage a workforce—virtual or otherwise.

- Embrace diversity, but continually repeat the purpose, mission, and values of the company.

- As manager, you are tasked with paving the way, removing any roadblocks, and encouraging your people.

The Well-Rounded Manager

Part 6 brings together everything you've learned. You discover how important it is to maintain personal balance, learn ways to appropriately handle people who are more than just workers on your team, and understand the difference between hard and soft skills.

Finally, I cover some of the many options you might face in your future as a manager, including what factors in your current role will probably affect the choices you have in the future and which ones play the biggest part in shaping what your next steps might be.

One thing we know for sure is that the future will be different from the past, and the more prepared and nimble you are, the better you will do. My goal in this book is to help you attain success now and also be prepared to grow and develop in the future for even greater success.

Employees Are People, Too

Your employees are people, and you need to build relationships with your staff. But there's a delicate balance between business and personal relationships. The difference isn't something that's easy to define in an employee manual or college textbook, but you do want to do it right.

In this chapter, I give you some practical advice on dealing with employees on a personal level. I'm not a human resources representative, nor am I a trained psychologist, but I have been around the block a few times and have learned many lessons—some the hard way.

In this chapter, my goal is to blend the experience I've had with a lot of coaching, mentoring, and unique insights. There are no cut-and-dry answers to the topics in this chapter. You'll probably set your own standards and guidelines, and that's likely the best solution. I hope my perspective in this chapter helps, too.

In This Chapter

- Your responsibility to your employees
- Helping your employees be well
- Dealing with friends and family
- Being a good steward of employee wellness

Your Responsibility

You are not responsible for helping your people make decisions about their personal lives. Nor are you their rabbi, priest, or pastor. You also are not, most likely, trained as a psychologist or psychiatrist, so it would be inappropriate for you to give spiritual or psychological advice to your employees in need.

Now, I realize you probably have an opinion and a belief about some subjects, but remember you get paid by your company to serve as a manager and help your people in their jobs. Ethically, you are responsible to deliver for the company—that's why they pay you. Resist going off on tangents.

LEADING THOUGHT

When dealing with people, remember you are not dealing with creatures of logic, but with creatures bristling with prejudice and motivated by pride and vanity.

–Dale Carnegie

Their Reasons; Your Reasons

Everyone does what they do for their own reasons. The same is true for your employees. As loyal to you as they might be, they're not doing anything *for you*. They're primarily concerned with their own welfare (keeping their job and getting paid).

By the same token, as manager, you do what you do for your own reasons. It's in your best interest to help your people be healthy and productive. You need them to be focused and perform efficiently so you can do your own job well. And you can help with that, to some degree.

It's been said that successful employment is "mutually satisfactory exploitation." There's a ring of truth to that, even if it does sound a bit harsh. It's a bit like the "one hand washes the other" metaphor. Or the simple idea embedded in the concept of capitalism—a company makes a profit by providing the consumer's desired products and services.

If either side of the equation doesn't provide some value, the whole thing is thrown out of balance. Workers have to produce a given amount of labor in the form of products and services, and the employer, in turn, provides compensation or a reasonable wage for that labor. There must be an equitable balance of give and take between worker and employer.

Staying Focused

You have to keep your focus on business, on how to be productive, and on how to help your people be productive. You don't have time to get caught up in extraneous matters.

Authority and responsibility go hand in hand. Your authority as manager bears with it certain responsibilities. You have the authority to decide what you'll pay attention to while at work. The challenge lies in knowing not only what to pay attention to but also having a clear understanding of what *not* to pay attention to.

When you have clear focus on the job at hand, you're not distracted by things that don't pertain to the job. If an issue isn't directly relevant to your work and your folks' performance, you can take some time to understand the situation but then avoid getting personally involved. Refer the worker to human resources or an outside professional instead. Getting personally involved in a worker's problem becomes a distraction, so do all you can to avoid it.

This doesn't mean you don't express any compassion or empathy. It merely means you focus mainly on your work. If you need to, turn back to Chapter 4 for a refresher on how to relate to the different styles of behavior. Use that information and recommended communication techniques to help your employee find a solution. Your goal is to help your employee maintain his or her pride, self-esteem, and dignity while at the same time directing them to seek assistance from others who are experts in the appropriate field.

For instance, if a worker has a child with serious behavior problems who is causing her to be late for work, your focus has to be on either finding a way she get to work on time—possibly adjust her schedule to mitigate the issue—or suggesting she find help outside the work environment to assist her.

You are not responsible for rearranging the production line or staffing so others are disrupted to accommodate the first worker's family problems. Look for possible solutions, but do not compromise productivity at work for yourself or for others. The problem is the worker's problem, not yours. If she can't get to work on time, she needs to find another job.

Life isn't fair, nor is it always compassionate. You have to remember that the objective of business is to produce a profit.

Happy, Healthy Workers

Your employees probably invest more time in their work than in any other single activity in their lives—more than the time they spend with their families, relaxing, sleeping, etc. As a manager, you have to be sensitive to this and not take advantage of your ability to require them to be at work and not with their families or other things.

> **LEADING THOUGHT**
>
> For what it's worth: it's never too late or, in my case, too early to be whoever you want to be. There's no time limit, stop whenever you want. You can change or stay the same, there are no rules to this thing. We can make the best or the worst of it. I hope you make the best of it. And I hope you see things that startle you. I hope you feel things you never felt before. I hope you meet people with a different point of view. I hope you live a life you're proud of. If you find that you're not, I hope you have the courage to start all over again.
>
> —Eric Roth, *The Curious Case of Benjamin Button*

Finding Balance

The most productive worker is the happy worker. Your employees need to love what they do, first and foremost. Then they need to know, and believe, you value them and honor the fact that they have a personal life as well as a work life.

Many times I've seen companies determine how much an employee is "worth" based on the number of hours they put in at the office. "The best workers are here before start time and stay as late as necessary to get everything done," they claim. I disagree.

The best workers have found a balance between their work life and their personal life. Those who spend an inordinate amount of time at work often have problems at home they're trying to avoid or they're incompetent at their job. There are exceptions to this, of course, but this is the conclusion I've come to based on my 20+ years of coaching CEOs and executives and helping them figure out how to get control of their lives and maximize their results.

A workaholic will burn out, produce poor-quality work, and compromise their health and personal life. This isn't a formula for success or fulfillment. Often it's a person's reaction to a fear-based mentality. When you see this happening to your people, provide an intervention to get their attention and help them change their ways. This can be done through coaching or training.

In the ideal situation, a person really loves what they do. They have a vision, purpose, or mission that's big and involves others, and they really get emotionally committed to their work. That's all great, and I advocate having a passion for your work.

However, studies, real-life examples, and my own experience all have shown that a balanced person is happier, healthier, and more productive.

How Can You Help?

You can become a friend as well as a boss to your employees and let them know you care as you give them feedback. Encourage them to get involved in sports, attend social events, and spend time with their family.

And don't underestimate the impact you'll make when you approach an employee and say something as simple as, "Joe, you have been working too many hours. Here's a gift certificate for you and your wife to go out to dinner. Leave now."

When you see Joe a few days later, ask him how dinner went. After he shares the joy, explain that you want him to read a book, listen to a CD, or go to a seminar about work-life balance and you'll pay for it (with company funds). What do you think his wife's reaction will be?

When people know you care, they'll appreciate it and become more dedicated and loyal. It's just natural. You give before you get. But don't give just to get; give because it's the right thing to do.

Friends and Family

Mixing friends and family in the workplace can lead to lots of potential problems. In general, I recommend you don't hire good friends or family, period. Many times I've had to be the mediator in situations in which serious problems have arisen because of workplace friendships or relatives working in the same company.

But when it can't be avoided, the following sections help you deal with and manage these relationships to avoid the appearance of favoritism or any other issues.

Manager and Friend

The best employees have a positive attitude and are likable. And it's good when your relationship with those you work with includes friendship. One of the main reasons people leave companies is because they don't feel included and they have no friends at work. By the same token, one of the main reasons people stay at a particular job is because of the friendships they've developed and value at work.

LEADING THOUGHT

Real friends are priceless. Fake friends are cheap. Friends and business don't mix because one considers friends cheap while the other considers them priceless.

—Jay Deragon

On the other hand, when work decisions are made because of friendship rather than performance, problems can arise. Objective measurement will always help you make the right decision. If you're going to pursue and maintain friendships with your coworkers or direct reports, it's best to have friends who understand the value of good metrics, aren't easily offended, and appreciate the unique situation you face.

When friend coworkers achieve success in spite of extra-sharp requirements, they can actually influence their own coworkers to be more loyal and work harder. Sometimes they'll even become heroes to the rest of the workforce because people will respect them for working extra hard to get ahead.

Coworker and Relative

You might face the same dilemma when a relative is hired into your company. I always encourage CEOs I coach to be harder on relatives than they are on other workers. As with friends, if you're perceived to favor or be partial to a relative, the morale of the whole organization could be negatively impacted.

Recently, I coached a CEO of a small company who was having performance issues with his wife's son, who also worked in the company. The CEO obviously cared for the young man, but he was struggling with how to help him perform better while still keeping the peace between the boy's mother—his wife.

Morale was going down in the company because everyone knew who the young fellow was, and his lack of performance was causing problems with his customers and coworkers. His mother was concerned because her son needed the income to live, and if he didn't have a job, he might lose his car, too.

You can imagine how difficult and sensitive this situation was. The CEO and I spent lots of time together trying to figure out how to make it work.

Finally, the negative metrics and complaints lodged against the young man reached a tipping point. The CEO thought he should let the young man go. But because the company was a small one and the mother was one of the owners, she disagreed and felt the company job was a good way to help support her son.

What would you do in this situation?

> **LEADING THOUGHT**
>
> The man who does more than he is paid for will soon be paid for more than he does.
>
> —Napoleon Hill

Please be careful—or better yet, make a rule that you will not hire relatives of close friends. If it's too late and you're already working with relatives or close friends, be sure to use measurements for performance that are open, honest, and transparent to everyone. And no secrets; they only cause problems.

If it doesn't work out and you have to let them go, remember to say, "I love you, but I'll miss you."

Dealing with Performance Problems

My high school chemistry teacher's favorite saying was, "Figures don't lie, but liars can figure." If you're using honest, accurate, and transparent figures to measure performance and a friend or family member isn't performing well, you must set a time to have a meeting with the employee. This probably won't be easy.

You need to approach this meeting in the same manner you would with any worker. If you've been studying the principles in this book, especially in Chapter 4, you know what you have to say. You also know how you have to say it.

The person isn't cutting it, and they must improve or you'll have to let them go. That's the basic message you need to send, but dress it up to fit the person's preferred communication style.

Be open and honest as you discuss the performance issues. You should mention that this is especially hard because you're good friends. You must remain calm and not personalize anything or create an emotional event. It may be appropriate to have a third party join you in this meeting. That will emphasize the reality and intensity of your concern.

> **LEADING THOUGHT**
>
> If you speak your mind and if it is true what you're saying, then I think the integrity of what you're saying carries through.
>
> —Bill Cosby

The communication skills I've discussed throughout the book are not for occasional use. You should make them a part of who you are, day in and day out. You should be the same person at work and at home, whether you're talking to a friend or a new worker. That consistency is a hallmark of integrity.

Wellness

Your life will change dramatically if you lose your health. It's that simple.

Many routines and disciplines can be beneficial for your health. Focus on nutrition, exercise, sleep, relaxation, and mental alertness, and emotional well-being to maintain or improve your wellness.

The same is true for your employees. You can't preach "do as I say, not as I do" and expect your direct reports to take you seriously. As you pay attention to what you eat, the lifestyle benefits you include in your own life, and more, you'll lead by example and soon, hopefully, have your employees following suit.

Let's briefly review the critical elements of each area.

Nutrition

"You are what you eat," my mother would say. There's some truth to that saying, as it turns out.

It's important to be conscious of what you put into your mouth. Several common diseases or ailments can be mitigated or even prevented by a sound discipline of nutrition. The leading causes of death in the United States relate to heart disease, cancers, and diabetes—all of which can be at least partially avoided or lessened by good nutrition. What's more, eating good, fresh, whole foods makes you feel much better, gives you more energy, and makes you look better.

With the plethora of new diet books coming out every day, I only want to suggest here that you need to get focused on your nutrition if you aren't already. Eat lots of green vegetables, decrease the amount of red meat you consume, and reduce your intake of starches and sugars. Watch your portion size, too; keep it small. Finally, be sure you drink lots of water.

The best way I've found to control what I eat is by using an app on my smartphone called *Lose It!* (Many others are available if you want to check out different options.) This free app gives me the capability to record what I eat and also factor in my exercise. (Remember the management axiom: "if you can't measure it, you can't manage it.")

Exercise

There's no getting around it—you have to exercise. Daily. Ideally, you should get 30 to 45 minutes a day of vigorous exercise. You can do this by walking or simply climbing stairs.

One of my Ernst and Young clients in Los Angeles has started a whole troop of executives who daily transverse the stairs in their high-rise office building. This is great exercise, convenient, and fun because they all do it together. Can you start something similar in your workplace?

LEADING THOUGHT

If we could give every individual the right amount of nourishment and exercise, not too little and not too much, we would have found the safest way to health.

—Hippocrates

Another client has incorporated exercise in all their events for charity. They compete with other firms in swimming, volleyball, or golf, and the proceeds go to charity. It's great PR, fun for all, and healthy for the employees and their families at the same time. This also gets executives to band together and practice so they can compete well. This develops camaraderie, boosts health, and builds personal and organizational pride.

I mentioned walking or climbing stairs earlier, but that's not all you can do to get some exercise. Anaerobic exercise is strength training, aerobic exercise is using oxygen for endurance training, and stretching and flexibility are also important. You can do all of these groups either at the gym, in a yoga class, or with your work colleagues.

Ask around and find a buddy to work out with you if you want. A little accountability helps you keep up the routine. And you'll be happier, healthier, and feel terrific.

Sleep

Sleep is essential, and deep sleep is the most important. With lack of sleep, you compromise your memory; inhibit your ability to learn; and probably become moody, impatient, and easily annoyed. And believe it or not, studies have shown that without enough sleep, you actually can gain weight!

Your basic health is also compromised when you don't get adequate sleep. You could develop hypertension, or high blood pressure, or adversely affect your hormones, immunity to disease, and heart health.

 MANAGER MINEFIELD

Lack of sleep has been linked to most major causes of death: heart attack, high blood pressure, stroke, obesity, and accidents.

Additionally, with lack of sleep, you develop the habit of *microsleep*, during which you sleep for just a few seconds or minutes and are not even aware that you fell asleep. This is how people end up in car crashes, miss a part of TV shows, or don't remember their spouse or a lecturer saying something. Microsleep is involuntary, and often the sleeper is totally unaware they've even dozed off.

When you get the recommended 7 or 8 hours of sleep each night, you can expect better health, a more robust sex life, a reduction of chronic pain, and a safer life because of the lower risk of being involved in an accident. Sufficient sleep improves how you look, gets rid of those bags under your eyes, extends your life expectancy, boosts your stamina, and increases your creativity.

And if it does all that for you, it can do the same for your employees.

Mental Alertness

The more you read and exercise your brain, the longer you'll live. The more informed you are, the healthier you'll be. The more knowledge you acquire, the better the odds you'll get promoted, earn more money, and have a more fulfilling retirement.

Yes, they say ignorance is bliss, and for some, it probably is true. If you're so dull that you don't know what's going on in the world, you probably will be complacent and blissful. However, this only lasts until you're taken advantage of, exploited by hucksters, or used as another person's pawn.

Knowledge is power and freedom. Learn all you can, for as long as you can, to avoid your brain going into early retirement.

Emotional Well-Being

As you've learned, the trigger for all decisions you make is based on your emotions. You might know you can do a thing, but if you don't make the scary and emotional decision to try, you'll never do it. Then maybe you try it, and it doesn't work out. So do you just quit then? Many people do. However, if you have the emotional will to try again, you'll ultimately overcome and win.

Athletes who consistently win in their sport know how important the will to win is. Some call it the "fire in the belly." When you meet someone who has the "I will not be denied" attitude, not only are they totally disarming, but they also are inspiring and just seem to be like a magnet. People support them, encourage them, scream and yell and root them on. They "emotionally" help them win.

You can be your own emotional cheering section. But getting your emotions in check in a healthy, positive place, you can do just about anything.

 LEADING THOUGHT

You can conquer almost any fear if you will only make up your mind to do so. For remember, fear doesn't exist anywhere except in the mind.

—Dale Carnegie

Your employees are people who represent a kaleidoscope of different experiences. Some have had good fortune, a wonderful childhood, and loving family. Others have had some really bad and unfortunate circumstances. One thing is certain among them all: they're each unique.

As their manager, their leader, they're relying on you to provide for their best interests, for their wellness. It's your responsibility to have a positive and optimistic vision of the future; to nurture your employees emotionally; and to set an example of a caring manager who lives a life of integrity, seeking the best interests of your people.

You have a wonderful and awesome responsibility. Do it well.

The Least You Need to Know

- Everyone has an agenda, or a reason they do what they do. It most often has to do with personal gain or pain avoidance.

- You must strive for integrity; you should try to be the same person at work, at home, and at play because character counts.

- Have empathy and care for people, but don't mix business decisions with friendship or family.

- Balance of the physical, social, mental, and emotional aspects of your life (and your employees' lives) is critical to your success.

CHAPTER 23

Managing as If Your Life Depended on It

Remember the last time you were on an airplane? Do you recall that as the flight attendants were explaining the safety procedures, they instructed you to put on your own oxygen mask first, before you help your child? This is because you can't help your child—or yourself—if you're starting to lose consciousness because of lack of oxygen. Helping yourself first might seem selfish, but it's actually life-saving.

Everything I discussed in the previous chapter on helping your employees also applies to you as a manager. You need to be concerned for your people, but you need to focus on yourself, too. If you don't, no one else will. To do this, you need discipline, a clear vision of what you want to become, and the will to persist toward your goal even when it seems like you're fighting against all odds. I assure you, it can be done.

In this chapter, I give you many ideas and practical techniques so you can do it with grace. I suggest a few exercises and processes for you to delve into and become introspective. I've used each of these exercises with scores of executives I coach, and they've found the time and effort it takes to really work through them to be very worthwhile. I hope you do as well and then share them with the people you care about, at work and in your personal life.

In This Chapter

- Managers are people, too
- Balancing your work and your life
- How to unplug during time off
- Staying interested and interesting

Let's Get Real

Recently, I spoke to a group of financial executives and enjoyed a delightful dinner. These folks were real, unique, and fascinating.

One lady was the emotional dynamo of the group and worked directly with the chairman. She is a financially wealthy senior citizen and loves working with people. Her husband is in a rest home with Alzheimer's disease. The chairman is a highly decorated Marine and formerly the leader of the Marine Corp Silent Drill Team. He arrived in a Bentley. The fellow next to me at dinner was a former executive with Target and now is doing things he never dreamed of as a result of his success in financial services. He loves to write poetry. Then there was the fellow about to complete his PhD while working full-time.

The entire group was composed of hard-working, quality people all doing very well. They reminded me that life isn't easy. To be successful requires diligence, supreme effort, and a bit of luck, too.

> **LEADING THOUGHT**
>
> There are no secrets to success. It is the result of preparation, hard work, and learning from failure.
>
> —Colin Powell

The focus of our meeting that night was planning. This group has a big convention coming up in Las Vegas and they were reviewing agendas, suggesting changes, and making sure everything was covered. In short, they had met to "inspect what they expect."

As you read this chapter, I would like you to approach it as an opportunity to inspect what you expect from your own life. Why are you doing what you're doing, and what are your plans for your future?

If you and I were sitting at a table over a cup of coffee, I would be low key and a bit inquisitive. Probably after some small talk, I would say something like I did to the former Target executive sitting next to me at dinner that night: "So what's your real passion in life?" To this, he perked up and started telling me about his love of writing. He had been a literature major in college and had dreamed about having more time to write throughout his career.

Ask yourself that simple question now: *What is my real passion in life?*

You are like everybody else and yet you are totally unique. Everyone has dreams, goals, and a list of things they want to do that maybe aren't on the front burner right now because they have to earn a buck instead. But the closer you can get the way you earn a living to align with your dreams and goals, the happier you'll be.

Hopefully, you're in management because you love helping people; take pride in accomplishing great things with other people; and like the challenge of having to grow, develop, and improve. It's important to remember that the most powerful way for you to learn is to make a mistake and deliberately decide to learn from it. When working with others, realize it will gain you all kinds of credibility and respect if you have the courage to admit you made a mistake, apologize to those affected, and make a point to learn from the situation.

It's also important to admit to your people that you're struggling with trying to do everything and you appreciate their understanding and patience. Don't hesitate to request their feedback and help as you try to become better at your job. There's virtue in coming to grips with your vulnerability and being a bit humble. You aren't the answer man or woman, nor do you know *everything*. Admit it.

Monitor you own energy level and your own productivity, and measure your own activities daily. As you do, you'll notice that you run in cycles. There are times during the day when you're more productive, other times when your productivity lessens, and occasionally you need to take time to reflect. In my coaching and mentoring practice, I continually surprise and delight those I'm working with when I tell them to slow down, take a deep breath, and seriously take time to reflect. It's a very valuable habit to develop.

During your reflective times, be sure you have a pen and journal handy or open a new word-processing file on your computer. It's helpful to periodically review where you've been, what has worked well for you, and what you need to modify in the future. Journaling is useful for reviewing the past, seeing a record of your progress, and looking over all the things you've learned.

By continually crafting and refining your dreams, and goals you'll become more and more inspired.

Defining Your Values

Values are an excellent way to determine which way to go when making decisions. In order for this concept to be useful, you need to clearly know and define your values and what priority you place on each. In your journal, make a list of all the virtues, principles, or characteristics you value.

Here are a few possible values to get you started; feel free to add to this list and mark out those values that don't resonate with you:

Love	Integrity
Power	Dependability
Family	Harmony
Achievement	Privacy
Friendship	Money
Calmness	Teamwork

Values are personal, and you need to be true to yourself when making your list. Values aren't something you seek or adopt because someone else thinks they're important; this is your life, and your values must make sense for your life and how you want to live it.

> **LEADING THOUGHT**
>
> Your beliefs become your thoughts,
> Your thoughts become your words,
> Your words become your actions,
> Your actions become your habits,
> Your habits become your values,
> Your values become your destiny.
>
> —Mahatma Gandhi

By asking yourself which values you care about and which ones are not as important, try to narrow down your list to the seven or so core values you relate to and want to incorporate into your life. The next step is to prioritize your short list.

The best way I've found to do this is by working with another person. Give them your list, and have them ask you to choose between two items on it. For example, when deciding between family and money, he or she might ask you, "Which is more important to you, family or money?" Let's say you pick family. Then they ask, "Between family and love?" You might need to think about this one. Is love bigger or more important than family? What do the two words mean to you? Pick one, and continue on until you have your seven values picked.

Then it's time to prioritize your seven. Reflect on them a bit as you do rank them in priority order, from 1 to 7. You can think about them some more after you've ranked them, to be sure the list accurately reflects and represents your core values.

At this point, congratulations. You've just made a significant step forward in defining your life and where you want to go. Ready for the next exercise?

Prioritizing Your Life

Now let's prioritize the various areas of your life. Use the same process you used for values earlier. Here's a potential list of life areas to get you started:

Spiritual	Personality
Fitness	Career
Financial	Hobbies
Social	Service
Family	Knowledge

As you look over this list and add to it or eliminate from it based on who you want to become, it helps to define what each of these areas means to you. I'll get you started with a few possible definitions:

Spiritual   Your relationship with God, your church, your synagogue, or your personal belief system.

Fitness   Your health, weight, body mass index, or ability to exercise.

Financial   Your personal investment program, retirement plan, or personal money management issues.

And so on.

Once you have your own list, put the various areas in order of priority as you did with your values.

Next, determine an activity you can do on a daily basis that will advance that area of your life. Again, here are a few examples to help you develop your list:

Spiritual   Read your Bible, meditate, or attend a religious meeting.

Personality   Read a book on personality, go to a seminar, or spend time with affirmations and positive thinking exercises.

Service   Volunteer at a soup kitchen, give seniors a ride to the mall, help out with Meals on Wheels, or tutor a student.

Knowledge   Read a chapter per day of a book, watch or listen to a webinar, or study industry journals and research.

The third part of this exercise is your Be—Do—Have List. (Remember that from Chapter 2?) In your journal, write down all the things you want to be. Here are a few examples of possible Be—Do—Have items:

To Be   Be more charming. Be more relaxed. Be more caring. Become more disciplined. Become an active listener.

To Do   Do my exercise. Do a research project. Write a book. Sail across the Atlantic Ocean.

To Have   Have a million dollars in my investment account. Have a new boat. Have 200 fine wine bottles in my wine cellar.

Then narrow down and prioritize this list as you've done with the others. I think you'll find it's much easier to do the To Do and To Have lists as opposed to the To Be list. However, I think the To Be list is the most important.

MANAGER MINEFIELD

Remember that *being* is different from *having*. There's a great book called *To Have or To Be?* written in 1976. In it, author Erich Fromm included many thought-stimulating ideas and concepts. One is that suicide rates are highest where people have the most material goods. Seems *having* isn't so satisfying.

Applying Your Lists to Your Life

Lists are useful to have when you put them to good use. So that's the next step—applying your lists of values and ideal areas of your life to your actual life. This is best done by defining a specific activity or activities you can do to advance a particular item on your list.

One of the easiest items to do this with is physical exercise. If you want to get in better shape, it probably relates to your values because you value your health. It relates to your life areas if you put "Fitness" near the top of your list of ideal life areas. And it relates to your Be—Do—Have list because you want to do exercise and be healthy.

Let's say you want to start with walking. Start by thinking when, in your ideal week, would be the best time to walk? Early morning? After work in the early evening? Whenever is best for you, block out just a few minutes at first, and gradually increase the time and frequency you plan to walk.

Now, because you are continually reviewing your lists, dreams, and goals, you realize that if you schedule your walking in the evening, you might be able to convince your spouse to join you. This would then help with your other goals of becoming a better listener and spending more time with your spouse. It also will get your spouse to start exercising, lose a few pounds, and improve your communication. You can see how this can become pretty exciting.

In business, you use written goals and design strategies to meet objectives, measure performance, and achieve results. Why not apply these same principles to your personal life? If you have children, have you created a plan for their development that includes all their life areas, such as learning, exercising, or becoming more socially aware by joining a club or Scout group? What about their personal development, knowledge, spiritual life, etc.? Do you design vacations to be educational as well as fun and relaxing?

Don't hesitate to apply what you've learned in your professional life as a manager to your personal life and your family. You could improve communication with your family and friends, improve your health with increased activity, solidify a plan for your children's futures, and many other things that align with your values.

 LEADING THOUGHT

Life is either a daring adventure or nothing at all.

—Helen Keller

Making the Most of Your Personal Time

To stay healthy, energetic, and vibrant, you need to have periods of rest, relaxation, and repose. Downtime is good, and learning to unplug and relax is vital to being productive when you are at work. To maintain a healthy work-life balance, you need to plan for some time to unwind and regroup when you're not at work.

Scheduling Time with Family

If you have a family, I recommend you hold family meetings on a regular basis. If you have a significant other, schedule a date night at least weekly. On my calendar, for example, every Friday afternoon and evening is reserved for date night. If an important meeting or appointment comes up, I'll change my schedule if I can't arrange to change the meeting, but this doesn't happen very often.

Your family meeting or date night should be a modified version of the one-to-one appointments I recommend you conduct with your direct reports. Focus mostly on asking questions, share your updates on work and personal issues, discuss and plan your future together, and strive to include some learning or education.

Because this is a completely different environment and focus from what you do at work, it'll be stimulating and relaxing if you know how to communicate well. (If you're having issues communicating with family members, review Chapter 4 again.)

Participating in Clubs

Another way to relax is to join a service club. I was a member of Rotary for many years when I started my career with Merrill Lynch. We would meet for lunch every Thursday, and if you missed, you were encouraged to make up the time by going to another Rotary club. This was a fun thing to do, especially when I was traveling internationally. I "made up" in clubs all over the world.

The Rotary motto is "Service above self," and I actually practiced living that motto. I volunteered with international students, at special events, for speaking engagements, and served on the board. Be sure you live the motto of any club you join. Part of the experience is helping others and giving of your time, talents, and energy.

One week at Rotary, we honored a bank president who had just received a citizen of the year award for his contribution and service to several organizations. I happened to be sitting right next to him. I was in my early 30s at the time, and he was in his 60s. When he came back to his seat, I said congratulations. He paused, took a deep breath, said "Thanks" and then, "Dave, I don't know if it was really worth it. I hardly know my two daughters." It's important to give of yourself, but remember to maintain a balance. Don't give so much—to either work or your personal life—that you'll regret it.

LEADING THOUGHT

You have to learn from the mistakes of others. You won't live long enough to make them all yourself.

—Hyman Rickover and Eleanor Roosevelt

If you join a service club with the objective of promoting and selling your services or products—which is common for many—I believe you are compromising your integrity. After all, it's called a service club for a reason. Some of the doctors in clubs I frequented would have their office page them early so they could leave right after they ate. The same ones did it every week.

Gathering with Like-Minded Peers

Benjamin Franklin was famous for many innovative ideas. One of which was to form a Junto, a weekly group meeting of diverse businessmen with the purpose of participating in mutual development; sharing ideas; and discussing morals, politics, and philosophy.

Similar mastermind groups and executive forums are now common. I suggest you form a group of your own. Be sure to invite participants from diverse businesses so you can build relationships, share information, and help each other improve. This is a wonderful way to expand your network with a purpose.

When I wrote my first book, *The CEO Code*, I formed a group of colleagues to meet once a month for breakfast, during which time we discussed ideas and built relationships. It was such a smashing success, we still meet once a month. The name of our group is Maestro Network, and our purpose is "Relationships, Resources, and Results." Each month, various people come and go depending on their commitments and schedule. I highly recommend the concept.

Getting Away from It All

All these options for relaxation and diversion are local and can be incorporated in your normal work week. Vacations are another alternative that take you away and get you out of your "normal."

When I finished my service with the U.S. Air Force, I started thinking about goals and my future. One of my goals was to own a cabin in the woods. This became a reality in about 2 years when I bought a condo in Mammoth Lakes, a ski resort in the high Sierra Mountains in California. That turned into several properties; lots of skiing, hiking, and fishing; and a wonderful place to get away. This lasted for more than 30 years, until I finally decided to sell, partly because of the feeling of obligation or almost guilt to use the mountain home.

You don't have to own a cabin in the mountains to get away and enjoy a vacation. Book a week in a beach resort. Plan a week of backpacking through European countries you haven't visited before. Buy tickets for a Mediterranean cruise.

Do what's best for you and your family and what will make you feel the most relaxed. If you just can't help yourself, you can analyze your vacation-destination decision the same way you would a business decision.

Being Interested and Interesting

What makes for an interesting person? Do people find you to be fascinating and stimulating? Or boring and dull? Does it really matter?

I think for the truly dull and boring person, it really doesn't matter. These folks don't seem to care what others think of them. I'm not sure why some people choose to be boring, but I suspect it has to do with fear and scarcity as a mind-set. Whatever the theory, it probably derives from their past experiences.

 **LEADING THOUGHT**

The man who does not read good books has no advantage over the man who cannot read them.

—Mark Twain

My assumption is you would not be reading this book if you were determined to be dull and boring. Therefore, let's leave the boring point of view and focus on how to be interested and interesting.

Showing Interest

The quickest and easiest way to be interested, and show it, is to be a good listener. Few people enjoy a better topic of conversation than talking about themselves. If you listen well, pay close attention, and find something unique, worthwhile, or relevant in what they say, you can express a genuine interest in them.

Ask questions to help you understand their point of view, their background, and their future plans and goals. Dig to discover everything you can about the other person, and this curiosity will stimulate your genuine interest. The more they're able to relate to you because of your rapport and receptivity to their information, the more interested you'll be—and that will show.

Simple responses like "Wow!" "Really?" "Tell me more," or "That is really unique," demonstrate your interest. You also want to give the other person full eye contact and focus your body language on them. Lean in, don't fidget, be calm, and concentrate focus on the other person.

MANAGER MINEFIELD

When you shift the conversation to yourself or to things you've experienced that they haven't, the less interested you'll appear to be.

Making a Connection

For you to be interesting to another person, you have to be able to make some kind of an emotional connection to them. By listening and concentrating on the other person when they talk, you'll be able to pick up something they're interested in so you can tie it in to something you like and make that link.

You also want to observe and then model their tone, cadence, and style of talking. This will make them more comfortable and, therefore, more likely to be relaxed and open. It's just a matter of being respectful, sensitive, and flexible enough to accommodate their manner of speaking and style.

The more interests, hobbies, knowledge, and experiences you have, the higher the probability you'll be able to relate to other people and share interesting perspectives. It's in your best interest to be well informed—not only to be interesting but also because an informed manager is able to see and discover unique and plentiful options to solve problems, relate to people, and be successful.

There was a survey done of elderly people and they asked them, "As you look back on your life do you have any regrets, are there things you wished you had done that you didn't?" Amazingly there were three common answers that kept coming up. The folks questioned wished they had …

1. Taken more risks.

2. Done something with their life they really cared about.

3. Taken more time to reflect on what life is all about.

LEADING THOUGHT

Find a job that you love doing and you will never have to work a day in your life.

—Confucius

To be the best *manager* you can possibly be, you need to become the best *person* you can possibly be. If you just try your best, are patient with yourself, and persist, you'll achieve goals beyond your wildest dreams. Do your best!

The Least You Need to Know

- Know and follow your passion. If you do what you love, you won't work a day in your life.

- Remember that you learn more from your mistakes than your successes.

- Take time to reflect and clearly define your life plan. Start with your values, prioritize your list, and then implement them.

- Watch where you spend your time (and your money); it will show you what you truly value.

- Seek wise counsel and friendship from people you admire on a regular basis.

CHAPTER 24

Managing the Larger World

Life is so much bigger than most people ever realize. Thanks to new technology, faster transportation, and international trade, we truly live in a global economy. More and more, you are influenced by what happens in other parts of the world. Some of those developments are good, and some aren't. But like you are influenced by such developments, realize that your behaviors also influence others beyond your neighborhood, your personal acquaintances, or and your company.

A simple little promotional video uploaded to YouTube, for example, is available around the world in a matter of minutes—sometimes even seconds. Products, information, ideas, and even, unfortunately, viruses can spread like wildfire around the globe.

You have a responsibility to deliberately design and create exactly what type and size of impact you're going to make— on your coworkers, on your community, and on your planet. It might sound like a cliché, but it's true: one person really can make a difference.

In This Chapter

- Developing the mind and heart of giving
- Walking the talk of corporate social responsibility
- Investing in community service
- Sharing what you know
- Serving your professional community

In this chapter, I suggest a few areas to consider as you determine what legacy you want to leave. Just like emotional intelligence, it all starts with being aware of yourself and growing from that comfortable and well-known person you've been all your life. It all starts with you, and what happens really depends on you as well.

Sure, a lot depends on luck and circumstances, too, but they say luck is when preparedness meets opportunity. The more prepared you are, the easier it is to see and exploit an opportunity, crisis, or everyday experience to your benefit. Let's start with the way you think.

To Have or To Be?

As you develop and mature your worldview, you'll find the joy and challenge of becoming a more vibrant, knowledgeable, and informed person. You'll undoubtedly advance beyond the basic desires of having things, being a spectator, and living a life of simple daily routines. As Helen Keller said, "Life is either a daring adventure or nothing." You'll find lasting satisfaction and excitement in the world of ideas, of giving, and of becoming, but not in the tedium of owning trinkets and toys.

You've probably seen the bumper sticker, "He who dies with the most toys wins." Some people think this is truly their ultimate goal, that having "the most toys" means they've made it, that they've succeeded. So be it. But you know better.

> **LEADING THOUGHT**
>
> I've never worked to make money. I understand we've got to eat and all that, but I never said I want to be a multimillionaire or a billionaire. To me, that's of no significance. I work to have the accomplishment.
>
> —Bob Parsons

Be more interested in how you can grow and improve personally and then develop goals that orient around giving and helping others. I encourage you to think in terms of significance rather than merely success. Significance has a lasting impact on others and is a manifestation of getting beyond yourself and selfish thinking. It's the desire to make the world a better place, to contribute to others, and to leave a lasting legacy.

Donating Your Money

Traditionally, people think of money as a way to leave a lasting legacy. Colleges, hospitals, and charities make a heroic effort to get wealthy businesspeople to donate to their cause and name buildings, schools, and foundations after the donors to appeal to their ego and sense of accomplishment. A local university in Orange County, California, for example, has named every building and each school—law, theater, and music—after a different wealthy donor.

The government, some service clubs, and well-meaning individuals give donations of money to help others. It's efficient, easy to do, and does help.

But there are more meaningful ways you can share and give to help others.

Giving Your Time

If you want to make a real difference, give of your personal time more than you simply donate money. Time is the essence of what life is made of, and when you share your time, you're giving of yourself, of your life, to help another. Think of Mother Teresa, the U.S. military, or emergency responders in towns and cities all across America. They selflessly give (or gave) of themselves in their work.

You can do the same by helping someone across the street, carrying a senior citizen's groceries, or helping a coworker with a personal problem.

The Boy Scouts are famous for doing one good deed each day. Think about what you might do for someone in need. You'll find the act of helping another gives you great joy, a feeling of satisfaction, and a strong desire to do it again.

 LEADING THOUGHT

My favorite things in life don't cost any money. It's really clear that the most precious resource we all have is time.

—Steve Jobs

Sharing Your Ideas

Sharing ideas, knowledge, and experience is another way to leave a legacy and help people in the process. This may be a formalized process like mentoring students or coworkers or working with a local organization.

When you share your ideas, you have a lasting impact, you give of yourself, and your contribution is uniquely yours. It takes time, focus, and creativity to share good ideas with others, but a good idea truly can change the entire direction of a department, a company, or even an industry or a nation.

In the nineteenth century, Hungarian doctor Ignaz Semmelweis noticed high infant death rates and realized it was because of germs and infections carried by the dirty hands of the doctors who touched the babies after working with other sick or dead patients. By simply having doctors wash their hands, the infant mortality rate dramatically fell. Now cleanliness is understood, and high standards are demanded in all hospitals.

I recently spoke to a local startup organization called PlantASeed.org founded by a CPA and several businesspeople, the purpose of which is to create mentoring programs for students. You could start your own similar organization or volunteer to help others through an established group. Think how powerful your ideas might be if they were applied well.

Lending Your Talent

Talent is a unique and wonderful gift. My son had a serious on-the-job accident that required hand surgery. While I waited at the hospital for several hours, I noticed an elderly man sitting at the receptionist desk reading. I could tell he clearly had a vision problem because he held the book about 6 inches away from his eyes.

Once, I went to him to ask a question. After he answered my query, he asked me why I was there. I explained that my son was an artist whose hand had been crushed, and we became engaged in a conversation. He started to tell me about his relationship with his father many years ago.

The man loved music and took violin lessons, but his father did not approve and instead wanted him to be an attorney. So the man attended and graduated from law school in New York. His love was still music, though, and he wanted to play the violin. After graduation, he left New York and came to California, where he ultimately became the first violinist in a major orchestra. He lived his life fulfilling his musical dream.

Suddenly, as he told his story, he glanced at his watch and stood up to leave. He needed to take a young Chinese piano protégée to the airport for her flight to New York, he quickly explained, because she was performing at Carnegie Hall in a few days. He was still giving to others while maintaining a passionate focus on music and musicians.

> **LEADING THOUGHT**
>
> Hard work without talent is a shame, but talent without hard work is a tragedy.
>
> —Robert Half

If you can figure a way to focus on your hobbies, talents, and gifts while giving to others, you'll be forever joyful. You might share your money, your time, your ideas, or your talents—or a combination of these. You can still keep your job as manager and continue to advance in your career. But if you will carve out a little *time* to give to others along the way, not only will you personally benefit with feelings of joy and satisfaction, you also will be leaving a legacy for others.

The Importance of Corporate and Social Responsibility

Stakeholders are people with a vested interest in your company such as investors, creditors, suppliers, employees, the government, and the community. Without the support of each of these groups, your company would have difficulty functioning or even existing. It's foolish to ignore or slight any of these groups. It's far better to embrace and join forces with each group to not only help the company but also to make a positive contribution to each group.

As a manager, you need to understand your company's value structure and priorities and work at coordinating those with the interests of each stakeholder group. It helps to think of each group separately when you're making decisions. Ask yourself what the impact of your decision will be on each group.

You nurture your relationships with your stakeholders over time and based on your interchange with them. You need to figure out ways to touch base with each group to get an understanding of their point of view as well as to develop rapport.

Many years ago, I was an investment broker with Merrill Lynch. This meant I dealt with wealthy people in the community, financial institutions, and service clubs. I gave investment lectures in schools, at the local hospital for the hospital foundation, and in financial institutions. This all helped me develop my reputation as well as gradually find clients.

One day I was asked to visit the local Rotary Club. I did, and when asked, I agreed to join the club. The Rotary membership was diverse—doctors, lawyers, educators, bankers, gas station owners. and a wide range of small businesspeople as well as the local college president.

My wife was in education and frustrated with the bureaucracy, so I suggested we build our own school. At Rotary one day, I mentioned to a real estate agent that I was looking for some land for a school. This turned into a wonderful chain of events, and I ended up buying 6 acres adjacent to a major freeway.

Because of my networking with all the different business, government, and financial people in the community, I personally knew someone for every phase of the project. When I walked into the city council meeting for city approval, every person on the board knew me by name and greeted me cordially before the meeting began.

But situations like this don't happen overnight. It takes time, sincerity, and integrity to build quality relationships. Determine exactly who and what you're interested in relative to the several stakeholder's groups, and design a plan for how to get to know them. You could join your local service club, charitable group, or community/government group. Whatever approach you take, it pays to be a concerned citizen and an engaged member of your community. As you get involved, you'll discover ways to make a contribution.

> **LEADING THOUGHT**
>
> Courage means to keep working a relationship, to continue seeking solutions to difficult problems, and to stay focused during stressful periods.
>
> —Denis Waitley

Don't get involved in something you're not emotionally interested in being a part of. And don't go with the goal of looking for a payback or return. When you participate simply to make connections or get favors or business, people see through it and quickly disregard you or consider you a huckster.

Instead, get involved where you can make a quality contribution. Join appropriate committees and projects where you can demonstrate and share your management skills to get things done for the group. People are always looking for leaders and volunteers. Choose wisely, and when you decide where you'll participate, get involved and make a significant contribution.

The way you demonstrate your dedication and leadership will be the way people will perceive who and what you are. Your mind-set should be to give, give, give. There's a great joy and benefit to having a mind-set of giving and letting that mind-set influence your behavior. The real magic is when you can give without expecting anything in return.

Decide what gifts you have to share and where your interests are, and find a way to participate and make a contribution. If you love music, for example, look into the local symphony, choral groups, or school music programs. If you enjoy technology, find local computer clubs, go online and discover technology groups, or participate in discussion boards on websites you enjoy. If you have a heart for helping people, look into local charities, Goodwill, the Salvation Army, or homeless shelters and food banks. All kinds of opportunities are available.

If you're part of a larger organization, you might want to become a volunteer in the Red Cross, United Way, or your local hospital. If you have difficulty finding groups to participate in as a volunteer, start your own volunteer organization.

Some of your giving can be very personal. I have a friend who I've known for more than 30 years. It turns out he has developed a special type of dementia that necessitates he live in a retirement home and is no longer able to live at home with his family. I periodically call him and stop by to have a cup of coffee or give him a ride to a Starbucks. He loves it and is happy to "have an outing." As we visit and have outings, that's a little less time his family has to worry about him. And it lets him, and his family, know people still care.

Sharing Your Knowledge

It takes time and experience to develop knowledge and, ultimately, wisdom. But when you can share and apply your knowledge to help others grow and develop, you can't imagine how good that feels.

The most important area for sharing knowledge and wisdom is with your family and in particular, with your children. The only way this will work is if you've nurtured a positive and giving relationship with your family over the years of living together. I've found that having regular one-to-one meetings with my family is the best way to develop those relationships. It might be over a casual breakfast, a long walk or drive, or when you go to an event with just one other family member. If you have several children, I recommend you set a special regular time to meet with each child separately. Make it your special time together.

With your coworkers and employees, it's easier to set a time and focus on business, knowledge, or personal development. As a manager, you can establish routines that others will adhere to because they want to keep their job.

This isn't a meeting to "correct" the other person. Rather, it's a time to share successes, address concerns, and gently include advice where appropriate. Resist the temptation to force-feed or preach at another person. This will only land on deaf ears unless they want your advice.

Many schools have mentoring programs through which businesspeople can help up-and-coming students. Programs are also available to help students in special programs such as music, technology, or athletics. You might want to coach a kids' sports team, volunteer in a scouting program, or work with exchange students. The choices are endless.

> **LEADING THOUGHT**
>
> The only real security that a man can have in this world is a reserve of knowledge, experience, and ability.
>
> –Henry Ford

Many of my clients are on the board of directors of various nonprofit organizations and contribute to the organization their special business knowledge whether it's tax, the law, marketing, or another discipline. This benefits the organization, of course, but it also gives my clients connections with other business and professional executives. These can easily develop into long-term friendships and sometimes even business opportunities.

Serving Your Industry

Most industries have various professional associations and groups through which people can gather, share information, and make connections. Painters have the Painting and Decorating Contractors Association (PDCA), established in 1884. Builders have the National Association of Home Builders (NAHB), established in 1942. Specific disciplines in engineering—electrical, professional, civil, energy, computer, and mechanical—all have associations, too.

There are thousands of associations out there; surely you can find one that fits your interests. You might start by searching online. (Remember to use long-tail searches—spell out your search request in detail and enter the whole phrase in the search box.)

Once you find a local group that interests you, call or email them. Ask if you can visit the group, if they could send you more information on the group, or if they could refer you to some local members to whom you could talk to about joining. Many associations are happy to have you visit with no obligation other than to pay for the meal, if that's part of their format. Most will invite you to attend for free.

Take your time as you look for associations and organizations to join. Don't just jump into the first group you visit because of some emotional reason, like they're super friendly and make you feel wanted. Every group has friendly people. In fact, if they don't welcome you with open arms, move on to the next group.

Ideally, you've made a list, or will develop one, outlining why you want to join a group. Include what you plan to give—time, knowledge, leadership, contacts, etc. Also list what you hope to gain—education; connections; industry information; political influence at the local, state, or federal level, etc. It's your list, so get creative.

Be very deliberate and thoughtful as you consider the associations you've found. Exactly why do you want to join a group? How much of a commitment are you able and willing to make? Will this group help you reach your goals? Do you like the people, and do they seem to enjoy you? Are the time, financial, and emotional commitments worth the potential outcome?

I suggest you not take on any responsibility with your new group until you have a good feel for who the people are and how things work. This likely will take a few months. During that time, look for those areas that are meaningful to you and evaluate what you see.

When I first joined Rotary, there were over 100 members in the club, and most were small-business owners. I was a stockbroker with Merrill Lynch. At first, I just helped out on projects and got to know people. After a year or so, I got involved in international student exchanges and even had an opportunity to host a student from India and another from Germany in our home for a year. This proved to be a great experience, and we learned a great deal about the students, their family, and their culture.

I also had an opportunity to share my speaking skills at meetings and special events. Helping out on the program committee gave me an opportunity to meet many people. I remember inviting and then introducing Regis Philbin to speak to our club. At the time, he was a local TV host in the Los Angeles market. When you get out and about, you'll meet interesting people and learn so much.

One of the biggest mistakes I see people make is getting so involved with their jobs and their company that they forget to stay connected with the "real world" outside their work. This can be very damaging to your career and your personal development. You don't want to develop tunnel vision and limit your point of view.

LEADING THOUGHT

By working faithfully eight hours a day you may eventually get to be boss and work twelve hours a day.

–Robert Frost

I've worked with scores of partners at large, international accounting firms. Last year, my wife and I were travelling by train from Helsinki, Finland, to St. Petersburg, Russia, en route to join a river cruise. On the train, we happened to sit by an American couple. As we got to know each other on the ride, the husband mentioned he had recently retired from one of the big four accounting firms—one of my client firms.

Jokingly I said to the wife, "Are you enjoying having him home?" She rolled her eyes and moaned. (It's very typical for a big accounting firm's partners to work 60 or more hours per week, so having him home and retired was probably a very big change for both of them.) He then jumped in and explained that he's looking for a teaching job so he can get out of the house.

Sharing by teaching is powerful. When you teach, you establish yourself as an expert. By volunteering to counsel and consult with other industry people, you force yourself to stay current, be well disciplined, and maintain a professional image and reputation within the industry. Not only is this invaluable for you personally, it also helps others and positions you as a leader within your chosen field.

If you join a philanthropic organization, you might start by helping with membership and new members. This is a smart strategy to employ at the beginning of your tenure with a group because it will position you as a positive force for shaping the group. Additionally, you'll be able to meet new people and establish a platform of experience, knowledge, and expertise. You'll also project an attitude of giving and sharing.

One of the primary goals every organization I have ever participated in is to grow the membership. If you can help the group grow, you'll earn the respect of the other members. It's the most tangible way you can position yourself as a leader and positive influencer as a new member of a group.

As you develop relationships and understanding of the needs, strategy, and objectives of your industry group, you can contribute your special skill sets and knowledge to help achieve those goals. This will naturally propel you into more and more leadership roles.

A young professional I know recently became the California representative to a national medical organization, simply because he applied. He just returned from the national conference in Washington, D.C., and was thrilled with what he learned and the new people he met.

Can you become a national representative for your industry? You can if you make a plan to do so and take the initiative. Imagine who you might meet, what you might learn, and the positive impact you'll make on your career.

The beauty is that all of this starts by giving. The more you give, the more bountiful your life will be.

The Least You Need to Know

- You can impact the global community if you are aware, decide to commit, have a clear vision, and take action.

- Money is the easiest, most efficient, and convenient way to give to others; your time is the most expensive but also has a much bigger payoff for you and for the recipient.

- Sharing your ideas and talents can be beneficial even if you only make a small contribution to one individual.

- Focus on what makes you unique and what brings you joy before you determine how you might share with others. Come from your strength.

- Develop a plan for why, how, when, where, and exactly what you might enjoy giving and to whom you would enjoy contributing.

CHAPTER 25

Taking Your Management Career to the Next Level

As you develop your skills in management, you'll either love it or not. Hopefully, you'll enjoy working with people, helping them grow, and creating dynamic results. The skills you're learning and practicing as a manager will naturally prepare you for advancement within your current organization or any other.

As you work on your present managerial job, you might be thinking about getting a promotion, seeking advancement, or possibly even starting your own company. All this is possible if you really want it, are willing to work for it, and really apply yourself.

In this last chapter of the book, I give you an overview of the many things you can do, tips on how you might expand your thinking, and help you think about what the future may hold for you. After all, according to the adage, "You're either green and growing or ripe and rotting." This chapter is a summary of the most important things you'll want to do and pay attention to as you continue to be "green and growing" and develop your skills and your future career.

In This Chapter

* Being earnest about your career
* Planting your career goals
* How to track your achievements
* Staying nimble in a world that demands it
* Keeping yourself market-ready
* Aiming for the leadership ranks

Making It a Career

Professionals are apparent to all by the clothes they wear, their posture, the way they speak, and their ability to influence others because of their confidence and demeanor. They have the look. Even more important, they have the track record.

For example, a reporter from *U.S. News & World Report* interviewed me about the chances students in business graduate schools have of later becoming CEOs of Fortune 500 companies. If you just look at the thousands of students graduating every year and compare that to Fortune 500 companies—most of which don't have openings in the CEO job slot—the statistics are not in favor of getting one of the jobs as CEO.

It can be done, but what does it take?

Creating a Winning Track Record

From my experience, the single most important characteristic a candidate needs to land the CEO slot is a consistent success pattern. Think about it for a minute. If you owned a company, you'd want someone to run it who knows and has experienced success, right? You probably wouldn't hire someone who had a few or many failures—nor would you want someone who didn't look, act, and behave like a CEO. You'd be looking for a winner.

Right now, today, you are building your track record. Is it a winning track record?

> **LEADING THOUGHT**
>
> Choose a job you love, and you will never have to work a day in your life.
>
> —Confucius

You want to win and succeed in all of your endeavors. Therefore, make up your mind right now, if you haven't already, that you are going to apply yourself, give your very best effort, and succeed. It all starts in your brain and then gets manifested in the rest of your body until it controls your actions.

As I discussed earlier in this book, this kind of confidence comes from being sure you know and are using your talents and strengths. Success won't mean anything if you don't derive great joy from doing what you do.

Thinking About the Big Picture

Becoming a CEO also requires thinking about the big picture. This isn't just a job; it's the way you have chosen to spend your life.

You probably work 8 or more hours a day, which means you're investing a majority of your life in your work. You're also influencing the people who work for you because they're investing their lives in the work you're leading. Therefore, be sure the work you do is worthwhile and significant and provides rewards for all concerned. When you have that kind of balance and involvement, it makes for a happy workplace.

As a manager, you also must think of the legacy you're leaving your employees. What memories of you will they carry with them? Were you able to communicate how much you cared for your employees? Did you listen well? Were you thought of as competent at your job? Did you ask them for input, giving serious consideration to an idea and explaining why or why not you decided to use it? Did you treat your employees with dignity and respect, making sure to never raise your voice in anger?

People will remember the way you made them feel. The emotional memory is always strongest, and they'll talk about the results to their lives because of knowing you. "He gave me a chance." "She believed in me and made me believe I could do it when I doubted myself." "He's the best boss I ever had." These feelings go beyond the workplace and carry over into your employees' personal lives, so be sure your legacy is one of both success and caring.

LEADING THOUGHT

To laugh often and much; to win the respect of intelligent people and the affection of children; to earn the appreciation of honest critics and endure the betrayal of false friends; to appreciate beauty, to find the best in others; to leave the world a bit better, whether by a healthy child, a garden patch or a redeemed social condition; to know even one life has breathed easier because you lived. This is to have succeeded.

—Ralph Waldo Emerson

Getting a Bountiful Management Harvest

Building your management career is like growing a bountiful garden. The joy and hard work needed to make a garden thrive can also help you develop your management skills. Let me walk you through how this works.

Preparing the ground—getting your mind ready   The ground is where the garden grows, so the soil must be turned over and the weeds, old roots, and rocks removed. In the business world, the ground is your mind. You should prepare your mind to go to work with plans of action and their importance to be sure you're focused and not distracted by extraneous thoughts. What are the old roots and rocks in your life that need to be removed? Any personal distractions can hinder your progress—family complications, health problems, excess weight, emotional issues—you name it. Figure out a way to eliminate the problem.

Planning the garden—working on your approach to the job   Based on the amount of sun, the soil, and the time of year, you need to plan what you'll plant and how far apart each row will be in your garden. As a new manager, you first need to focus on the basics. You'll be in an environment that probably isn't perfect for learning how to be a manager. What are you going to do to supplement your learning; coaching; and knowledge of the job, your people, and the company? In what areas do you need extra support—training, technical skills, human resources, communication, leadership? Match your personal resources with the reality of how the company and your new team can help you.

Planting—feedback and setting expectations   Most gardens start with seeds or small, fragile seedlings. And you probably will plant more seeds than you expect to ultimately have as plants. When you start as a manager, you and your people are learning together. Therefore, be sure you give and get feedback on a regular basis so everyone knows what's working and what isn't. Give each person room to grow, and set realistic expectations of what can be accomplished.

Water and fertilizer—taking care of your employees   Plants need the right amount of water and nourishment. Too much water can rot the roots, and too much fertilizer can burn the plants. Similar to this, your people need care and feeding in the form of knowledge, caring, and reinforcement/rewards. Your career needs the same type of continual support and freedom. It's a balance between task behavior and relational behavior, as discussed earlier.

In a garden, weak plants need to be removed, weeds need to be picked, and light pruning must be done to keep the growth healthy. Like strong plants that flourish with sunlight and room to grow, your talents and your staff's talents need to be capitalized on to get the best growth. Rewards and praise are appreciated and vital, yet occasionally a course correction or behavioral tweak help you and your people stay focused and productive.

Harvesting—managing change   Picking the fruit or cutting the flowers in a garden is a process that occurs over time. When you pick fruit and flowers, you help the plants generate new fruit or flowers faster. If fruit or flowers are left on the plant or vine, they sap the plant's energy and diminish its yield. In the same way, as you and your employees become more and more productive, there's a time to help them earn new responsibility, move to another section, do cross-training, or learn additional duties. All these activities help you and them grow and yield more results.

Like a garden, growth in management is continual. Stay green and growing!

Tracking Your Achievements

Earlier in the book, I recommended keeping a journal. This is a useful and rewarding habit to get into. In fact, Peter Drucker and Edward Deming, both icons in management development and history, encourage executives to keep track of their accomplishments, shortcomings, and things they want to change, and a journal is a good place in which to record these thoughts. Good records are important for the changes and required qualifications you'll undoubtedly have in the future.

Your journal can be a notebook, a three-ring binder, or a word processing file on your computer. In it, keep each certificate, employee review, recommendation, and award you earn. (If you keep an electronic journal, you can scan the paper versions of these items and insert them into your files.)

It's also important to keep the records of your employment, including your start and finish dates and any promotions. Be sure you also record any training you've participated in, including the flyer that details what was covered in the course or seminar. As your career develops, you'll be required to know this information when there's a change in your job or department or when you go to a new company. And with some heavily regulated industries, such as the securities industry, it's critical to have up-to-date and detailed records for any tests, investigations, and approvals you might need to qualify for a job.

> **SKILL BUILDER**
>
> If you were in the military, be sure you keep your Form DD 214, which shows you received an honorable discharge. I needed mine just a few months ago, and it's now several decades since I was in the military.

In the same journal, or maybe in another journal, you keep track of your goals and the worksheets you use to measure your progress. Keep a list of the goals you've accomplished. I've done this, and it's been very rewarding to go back and see what I've done over my career. It also can give you confidence and faith in yourself so you can tackle your next hurdle.

At the end of every year, as you review the journal pages you kept during the last 12 months, ask yourself three critical questions based on what you've recorded:

1. What do I want to continue doing?

2. What do I want to stop doing?

3. What do I want to start doing?

Periodically, such as at the beginning of the year, plan a strategy session with yourself and review the year you just completed using documents, graphs, and your metrics. Then plot out how you're going to conquer the new year using new graphs, charts, and metrics. Include pictures of your goals so you have an emotional component to help you stay focused and motivated.

When you keep good records, you can review exactly what you were successful with during the past year, what you need to work on to find success, and ideas or goals you might have for the future. If you only rely on your memory or a scattering of random notes and papers, you'll get sloppy results.

Now that you've decided to become a professional manager, sloppy doesn't cut it. Get organized, clean up your records, and establish a professional filing system for both what you've done and what you plan to do in the future.

Staying Flexible

As a manager, you have the choice of being a tall and unyielding oak or a lithe willow. Think of what the wind could do to each of these trees. The oak will stand tall and rigid until it breaks or the wind stops. The willow will flex and bend and remain pliable in a storm. If you're unyielding and unbending like the oak, and if you're not flexible like the willow, you run the risk of breaking when conditions get rough.

When you're flexible, you're easier to get along with and people are more apt to come to you with problems or questions. When you're rigid, you annoy people and many people will avoid you rather than have to deal with your lack of tolerance. The choice should be a simple one: be flexible, or be a stubborn bull people avoid. Remember that sometimes it's tactically advantageous to give in on a small issue or battle and save your big guns to win the war.

MANAGER MINEFIELD

There's a distinct advantage to being flexible, but many people don't have the emotional intelligence to be flexible and relaxed. If you do, use it to your advantage without belittling those who can't handle change so well.

If, for example, someone you're scheduled to get together with is late for your meeting or has to reschedule at the last minute, don't get upset. Roll with it and stay calm and cool. It's no big deal. If you're flexible and remain cordial and relaxed while you accommodate their disruption, you'll be the good guy in this situation. They'll remember that the next time they have a question or issue and need someone to talk to about it.

There are much better ways to deal with people who have trouble following schedules, meeting deadlines, or staying in line than making a big deal out of the issue. If you keep a level head and stay in control of your emotions, people around you will remember that, and how easy you are to get along with.

The Importance of Being Prepared

The Boy Scouts got it right: always be prepared. As a manager, you should plan and prepare for everything you can imagine that might go wrong and have a solution ready to implement if it happens. Being prepared has saved my life on more than one occasion   literally. I spent a lot of time in preparation when I was flying combat in the RF-4C Phantom II in Southeast Asia.

As a reconnaissance pilot during the Vietnam War, I flew hundreds of combat missions over Vietnam, Cambodia, and Laos. The typical flight was between 2 and 3 hours, at low altitudes, and at night. Because we flew fast, low, and at night, the flights required a lot of precision and planning beforehand. I would typically spend an hour or two plotting each flight. Fortunately, I never missed a target and was never hit by antiaircraft fire or a missile, although many were shot my way.

> **LEADING THOUGHT**
>
> Give me six hours to chop down a tree and I will spend the first four sharpening the axe.
>
> —Abraham Lincoln

These flights, and the preparation they required, taught me a few lessons. I learned that planning well in advance is absolutely essential—it could mean the difference between life and death. I learned that approaching the target the most difficult way is actually safer because the enemy isn't expecting you to bypass the easy way. I learned to never fly over the clouds because if you do, and you see a missile that's been fired at you come above the clouds, it'll be too late to maneuver out of the way. And I learned never to fly in a straight line for more than 50 seconds—it takes the enemy just over 50 seconds to acquire a radar lock-on. These and other lessons became valuable to me and to the other pilots who flew similar missions.

The best CEOs today have written guidelines of lessons they've learned in business—the things they will or will not do based on their own experiences and principles they learned from the mistakes of others. Like these managers, I suggest you start your own list of principles and guidelines of how you intend to successfully build your career and what lessons you've learned.

Here are some to get you started:

- Always do intensive planning.

- Anticipate obstacles, and be prepared to handle them.

- The hard course is often the best chance of success.

- Be flexible and nimble to confuse and overcome.

- Practice so you can do precisely what you intend to do.

If you're well prepared, odds are good you'll succeed.

Becoming a Leader

Leadership is a skill set that can be defined in many ways. For example, Paul Hersey says leadership is influence, while Peter Drucker says a leader is someone who has followers. No matter how leadership is defined, here a few of the ways leaders inspire and motivate:

- Leaders set the vision and are concerned with what and why.

- Leaders focus on the longer view and foment change within the organization.

- Leaders develop, innovate, and originate at an organizational level.

> **LEADING THOUGHT**
>
> Go to the people. Learn from them. Live with them. Start with what they know. Build with what they have. The best of leaders when the job is done, when the task is accomplished, the people will say we have done it ourselves.
>
> —Lao Tzu

It's impossible to completely differentiate between management and leadership because they include many of the same things. However, management has a closer focus, is more hands-on, and gets more involved in systems and procedures.

As you become more and more involved in leadership, you'll notice your concerns will become longer-range and focused on the company and interfacing with your industry as opposed to one department or a small group.

The natural progression for you as a manager is to gradually accept more responsibility for larger and larger parts of the company. You'll likely begin to have other managers report to you, which gives you a distinct advantage because you know how things really work because you, too, have been in management. You know how to make things happen internally with various departments within the organization. Little by little, you'll see your leadership grow as you take on these new roles.

Your Future as a Manager

We've covered a lot of ground in these pages. I heartily suggest you become very deliberate with planning. Plan how you're going to develop your people, make your team productive, and grow your own career.

Be sure you master the concepts in Chapter 4 on how to communicate. That's the single biggest problem many managers wrestle with nearly on a daily basis.

And get into the habit of having one-to-one meetings with all your direct reports. Quality, focused meetings accelerate your workers' growth, minimize your headaches with people problems, and dramatically improve production results.

> **LEADING THOUGHT**
>
> First comes thought; then organization of that thought, into ideas and plans; then transformation of those plans into reality. The beginning, as you will observe, is in your imagination.
>
> –Napoleon Hill

I wish you the very best of success in your management career.

The Least You Need to Know

- Strive to build a winning track record. People will hire a person with a success pattern.

- Always be thinking and acting with your legacy in mind. What good have you done both for yourself and your employees?

- Plan your life like a garden—deliberately and with lots of care. Success takes consistent nurturing.

- Prepare for everything you can imagine that might go wrong, and have a solution ready to implement.

- Gaining experience and expertise as a manager will lead you to become a better leader.

Glossary

ability   The knowledge and skill to accomplish a task.

activity   A task, duty, or function requiring personal involvement, commitment, and time allocation. Phone calls, meetings, filing, planning, discussions, and inspections are all activities.

affirmation   A positive statement of a condition or mind-set that's made in the first person, present tense, to declare a desired condition, belief, or outcome.

as-needed production   A method whereby you only order and receive the goods you require for a limited time, and you avoid having to buy in bulk or large quantities.

assessment   A test to define various characteristics of a potential hiring candidate. IQ, EQ (emotional intelligence), behavioral style, personality, aptitude, and skills can all be evaluated with assessments. You can also benchmark the assessment with results from both your best and least attractive employees.

attitude   A person's demeanor; point of view toward themselves and others; or manner of thinking, speaking, and acting in a positive or negative manner.

baby boomer   A member of the generation born between 1946 and 1964. Commonly called the "me" generation, boomers grew up during the Vietnam War, civil rights demonstrations, and man launching into space. Divorce rates rose dramatically among the boomers, and they pursued money, material goods, and personal gratification.

balance   Proportionally mixing several areas in one's personal life such as career, family, health, spiritual, and social.

balance sheet   A statement of all assets minus liabilities with the remainder being equity at a fixed date in time.

body language   The way people reveal how they feel, what they're thinking, and what their goals are using their posture, movement, tone of voice, facial expressions, and eye movement. Everything is revealing, even a person's rate of breathing and heart rate.

communication   The act of giving and receiving information, feelings, and intentions with another.

control   The act of accurately accumulating performance data; evaluating that data; and making necessary adjustments of time, people, resources, and focus to achieve specific results.

delegation   A process that enables others to learn and develop skills by helping you accomplish necessary and worthwhile tasks. This is not "dumping" unpleasant or useless tasks to others.

delta (Δ)   A Greek letter that's also used as a mathematical symbol to represent change or difference.

effective   The act of doing the right or correct things to accomplish the objective.

efficient   The act of doing whatever you're doing quickly and well.

emotional intelligence (EQ)   The ability to be aware of self and others, to influence self and others, and to lead and control the emotional dynamic of any relationship.

execute   To make something happen by your personal involvement and effort in the specified task.

feedback   Sharing with another worker how they performed, what they did well, how they might improve, and what could be changed to improve the outcome.

Generation X   A member of the generation born between 1965 and 1980. Divorce rates have continued to rise in this generation; both spouses typically work; and kids are more casual, free, and independent. They're skeptical of and not impressed with authority, yet they strive for education, balance, and good jobs.

generational difference   The varying points of view of different generations on topics such as change, values, attitude toward discipline, competitiveness, self-reliance, trust, and adaptability.

habit   A repetitive act, thought, or behavior that's done without conscious thought to accomplish the fulfillment of a known or unknown need.

income statement   A record of sales revenue over a period of time (quarter, half year, or annual) minus expenses. The result is gross income for the period.

integrity   A trait that indicates you know what you believe and you're able to express and explain those beliefs verbally and in writing. Most importantly, your behavior demonstrates your beliefs and values.

just-in-time production A method used to minimize inventory or parts and goods. You get the parts or goods precisely when you need them in the manufacturing process and eliminate the need to inventory large quantities of parts.

key function indicator (KFI) or **key performance indicator (KPI)** A measurement that's easy to measure frequently that indicates the direction, volume, and quality of a given task. Appointments for sales, units for production, and complaints for customer service are some such measurements.

laissez-faire A leadership style under which all the rights and power to make decisions is fully given to the worker.

leadership The act of influencing others by your behavior and example to attain your and your organization's vision and mission. A leader must effectively manage him- or herself as well as others.

leveraged buyout (LBO) The purchase of a company by investors who then restructure the finances, operations, and people to maximize their investment profits. They often refinance the company with debt to recapture their initial investment and have the company pay off the debt incurred.

locus of control The way a person views his or her life and what controls the outcome, be it internal, wherein a person believes he or she has personal control of their own circumstances, or external, wherein a person believes external circumstances determine his or her future and results.

manage by walking around (MBWA) A simple management technique in which you literally walk around and interact and engage with your employees.

management A group of leaders whose goal it is to accomplish a specific objective by guiding, controlling, instructing, coaching, monitoring, and leading their team(s).

manager A person who guides, coaches, and controls a group of people who are focused on common goals or outcomes.

measurement The process of taking account of specific actions, tasks, and outcomes on a consistent and accurate basis to determine and then evaluate the results to improve the outcome in the future.

millennial A member of the generation born before and after the turn of the twenty-first century. This group has grown up during worldly disruptions like terrorist attacks, AIDS epidemics, and school shootings, and divorce has become the new normal. Education is emphasized, tolerance is expanded, and the internet is omnipresent.

Moore's law   An observation that states that over the history of computing hardware, the number of transistors in a dense integrated circuit doubles approximately every 2 years.

motivation   The reason why people do what they do, or their purpose to action.

one-to-one meeting   A regularly scheduled meeting between two people during which progress, suggestions, and status of the person's performance is reviewed while rapport and confidence are built between the two individuals. It's primarily a positive event.

parking lot   A written list of ideas, topics, and agenda items that are mentioned in a meeting and deemed worthy to discuss but are not directly related to the current meeting. They're written down and addressed at the end of the meeting or some other time.

plan   The act of determining objectives; allocating resources; and designing methods, tactics, and strategies to take deliberate action and achieve measurable results.

politics   Relating to and interfacing with others in order to influence outcomes or decisions and advance personal agendas.

proactive   Taking action without having to be told to do something. It's the state of mind wherein an individual takes initiative without requiring outside stimulation.

profit   The money that remains in the business after all taxes, costs, and expenses have been paid.

relationship behavior   A form of behavior you as a manager have with your employees. Relationship behavior is listening, encouraging, clarifying, and giving emotional support. *See also* task behavior.

result   A measurable and tangible outcome that directly relates to and positively impacts the bottom-line profit of the business.

rules of engagement   The agreed way you as a group will behave and interact during a meeting.

self-disclosure   The revealing to another of some personal or intimate information about oneself that's not commonly known.

significance   A lasting impact on society and other people that markedly improves their condition on a long-lasting and permanent basis.

skill   A developed performance ability, understanding, and knowledge for particular disciplines. For example, typing, driving, selling, engineering, operating machines, accounting, law, customer service, and research are all learned skills.

success   The progressive realization of predetermined worthwhile personal goals.

supervise   To be in charge of a team or group that's performing a task or objective to create a specific result as directed by management.

sycophant   A person who compliments, flatters, or praises an important person to win his or her approval or gain an advantage for themselves.

task behavior   A form of behavior you as a manager have with your employees. Task behavior is you telling your people the what, how, when, and where of doing tasks. *See also* relationship behavior.

traditionalist   A member of the generation born before 1946. The traditionalist's worldview was shaped by the Great Depression, two World Wars, and the Korean War as well as the growth of major corporations like General Motors.

willingness   When a person chooses to participate with enthusiasm to help advance the objective.

Resources

The following resources are available to help you learn more about management. I've included some groups to join so you can practice skills along with some books I believe are valuable for new managers.

Groups

These groups offer you the opportunity to meet and learn from other executives:

American Management Association
amanet.org
This site offers webcasts, podcasts, articles, and books.

Institute of Management Consultants USA (IMC USA)
imcusa.org
IMC USA is the certifying body and professional association for management consultants and firms in the United States. The site offers certification, education, and professional resources.

Maestro Network
linkedin.com/groups/Maestro-Network-4814434/about
Maestro Network, a subgroup of Consultants Link on LinkedIn, is a global organization of exceptional executives focused on building trusted relationships, sharing resources, and producing remarkable results.

Toastmasters International
toastmasters.org
Toastmasters International members learn to improve their speaking and leadership skills. Search for a club near you.

Books

These books about management are worth reading:

Case, John. *Open-Book Management*. New York: HarperCollins, 1996.

Champy, James. *Reengineering Management*. New York: HarperCollins, 1995.

Collins, Jim. *Good to Great*. New York: HarperCollins, 2001.

Drucker, Peter. *The Effective Executive*. New York: HarperCollins, 2002.

Gerber, Michael. *The E-Myth Revisited*. New York: HarperCollins, 1995.

Greenleaf, Robert. *The Power of Servant-Leadership*. San Francisco: Berrett-Koehler Publishers, Inc., 1998.

Hradesky, John. *Total Quality Management Handbook*. New York: McGraw-Hill, 1995.

Hunsaker, Phillip. *The Art of Managing People*. New York: Simon & Schuster, 1980.

Loehr, Jim. *The Power of Full Engagement*. New York: Simon & Schuster, 2003.

Rohlander, David. *The CEO Code*. Pompton Plains, NJ: Career Press, 2013.

Senge, Peter. *The Fifth Discipline Fieldbook*. New York: Doubleday, 1994.

Slywotzky. Adrian. *The Upside*. New York: Random House, 2007.

How to Read People

Have you ever asked yourself, *Why isn't everyone* normal *like me?* If you have, you're not alone. Most of recorded history is replete with stories of people trying to figure out why people behave the way they do and how to predict and handle others.

When you choose to ignore the differences in people and treat everyone the same way, you're only going to be successful a small percentage of the time. The way you or anybody behaves with other people is very complex. Many factors determine behavior, including past experiences, cultural background, environment, temperament, and even age.

Yet we all have developed behavioral patterns or distinct ways of thinking, feeling, and acting. If you learn to recognize these patterns, you can improve your ability to communicate with the infinite variety of people you encounter every day. You don't have to become a psychologist or a psychiatrist. Just remember what the late comedian Flip Wilson often said, "What you see is what you get." Each one of us is unique. Your task is to be able to recognize the differences and respond accordingly. Even though this is straightforward and a relatively simple method, it takes time and practice to make it a habit. Don't give up on learning it.

Look, Listen, and LEAN

One of the first people to record and analyze the different types of behavior in people was Hippocrates. He thought it had something to do with the type of body a person had. Some people believe it's all in the structure of a person's face, others rely on the place and time of birth, and still others feel environment has a lot to do with behavior. Is it nature or nurture? Maybe it's a form of intelligence or genetics.

I believe all these things have some truth and are worth considering. However, I'd like to share an elementary paradigm that has served me well for more than 20 years. It's simple to learn, and it really works. It goes like this:

> Look, listen, and LEAN.

Look

You'll discover many things by simply observing other people. Obviously, if you're communicating by phone, email, or text messages, you are limited in your communication quality because you can't see the other person. But if you can see the other person, you can learn many things.

Observe their total body language and demeanor. Don't get hung up on one thing or a specific minor part of the person's body language. Folded arms do not necessarily mean the person is closed off and stubborn. Maybe they're just cold. As you look at a person, let your intuition identify your feelings about that person. Do they appear comfortable, nervous, or distracted? What are their facial expressions?

A person's face can tell you whether they're an extrovert or introvert. Wide eyes and a smile indicate they're an I style (see Chapter 4) and probably friendly and emotional. A stern or blank face indicates either a C if they are low key or a D if they're intense and confident. You want to look for patterns, not just one particular thing. Of all the things you're looking at when you observe and communicate with another person, the most important is their eyes.

When a person looks down, it's probably a sign of thinking emotionally. If their eyes haltingly go back and forth, left to right and back to left, etc., their brain is analyzing and calculating. A glance up usually relates to activation of imagination and sometimes a false statement (lying). Sometimes a look down is a sign of respect or deferring to the other person, while looking away or to the side might mean fear, confusion, or insecurity. A direct and constant stare or eye contact can mean defiance, confrontation, or just trying to understand.

The easiest, most obvious, and yet very insightful part of reading people is to consider the total person and identify the behavioral patterns of each element of their body language. It's impossible for a person not to communicate something with their body language. Whether they move or don't move tells you something about how they're reacting to the situation. This takes practice and study, but it's well worth the effort.

Remember, the first and easiest way to start reading another person is to studiously look at them.

Listen

Believe it or not, you are able to listen with your ears as well as with your feelings and energy. It's been scientifically proven that people radiate energy, and you can become aware and sensitized to another person's energy. You probably already are and haven't really thought about it. But stop and consider it a moment: when you meet some people, don't you just get a feeling whether they're good, evil, or arrogant? Part of this is from the energy they radiate.

Your body is composed of chemicals and electricity. Water drops have a polarity, and because your body is 70 percent water, that water can be influenced by outside electrical forces. It's relatively easy to measure a person's electrical field with modern technology. But for you, it's important to realize your body is also sensitive to, and influenced by, the other peoples' energy fields. As a manager, it's your responsibility to positively influence others with your own energy field.

When you listen with your ears, don't forget to listen and feel the other person's energy. People express their feelings, ideas, and overall energy by their tone of voice, the cadence of their speech, and the way they verbally represent themselves. Notice how often they use the pronoun *I* as opposed to talking about others. Are they primarily interested in other people and things, or do they focus on ideas? Are their frames of reference in positive terms, or do they lament that they're always being taken advantage of, getting the short end of the stick, and in need of help and special attention?

Do they sound confident, secure, and in control, or are they weak, needy, and whiney? All these things give you an opportunity to understand where they're coming from, what their values are, and the direction they're trying to go in the future.

Also pay special attention to what they *don't* talk about. Do they avoid certain views, attitudes, or subjects? Listen and try to understand why they behave the way they do.

Remember, it's very difficult to learn and develop understanding when you're talking. Get comfortable with listening a lot and talking a little.

LEAN

The LEAN part of this paradigm is an acronym:

L = learn about them   You need to develop the intention of learning about the other person, understanding him or her, and being able to develop rapport. You can deliberately adjust your behavior to accommodate the other person by modeling the other person's body language, tone of voice, and cadence while not sacrificing your own identity or values. When you show another person you're interested in them by your total behavior, they will share.

E = empathy   This is mostly an emotional effort to be attentive, interested, and empathetic. This is not sympathetic; rather it's empathy: "I understand how you feel." You might not agree with the other person's feelings; however, you show empathy when you let the other person know you can relate.

If you have disdain, an attitude of superiority, or a lack of interest, you'll quickly learn that people aren't willing to share their real feelings and ideas with you. You'll know you're doing a good job of communicating when people share their deep feelings and thank you for listening to them. This means they trust you. You have a responsibility to honor that trust and respect them and their personal confidentiality.

A = ask questions   This is the magical tool that opens people and helps you understand them. I've discussed the art of asking questions a lot in this book. Practice asking questions and knowing what kinds of questions to ask, and see if you can become a master at asking the profound or right question. Keep them short and simple. Start with the weather and other small-talk questions. Avoid questions that merely require a "yes" or "no" answer, too. Instead, ask open-ended questions that encourage an explanation. As the other person responds, nod your head, smile, and say things like "Tell me more," "Can you give me an example?" or "Wow. How did that make you feel?"

N = nonjudgmental   This is critical. People will feel you being judgmental by the slightest of reactions. An uplifted eyebrow, the corners of your mouth drooping down, the quick eye stare, or the widening of your eyelids all indicate you're passing judgment.

No one enjoys talking to someone who looks down on them with even the slightest of negative judgment. It reminds me of the story in the Bible when the women was caught in adultery. Instead of judging her, Jesus said, "Let him who is without sin throw the first stone." (John 8:7)

Everyone is in the situation they're in because of their life experiences and the decisions they've made up to now. As a manager, you have a great opportunity to communicate and read your employees by becoming an astute observer of people. Work at developing the skill of being an active and interested listener. And then *lean* in to your people. Don't pull away, but instead lean in and relate by learning about them, showing empathy, asking good questions, and containing your impulse to judge. You can help them make better decisions in the future. In fact, it's your job.

The more you understand other people, their goals, and their fears, the better you'll be able to communicate. Effective communication requires more than talent. It takes trust, respect, understanding, empathy, and resolution. It's an art.

Making the Most of Conventions

Industry and association conventions are major events that you might sometimes attend to learn new ideas, connect with colleagues, and meet new people. As with meetings (see Chapter 14), you need to plan ahead for conferences to get the most out of them.

When I attend conferences with the National Speakers Association (NSA), the most valuable parts of the meeting for me are the discussions I have with colleagues over a meal or even in passing in the hallway.

The official stage show the NSA puts on is fun, but it's not always valuable as a takeaway. One significant reason to go to conferences is to have the time and chance to build relationships with people from other parts of the country—or in the case of the NSA, with speakers from other countries.

Any convention you attend should have an opportunity for you to learn and accomplish a specific business agenda. Before the convention, especially if you're traveling there, prepare yourself for what's to come:

- Review the agenda.

- Evaluate the speakers, breakout sessions, and training schedule.

- Do some research to find out who else is going to be there.

- Build your list of goals and define what you want to accomplish as a result of attending the meeting.

I'm a mentor to new members of the NSA, and I'm also on the board of directors of a charity affiliated with NSA. Before going to a meeting, I have a conference call with the person I'll be mentoring and check them out online as much as I can. This enables me to recommend specific people I know who they should meet; coach them on the politics and procedures of the organization; and schedule time to meet in person to share any information, guidance, or assistance they might benefit from having.

When you arrive at the convention, you're likely going in high gear, and you might find it difficult to meet people if you haven't set aside a time before the event that's mutually convenient for those you want to connect with.

Realize that everyone has an agenda at such events, and they have their own objectives to accomplish. When you meet someone you'd like to get to know better, offer to buy them coffee, a drink, or a meal in exchange for spending a few minutes getting to know them and "picking their brain."

Index

F